The Count of Monte-Cristo

(51)

The Count of Monte-Cristo

THE

COUNT OF MONTE-CRISTO

BY

ALEXANDRE DUMAS

WITH NEARLY FIVE HUNDRED ILLUSTRATIONS FROM DESIGNS BY G. STAAL, J. A. BEAUCE, AND OTHER EMINENT FRENCH ARTISTS

IN FIVE VOLUMES

VOL. IV

GEORGE ROUTLEDGE AND SONS
LONDON AND NEW-YORK
1888

THE DUEL IN THE SNOW.

TABLE OF CONTENTS

LIST OF ILLUSTRATIONS

CADEROUSSE RIDES WITH ANDREA CAVALCANTI.

THE COUNT OF MONTE-CRISTO

CHAPTER LXXIV

THE VILLEFORT FAMILY VAULT

TWO days after, a considerable crowd was assembled, toward ten o'clock in the morning, round the door of Villefort's house, and a long file of mourning-coaches and private carriages extended along the Faubourg Saint-Honoré and the Rue de la Pépinière. Among them was one of a very singular form, which appeared to have come from a distance. It was a kind of covered wagon, painted black, and was one of the first at the rendezvous. Inquiry was made, and it was ascertained that, by a strange coincidence, this carriage contained the corpse of the Marquis de Saint-Méran, and that those who had come for one funeral would follow two corpses. Their number was great. The Marquis de Saint-Méran, one of the most zealous and faithful dignitaries of Louis XVIII. and King Charles X., had preserved a great number of friends, and these, added to the personages whom the usages of society gave Villefort a claim on, formed a considerable body.

Due information was given to the authorities, and permission obtained that the two funerals should take place at the same time. A second hearse, decked with the same funereal pomp, was brought to Villefort's door, and the coffin removed into it from the wagon. The two bodies were to be interred in the cemetery of Père-la-Chaise, where

Villefort had long since had a tomb prepared for the reception of his family. The remains of poor Renée were already deposited there, whom, after ten years of separation, her father and mother were now going to rejoin.

The Parisians, always curious, always affected by funereal display, looked on with religious silence, while the splendid procession accompanied to their last abode two of the number of the old aristocracy, celebrated for traditional *esprit*, for fidelity to engagements and sincere devotion to principle.

In one of the mourning-coaches Beauchamp, Debray, and Château-Renaud were talking of the very sudden death of the marchioness.

"I saw Madame de Saint-Méran only last year at Marseilles," said Château-Renaud, "and should have supposed she might have lived to be a hundred years old, from her apparent sound health and great activity of mind and body. How old was she?"

"Franz assured me," replied Albert, "that she was seventy years old. But she has not died of old age, but of grief; it appears, since the death of the marquis, which affected her very deeply, she has not completely recovered her reason."

"But of what disease did she, then, die?" asked Debray.

"It is said to have been a congestion of the brain, or apoplexy, which is the same thing, is it not?"

"Nearly."

"It is difficult to believe it was apoplexy," said Beauchamp. "Madame de Saint-Méran, whom I once saw, was short, of slender form, and of a much more nervous than sanguine temperament; grief could hardly produce apoplexy in such a constitution as that of Madame de Saint-Méran."

"At any rate," said Albert, "whatever disease or doctor may have killed her, M. de Villefort, or rather, Mademoiselle Valentine,—or, still rather, our friend Franz, inherits a magnificent fortune, amounting, I believe, to eighty thousand livres per annum."

"And this fortune will be doubled at the death of the old Jacobin, Noirtier."

"That is a tenacious old grandfather," said Beauchamp. "*Tenacem propositi virum.* I think he must have made a bet with Death to outlive all his heirs, and he appears likely to succeed. He is the old Conventionalist of '93, who said to Napoleon, in 1814, 'You bend because your empire is a young stem, weakened by rapid growth. Take the Republic for a tutor; let us return with renewed strength to the battle-field, and I promise you five hundred thousand soldiers, another Marengo, and a second Austerlitz. Ideas do not become extinct, sire; they slumber sometimes, but only revive the stronger before they sleep entirely.'"

"Ideas and men appear the same to him," said Albert. "One thing only puzzles me, namely,—how Franz d'Epinay will like a grandfather who cannot be separated from his wife. But where is Franz?"

"In the first carriage, with M. de Villefort, who considers him already as one of the family."

Such was the conversation in almost all the carriages; these two sudden deaths, so quickly following each other, astonished every one; but no one suspected the terrible secret which M. d'Avrigny had communicated, in his nocturnal walk, to Villefort. They arrived in about an hour at the cemetery; the weather was mild, but dull, and in harmony with the funeral ceremony. Among the groups which flocked toward the family vault, Château-Renaud recognized Morrel, who had come alone in a cab, and walked silently along the path bordered with yew-trees.

"You here!" said Château-Renaud, passing his arm through the young captain's; "are you a friend of Villefort's? How is it I have never met you at his house?"

"I am no acquaintance of M. de Villefort's," answered Morrel; "but I was of Madame de Saint-Méran's." Albert came up to them at this moment with Franz.

"The time and place are but ill-suited for an introduction," said Albert; "but we are not superstitious. M. Morrel, allow me to present to you M. Franz d'Epinay, a delightful traveling companion, with whom I made the tour of Italy. My dear Franz, M. Maximilian Morrel, an excellent friend I have acquired in your absence, and whose name you will hear me mention every time I make any allusion to affection, wit, or amiability."

Morrel hesitated for a moment; he feared it would be hypocritical to accost in a friendly manner the man whom he was tacitly opposing, but his oath and the gravity of the circumstances recurred to his memory; he struggled to conceal his emotion, and bowed to Franz.

"Mademoiselle de Villefort is in deep sorrow, is she not?" said Debray to Franz.

"Inexpressibly deep," replied he; "she looked so pale this morning, I scarcely knew her."

These apparently simple words pierced Morrel to the heart. This man had then seen Valentine, and spoken to her! The young and high-spirited officer required all his strength of mind to resist breaking his oath. He took the arm of Château-Renaud, and turned toward the vault, where the attendants had already placed the two coffins.

"This is a magnificent habitation," said Beauchamp, looking toward the mausoleum; "a summer and winter palace. You will, in turn, enter it, my dear d'Epinay, for you will soon be numbered as one of the family. I, as a philosopher, should like a little country-house, a cottage down there under the trees, without so many cut-stones over my poor body. In dying, I will say to those around me what Voltaire wrote to Piron: '*Eo rus,*' and all will be over. But come, Franz, take courage, your wife is an heiress."

"Indeed, Beauchamp, you are unbearable. Politics have made you laugh at everything, and political men have made you disbelieve everything. But when you have the honor of associating with ordinary men, and the pleasure of leaving politics for a moment, try to find your affectionate heart, which you leave with your stick when you go to the Chamber."

"But tell me," said Beauchamp, "what is life? Is it not a halt in Death's anteroom?"

The Cemetery of Père-la-Chaise.

"I am prejudiced against Beauchamp," said Albert, drawing Franz away, and leaving the former to finish his philosophical dissertation with Debray.

The Villefort vault formed a square of white stones, about twenty feet high; an interior partition separated the two families, and each compartment had its entrance door. Here were not, as in other tombs, those ignoble drawers, one above another, where economy incloses its dead with an inscription resembling a ticket; all that was visible within the bronze gates was a gloomy-looking room, separated by a wall from the vault itself. The two doors before mentioned were in the middle of this wall, and inclosed the Villefort and Saint-Méran coffins. There grief might freely expend itself without the flirting couples or trifling loungers who came from a picnic party to visit Père-la-Chaise, disturbing by their songs, their shouts, or their running to and fro the mute revery or the tearful prayer of the mourner in the tomb.

The two coffins were placed on trestles previously prepared for their reception in the right-hand division belonging to the Saint-Méran family. Villefort, Franz, and a few near relatives alone entered the sanctuary.

As the religious ceremonies had all been performed at the door, and there was no address given, the party all separated; Château-Renaud, Albert, and Morrel went one way, and Debray and Beauchamp the other. Franz remained with Villefort; at the gate of the cemetery Morrel made an excuse to wait; he saw Franz and Villefort get into the same mourning-coach, and thought this *tête-à-tête* foreboded evil. He then returned to Paris, and although in the same carriage with Château-Renaud and Albert, he did not hear one word of their conversation.

As Franz was about to take leave of Villefort,—"When shall I see you again?" said the latter.

"At what time you please, sir," replied Franz.

"As soon as possible."

"I am at your command, sir; shall we return together?"

"If not unpleasant to you."

"On the contrary, I shall feel much pleasure."

Thus, the future father and son in law stepped into the same carriage, and Morrel, seeing them pass, became uneasy. Villefort and Franz returned to the Faubourg Saint-Honoré. The *procureur*, without going to see either his wife or his daughter, passed rapidly to his cabinet, and, offering the young man a chair:

"M. d'Epinay," said he, "allow me to remind you at this moment, which is, perhaps, not so ill-chosen as at first sight may appear, for obedience to the wishes of the departed is the first offering which should be made at their tomb; allow me, then, to remind you of the wish expressed by Madame de Saint-Méran on her death-bed, that Valentine's wedding might not be deferred. You know the affairs of the deceased are in perfect order, and her will bequeaths to Valentine the entire property of the Saint-Meran family; the notary showed me the documents yesterday, which will enable us to draw up the contract immediately. You may call on the notary, M. Deschamps, Place

VILLEFORT AND VALENTINE.

Beauveau, Faubourg Saint-Honoré, and you have my authority to inspect those deeds."

"Sir," replied M. d'Epinay, "it is not, perhaps, the moment for Mademoiselle Valentine, who is in deep distress, to think of a husband; indeed, I fear——"

"Valentine will have no greater pleasure than that of fulfilling her grandmamma's last injunctions; there will be no obstacle from that quarter, I assure you."

"In that case," replied Franz, "as I shall raise none, you may make arrangements when you please; I have pledged my word, and shall feel pleasure and happiness in adhering to it."

"Then," said Villefort, "nothing further is required; the contract was to have been signed three days since: we shall find it all ready, and can sign it to-day."

"But the mourning?" said Franz, hesitating.

"Fear not," replied Villefort, "no ceremony will be neglected in my house. Mademoiselle de Villefort may retire during the prescribed three months to her estate of Saint-Méran; I say hers, for she inherits it to-day. There, in a week, if you like, the civil marriage shall be celebrated without pomp or ceremony. Madame de Saint-Méran wished her daughter should be married there. When that is over, you, sir, can return to Paris, while your wife passes the time of her mourning with her mother-in-law."

"As you please, sir," said Franz.

"Then," replied Villefort, "have the kindness to wait half an hour; Valentine shall come down into the drawing-room. I will send for M. Deschamps; we will read and sign the contract before we separate, and this evening Madame de Villefort shall accompany Valentine to her estate, where we will rejoin them in a week."

"Sir," said Franz, "I have one request to make."

"What is it?"

"I wish Albert de Morcerf and Raoul de Château-Renaud to be present at this signature; you know they are my witnesses."

"Half an hour will suffice to apprise them; will you go for them yourself, or will you send?"

"I prefer going, sir."

"I shall expect you, then, in half an hour, baron, and Valentine will be ready."

Franz bowed and left the room. Scarcely had the door closed, when Villefort sent to tell Valentine to be ready in the drawing-room in half an hour, as he expected the notary and M. d'Epinay and his witnesses. The news caused a great sensation throughout the house;

Madame de Villefort would not believe it, and Valentine was thunderstruck. She looked round for help, and would have gone down to her grandfather's room, but meeting Villefort on the stairs, he took her arm, and led her into the drawing-room. In the anteroom, Valentine met Barrois, and looked despairingly at the old servant. One moment after, Madame de Villefort entered the drawing-room with her little Edward. It was evident that she had shared the grief of the family, for she was pale and looked fatigued. She sat down, took Edward on her knees, and, from time to time, pressed almost convulsively to her bosom this child, on whom her affections appeared centered.

Two carriages were soon heard to enter the courtyard,—one was the notary's; the other, that of Franz and his friends. In a moment the whole party was assembled. Valentine was so pale, one might trace the blue veins from her temples, round her eyes and down her cheeks. Franz was deeply affected. Château-Renaud and Albert looked at each other with amazement; the ceremony which was just concluded had not appeared more sorrowful than did that which was commencing. Madame de Villefort had placed herself in the shade behind a velvet curtain; and as she constantly bent over her child, it was difficult to read the expression of her face. Villefort was, as usual, unmoved.

The notary, after having, according to the customary method, arranged the papers on the table, taken his place in an arm-chair, and raised his spectacles, turned toward Franz:

"Are you M. Franz de Quesnel, baron d'Epinay?" asked he, although he knew it perfectly.

"Yes, sir," said Franz. The notary bowed.

"I have, then, to inform you, sir, at the request of M. de Villefort, that your projected marriage with Mademoiselle de Villefort has changed the feeling of M. Noirtier toward his grandchild; and that he disinherits her entirely of the fortune he would have left her. Let me hasten to add," continued he, "that the testator, having only the right to alienate a part of his fortune, and having alienated it all, the will will not bear scrutiny, and is declared null and void."

"Yes," said Villefort; "but I warn M. d'Epinay, that during my lifetime my father's will shall never be scrutinized, my position forbidding any doubt to be entertained."

"Sir," said Franz, "I regret much such a question has been raised in the presence of Mademoiselle Valentine; I have never inquired the amount of her fortune, which, however limited it may be, exceeds mine. My father has sought consideration in this alliance with M. de Villefort; all I seek is happiness."

Valentine imperceptibly thanked him, while two silent tears rolled down her cheeks.

"Besides, sir," said Villefort, addressing himself to his future son-in-law, "excepting the loss of a portion of your hopes, this unexpected will need not personally wound you; M. Noirtier's weakness of mind sufficiently explains it. It is not because Mademoiselle Valentine is

going to marry you that he is angry, but because she will marry; a union with any other would have caused him the same sorrow. Old age is selfish, sir, and Mademoiselle de Villefort has been a faithful companion to M. Noirtier, which she cannot be when Madame la baronne d'Epinay. My father's melancholy state prevents our speaking to him on serious subjects, which the weakness of his mind would incapacitate him from understanding, and I am perfectly convinced that at the present time, although he knows his granddaughter is going to be married, M. Noirtier has even forgotten the name of his intended grandson." Villefort had scarcely said this, when the door opened, and Barrois appeared.

"Gentlemen," said he, in a tone strangely firm for a servant speaking to his masters under such solemn circumstances,—"gentlemen, M. Noirtier de Villefort wishes to speak immediately to M. Franz de Quesnel, baron d'Epinay." He, as well as the notary, that there might be no mistake in the person, gave all his titles to the bridegroom elect.

Villefort started, Madame de Villefort let her son slip from her knees, Valentine rose, pale and dumb as a statue. Albert and Château-Renaud exchanged a second look, more full of amazement than the first. The notary looked at Villefort.

"It is impossible," said the *procureur du roi.* "M. d'Epinay cannot leave the drawing-room at present."

"It is at this moment," replied Barrois, with the same firmness, "that M. Noirtier, my master, wishes to speak on important subjects to M. Franz d'Epinay."

"Grandpapa Noirtier can speak now, then," said Edward, with his habitual quickness. However, his remark did not make Madame de Villefort even smile, so much was every mind engaged, and so solemn was the situation.

"Tell M. Noirtier," resumed Villefort, "that what he demands is impossible."

"Then, M. Noirtier gives notice to these gentlemen," replied Barrois, "that he will give orders to be carried to the drawing-room."

Astonishment was at its height. A kind of smile was perceptible on Madame de Villefort's countenance. Valentine instinctively raised her eyes, as if to thank heaven.

"Pray go, Valentine," said Villefort, "and see what this new fancy of your grandfather's is." Valentine rose quickly, and was hastening joyfully toward the door, when Villefort altered his intention.

"Stop!" said he; "I will go with you."

"Excuse me, sir," said Franz, "since M. Noirtier sent for me, it is my part to attend to his wish; besides, I shall be happy to pay my respects to him, not having yet had the honor of doing so."

"Pray, sir," said Villefort, with marked uneasiness, "do not disturb yourself."

"Forgive me, sir," said Franz, in a resolute tone. "I would not lose this opportunity of proving to M. Noirtier how wrong it would be of him to encourage feelings of dislike to me, which I am determined to conquer, whatever they may be, by my devotedness."

And without listening to Villefort, he rose and followed Valentine,

who was running downstairs with the joy of a shipwrecked mariner who finds a rock to cling to. Villefort followed them. Château-Renaud and Morcerf exchanged a third look of still increasing wonder.

CHAPTER LXXV

THE OFFICIAL REPORT

NOIRTIER was prepared to receive them, dressed in black, and installed in his arm-chair. When the three persons he expected had entered, he looked at the door, which his valet immediately closed.

"Listen," whispered Villefort to Valentine, who could not conceal her joy; "if M. Noirtier wishes to communicate anything which would delay your marriage, I forbid you to understand him."

Valentine blushed, but did not answer. Villefort approached Noirtier.

"Here is M. Franz d'Epinay," said he; "you requested to see him. We have all wished for this interview, and I trust it will convince you how ill-founded are your objections to Valentine's marriage."

Noirtier answered only by a look which made Villefort's blood run cold. He motioned Valentine to approach. In a moment, thanks to her habit of conversing with her grandfather, she understood he asked for a key. Then his eye was fixed on the drawer of a small desk between the windows. She opened the drawer, and found a key; and understanding that was the key which he wanted, again watched his eyes, which turned toward an old secrétaire, long since forgotten, and supposed to contain none but useless documents.

"Shall I open the secrétaire?" asked Valentine.

"Yes," said the old man.

"And the drawers?"

"Yes."

"Those at the side?"

"No."

"The middle one?"

"Yes."

Valentine opened it and drew out a bundle of papers. "Is that what you wish for?" asked she.

"No."

She took successively all the other papers out till the drawer was

empty. "But there are no more," said she. Noirtier's eye was fixed on the dictionary.

"Yes, I understand, grandfather," said the young girl.

She pointed to each letter of the alphabet. At the letter S, the old man stopped her. She opened the dictionary, and, proceeding as before, reached the word "secret."

"Ah! is there a secret spring?" said Valentine.

"Yes," said Noirtier.

"And who knows it?" Noirtier looked at the door where the servant had gone out.

"Barrois?" said she.

"Yes."

"Shall I call him?"

"Yes."

Valentine went to the door and called Barrois. Villefort's impatience during this scene made the perspiration roll from his forehead, and Franz was stupefied. The old servant came.

"Barrois," said Valentine, "my grandfather has told me to open that drawer in the secrétaire, but there is a secret spring in it, which you know—will you open it?"

Barrois looked at the old man. "Obey," said Noirtier's intelligent eye. Barrois touched a spring, the false bottom came out, and they saw a bundle of papers tied with a black string.

"Is that what you wish for?" said Barrois.

"Yes."

"Shall I give these papers to M. de Villefort?"

"No."

"To Mademoiselle Valentine?"

"No."

"To M. Franz d'Epinay?"

"Yes."

Franz, astonished, advanced a step. "To me, sir?" said he.

"Yes."

Franz took them from Barrois, and casting his eye on the cover, read:

"'To be given, after my death, to General Durand, who shall bequeath the packet to his son, with an injunction to preserve it as containing an important document.'

"Well, sir," asked Franz, "what do you wish me to do with this paper?"

"To preserve it, sealed up as it is, doubtless," said the *procureur du roi*.

"No," replied Noirtier, eagerly.

"Do you wish him to read it?" said Valentine.

"Yes," replied the old man.

"You understand, baron, my grandfather wishes you to read this paper," said Valentine.

"Then let us sit down," said Villefort, impatiently, "for it will take some time."

"Sit down," said the old man. Villefort took a chair, but Valentine remained standing by her father's side, and Franz before him, holding the mysterious paper in his hand. "Read," said the old man. Franz untied it, and, in the midst of the most profound silence, read:

"'Extract of the report of a meeting of the Bonapartist Club in the Rue Saint-Jacques, held February 5th, 1815.'"

Franz stopped. "February 5th, 1815!" said he; "it is the day my father was murdered." Valentine and Villefort were dumb; the eye of the old man alone seemed to say clearly, "Go on." "But it was on leaving this club," said he, "my father was killed."

Noirtier's eye continued to say, "Read." He resumed:

"'The undersigned Louis Jacques Beaurepaire, lieutenant-colonel of artillery, Etienne Duchampy, general of brigade, and Claude Lecharpal, keeper of woods and forests, Declare, that on the 4th of February, a letter arrived from the Isle of Elba, recommending to the kindness and the confidence of the Bonapartist Club, General Flavien de Quesnel, who, having served the emperor from 1804 to 1814, was supposed to be devoted to the interests of the Napoleon dynasty, notwithstanding the title of baron, which Louis XVIII. had just granted to him with his estate of Epinay.

"'A note was, in consequence, addressed to General de Quesnel, begging him to be present at the meeting next day, the 5th. The note indicated neither the street nor the number of the house where the meeting was to be held; it bore no signature, but it announced to the general that some one would call for him, if he would be ready at nine o'clock. The meetings were always held from that time till midnight. At nine o'clock, the president of the club presented himself; the general was ready; the president informed him one of the conditions of his introduction was, that he should be eternally ignorant of the place of meeting, and that he would allow his eyes to be bandaged, swearing that he would not endeavor to take off the bandage General de Quesnel accepted the condition, and promised, on his honor, not to seek to discover the road they took. The general's carriage was ready, but the president told him it was impossible he could use it, for it was useless to blindfold the master if the coachman knew through what streets he went. "What must, then, be done?" asked the general —"I have my carriage here," said the president

"'"Have you, then, so much confidence in your servant that you can intrust him with a secret you will not allow me to know?"—"Our coachman is a member of the club," said the president; "we shall be driven by a State-Councillor"—"Then we run another risk," said the general, laughing, "that of being upset." We insert this joke to prove that the general was not in the least compelled to attend this meeting, but that he came willingly. When they were seated in the carriage, the president reminded the general of his promise to allow his eyes to be bandaged, to which he made no opposition. On the road the president thought he saw the general make an attempt to remove the handkerchief, and reminded him of his oath. "True," said the general The carriage stopped at a passage leading to the Rue Saint-Jacques The general alighted, leaning on the arm of the president, of whose dignity he was not aware, considering him simply as a member of the club, they crossed the passage, mounted to the first story, and entered the meeting-room.

"'The deliberations had already commenced. The members, apprised of the sort of presentation which was to be made that evening, were all in attendance. When in the middle of the room the general was invited to remove his bandage. He did so immediately, and was surprised to see so many well-known faces in a society of whose existence he had till then been ignorant. They questioned him as to his sentiments, but he contented himself with answering that the letters from the Isle of Elba ought to have informed them ——'"

Franz interrupted himself by saying:

"My father was a royalist; they need not have asked his sentiments, which were well known."

"And hence," said Villefort, "arose my affection for your father, my dear M. Franz. A similarity of opinion soon binds."

"Read again," said the old man.

Franz continued:

"'The president then sought to make him speak more explicitly; but M. de Quesnel replied that he wished first to know what they wanted with him. He was then informed

of the contents of the letter from the Isle of Elba, in which he had been recommended to the club as a man who would be likely to advance the interests of their party. One paragraph alluded to the return of Bonaparte, and promised another letter, and further details, on the arrival of the *Pharaon*, belonging to the ship-builder Morrel, of Marseilles, whose captain was entirely devoted to the emperor. During all this time, the general, on whom they thought they could have relied as on a brother, manifested evidently signs of discontent and repugnance. When the reading was finished, he remained silent, with knit brow.

"'"Well," asked the president, "what do you say to this letter, general?"

"'"I say that it is too soon after declaring myself for Louis XVIII. to break my vow in behalf of the ex-emperor." This answer was too clear to be mistaken as to his sentiments. "General," said the president, "we acknowledge no King Louis XVIII., and no ex-emperor, we acknowledge only his majesty the Emperor and King, driven from France, which is his kingdom, six months ago, by violence and treason."—"Excuse me, gentlemen," said the general; "you may not acknowledge Louis XVIII., but I do, as he has made me a baron and a field-marshal, and I shall never forget that for these two titles I am indebted to his happy return to France."—"Sir," said the president, rising with gravity, "be careful what you say; your words clearly show us that they are deceived concerning you in the Isle of Elba, and have deceived us! The communication has been made to you in consequence of the confidence placed in you, and which does you honor. Now we discover our error; a title and promotion attach you to the government we wish to overturn. We will not constrain you to help us; we enroll no one against his conscience, but we will compel you to act like a man of honor even if you are not disposed to do so."—"You would call acting like a man of honor, knowing your conspiracy and not informing against you; that is what I should call becoming your accomplice. You see I am more candid than you."'"

"Ah, my father!" said Franz, interrupting himself. "I understand now why they murdered him." Valentine could not help casting one glance toward the young man, whose filial enthusiasm ennobled him. Villefort walked to and fro behind them. Noirtier watched the expression of each one, and preserved his dignified and commanding attitude.

Franz returned to the manuscript and continued:

"'"Sir," said the President, "you have been invited to join this assembly—you were not forced here; it was proposed to you to come blindfolded—you accepted. When you complied with this twofold request you well knew we did not wish to secure the throne of Louis XVIII., or we should not take so much care to avoid the vigilance of the police. It would be conceding too much to allow you to put on a mask to aid you in the discovery of our secret, and then to remove it that you may ruin those who have confided in you. No, no, you must first say if you declare yourself for the king of a day who now reigns, or for his majesty the emperor."—"I am a royalist," replied the general; "I have taken the oath of allegiance to Louis XVIII., and I will adhere to it." These words were followed by a general murmur; and it was evident several of the members were discussing the propriety of making the general repent of his rashness. The president again rose, and having imposed silence, said: "Sir, you are too serious and too sensible a man not to understand the consequences of our present situation, and your candor has already dictated to us the conditions which remain for us to offer you." The general, putting his hand on his sword, exclaimed, "If you talk of honor, do not begin by disavowing its laws, and impose nothing by violence."—"And you, sir," continued the president, with a calmness still more terrible than the general's anger, "do not touch your sword, I advise you." The general looked around him with slight uneasiness; however, he did not yield, but recalling all his strength, "I will not swear," said he.—"Then, you must die," replied the president, calmly. M. d'Epinay became very pale; he looked round him a second time; several members of the club were whispering, and getting their arms from under their cloaks. "General," said the president, "do not alarm yourself, you are among men of honor, who will use every means to convince you before resorting to the last extremity; but, as you have said, you are among conspirators, you are in possession of our secret, and you must restore it to us." A significant silence followed these words, and as the general did not reply,—"Close the doors," said the president to the door-keeper. The same deadly silence succeeded these words. Then the general advanced, and making a violent effort to control his feelings,—"I have a son," said he, "and I

ought to think of him, finding myself among assassins."—"General," said the chief of the assembly, proudly, "one man has always the right to insult fifty—it is the privilege of weakness. But he does wrong to use his privilege. Follow my advice, swear, and do not insult." The general, again daunted by the superiority of the chief, hesitated a moment; then advancing to the president's desk,—"What is the form?" said he.

"'"It is this: 'I swear by my honor not to reveal to any one what I have seen and heard on the 5th of February, 1815, between nine and ten o'clock in the evening, and I declare myself worthy of death should I ever violate this oath'" The general appeared to be affected by a nervous shudder, which prevented his answering for some moments; then overcoming his manifest repugnance, he pronounced the required oath, but in so low a tone as to be scarcely audible to a majority of the members, who insisted on his repeating it clearly and distinctly, which he did

"'"Now am I at liberty to retire?" said the general The president rose, appointed three members to accompany him, and got into the carriage with the general, after bandaging his eyes. One of those three members was the coachman who had driven them there. The other members silently dispersed. "Where do you wish to be taken?" asked the president.—"Anywhere out of your presence," replied M. d'Epinay.—"Beware, sir," replied the president; "you are no longer in the assembly, and have only to do with individuals; do not insult them unless you wish to be held responsible." But, instead of listening, M d'Epinay went on,—"You are still as brave in your carriage as in your assembly because you are still four against one." The president stopped the coach They were at that part of the Quai des Ormes where the steps lead down to the river. "Why do you stop here?" asked d'Epinay.—"Because, sir," said the president, "you have insulted a man, and that man will not go one step farther without demanding honorable reparation"—"Another method of assassination?" said the general, shrugging his shoulders.—"Make no noise, sir, unless you wish me to consider you as one of those men whom you designated just now as cowards, who take their weakness for a shield. You are alone, one alone shall answer you; you have a sword by your side, I have one in my cane, you have no witness, one of these gentlemen will serve you. Now, if you please, remove your bandage." The general tore the handkerchief from his eyes. "At last," said he, "I shall know with whom I have to do." They opened the door; the four men alighted'"

Franz again interrupted himself, and wiped the cold drops from his brow; there was something awful in hearing the son, trembling and pale, read aloud these details of his father's death, which had hitherto remained unknown. Valentine clasped her hands as if in prayer. Noirtier looked at Villefort with an almost sublime expression of contempt and pride.

Franz continued:

"'It was, as we said, the 5th of February. For three days there had been five or six degrees of frost; the steps were covered with ice. The general was stout and tall, the president offered him the side of the railing to assist him in getting down. The two witnesses followed. It was a dark night. The ground from the steps to the river was covered with snow and hoar frost, the water of the river looked black and deep. One of the seconds went for a lantern in a coal-barge near, and by its light they examined the arms. The president's sword, which was simply, as he had said, one he carried in his cane, was five inches shorter than the general's, and had no guard. General d'Epinay proposed to cast lots for the swords, but the president said it was he who had given the provocation, and when he had given it he had supposed each would use his own arms. The witnesses endeavored to insist, but the president bade them be silent. The lantern was placed on the ground, the two adversaries arranged themselves, and the duel commenced The light made the two swords appear like flashes of lightning; as for the men, they were scarce perceptible, the darkness was so great. M. le Général d'Epinay passed for one of the best swordsmen in the army, but he was pressed so closely in the onset that he stepped back and fell. The witnesses thought he was dead, but his adversary, who knew he had not touched him, offered him the assistance of his hand to rise. The circumstance irritated instead of calming the general, and he rushed on his adversary. But his opponent did not step back an inch, but received him on his sword. Three times the general drew back, and finding himself foiled, returned to the charge. At the

third he fell again. They thought he slipped, as at first, and the witnesses, seeing he did not move, approached and endeavored to raise him, but the one who passed his arm around the body found it was moistened with blood. The general, who had almost fainted, revived. "Ah!" said he, "they have sent some fencing-master to fight with me." The president, without answering, approached the witness who held the lantern, and raising his sleeve, showed him two wounds he had received in his arm; then opening his coat, and unbuttoning his waistcoat, displayed his side, pierced with a third wound. Still he had not even uttered a sigh. General d'Epinay died five minutes after.'"

Franz read these last words in a voice so choked that they were hardly audible, and then stopped, passing his hand over his eyes as if to dispel a cloud; but after a moment's silence, he continued:

"'The president went up the steps, after replacing his sword in his cane; a track of blood on the snow marked his course. He had scarcely arrived at the top when he heard a heavy splash in the water — it was the general's body, which the witnesses had just thrown into the river after ascertaining he was dead. The general fell, then, in a loyal duel, and not entrapped into an ambush, as it might have been reported. In proof of this, we have signed this paper to establish the truth of the facts, lest the moment should arrive when either of the actors in this terrible scene should be accused of premeditated murder or of infringement of the laws of honor.

"'Signed, BEAUREPAIRE, DUCHAMPY and LECHARPAL.'"

When Franz had finished reading this account, so dreadful for a son,—when Valentine, pale with emotion, had wiped away a tear,—when Villefort, trembling, and crouched in a corner, had endeavored to lessen the storm by supplicating glances at the implacable old man,—

"Sir," said d'Epinay to Noirtier, "since you are well acquainted with all these details, which are attested by honorable signatures,—since you appear to take some interest in me, although you have only manifested it hitherto by causing me sorrow, refuse me not one final satisfaction — tell me the name of the president of the club, that I may at least know who killed my father."

Villefort mechanically felt for the handle of the door; Valentine, who understood sooner than any one her grandfather's answer, and who had often seen two scars upon his right arm, drew back a few steps.

"Mademoiselle," said Franz, turning toward Valentine, "unite your efforts with mine to find out the name of the man who made me an orphan at two years of age." Valentine remained dumb and motionless.

"Hold, sir!" said Villefort, "do not prolong this dreadful scene. The names have been purposely concealed; my father himself does not know who this president was, and if he knows he cannot tell you; proper names are not in the dictionary."

"Oh, misery!" cried Franz; "the only hope which sustained me and enabled me to read to the end was that of knowing, at least, the name of him who killed my father! Sir! sir!" cried he, turning to Noirtier, "do what you can!—make me understand in some way!"

"Yes," replied Noirtier.

"Oh, mademoiselle! mademoiselle!" cried Franz, "your grandfather says he can indicate the person. Help me! lend me your assistance!"

Noirtier looked at the dictionary. Franz took it with a nervous trembling, and repeated the letters of the alphabet successively, until he came to M. At that letter, the old man signified "Yes."

"M," repeated Franz. The young man's finger glided over the words, but at each one Noirtier answered by a negative sign. Valentine hid her head between her hands. At length, Franz arrived at the word MYSELF.

"Yes!"

"You!" cried Franz, whose hair stood on end; "you, M. Noirtier!—you killed my father?"

"Yes," replied Noirtier, fixing a majestic look on the young man. Franz fell powerless on a chair; Villefort opened the door and escaped, for the idea had entered his mind to stifle the little remaining life in the heart of this terrible old man.

CHAPTER LXXVI

PROGRESS OF CAVALCANTI THE YOUNGER

MEANWHILE Cavalcanti the elder had returned to his service, not in the army of his majesty the Emperor of Austria, but at the gaming-table of the baths of Lucca, of which he was one of the most assiduous courtiers. It need not be said that he had carried with him every farthing that had been allowed for his journey and as a reward for the majestic and solemn manner in which he had maintained his character of father.

Andrea at his departure inherited all the papers which proved that he had indeed the honor of being the son of the Marquis Bartolomeo Cavalcanti and the Marchioness Oliva Corsinari. He was now fairly launched in that Parisian society which gives such ready access to foreigners, and treats them, not as what they really are, but as what they wish to be considered. Besides, what is required of a young man in Paris?—to speak its language tolerably, to make a good appearance, to be a good card-player, and pay in cash. They are certainly less particular with a foreigner than with a Frenchman. Andrea had, then, in a fortnight, attained a very fair position. He was entitled M. le Comte; he was said to possess fifty thousand livres per annum; and his father's immense riches, buried in the quarries of Saravezza, were a constant theme. A learned man, before whom the last circumstance was mentioned as a fact, declared he had seen the quarries in question, which gave great weight to assertions hitherto somewhat doubtful, but which now assumed the garb of reality.

Such was the state of society in Paris at the period we bring before our readers, when Monte-Cristo went one evening to pay Danglars a visit. Danglars was out, but the count was asked to go and see the baroness, and he accepted the invitation. It was never without a nervous shudder, since the dinner at Auteuil and the events which followed it, that Madame Danglars heard Monte-Cristo's name announced.

If he did not come, the painful sensation became most intense; if, on the contrary, he appeared, his noble countenance, his brilliant eyes, his amiability, his polite attention even toward Madame Danglars, soon dispelled every impression of fear. It appeared impossible to the baroness

that a man of such delightfully pleasing manners should entertain evil designs against her; besides, the most corrupt minds only suspect evil when it would answer some interested end—unless injury is repugnant to every mind.

When Monte-Cristo entered the boudoir, to which we have already once introduced our readers, and where the baroness was examining some drawings, which her daughter passed to her after having looked at them with Cavalcanti, his presence soon produced its usual effect; and it was with smiles that the baroness received the count, although she had been a little disconcerted at the announcement of his name. The latter embraced the whole scene at a glance.

The baroness was partially reclining on a causeuse, Eugénie sat near her, and Cavalcanti was standing. Cavalcanti, dressed in black, like one of Goethe's heroes, with japanned shoes and open white silk stockings, passed a white and tolerably nice-looking hand through his light hair, in the midst of which sparkled a diamond, which, in spite of Monte-Cristo's advice, the vain young man had been unable to resist putting on his little finger. This movement was accompanied by killing glances at Mademoiselle Danglars, and sighs addressed to the same party.

Mademoiselle Danglars was still the same—cold, beautiful, and satirical. Not one of these glances, nor one sigh, was lost on her; they might have been said to fall on the shield of Minerva, which some philosophers assert protected sometimes the breast of Sappho. Eugénie bowed coldly to the count, and availed herself of the first moment when the conversation became earnest to escape to her study, whence very soon two cheerful and laughing voices being heard, in connection with the first notes of the piano, assured Monte-Cristo that Mademoiselle Danglars preferred to his society and to that of Cavalcanti the company of Mademoiselle Louise d'Armilly, her singing governess.

It was then, especially while conversing with Madame Danglars, and apparently absorbed by the charm of the conversation, the count remarked M. Andrea Cavalcanti's solicitude, his manner of listening to the music at the door he dared not pass, and of manifesting his admiration.

The banker soon returned. His first look was certainly directed toward Monte-Cristo, but the second was for Andrea. As for his wife, he bowed to her in the way in which some husbands do to their wives, but which bachelors will never comprehend, until a very extensive code is published on conjugal life.

"Have not the ladies invited you to join them at the piano?" said Danglars to Andrea.

"Alas! no, sir," replied Andrea, with a sigh, still more remarkable than the former ones. Danglars immediately advanced toward the door and opened it.

The two young ladies were seen seated on the same chair, at the piano, accompanying themselves, each with one hand, a fancy to which they had accustomed themselves, and performed admirably. Mademoiselle d'Armilly, whom they then perceived through the open door-way, formed with Eugénie one of those living pictures of which the Germans are so fond. She was of a sufficiently remarkable style of beauty, or rather of exquisite gracefulness — a little pale fairy-like figure, with

large fair curls falling on her neck, which was rather too long, as Perugino sometimes makes those of his Virgins, and her eyes dull from fatigue. She was said to have a weak chest, and like Antonia of the "Violon de Crémone," she would die one day while singing.

Monte-Cristo cast one rapid and curious glance round this sanctum; it was the first time he had ever seen Mademoiselle d'Armilly, of whom he had heard much.

"Well!" said the banker to his daughter, "are we then all to be excluded?"

He then led the young man into the study, and, either by chance or manœuvre, the door was partially closed after Andrea, so that from the place where they sat neither the count nor the baroness could see anything; but as the banker had accompanied Andrea, Madame Danglars appeared to take no notice of it.

The count soon heard Andrea's voice, singing a Corsican song, accompanied by the piano. While the count smiled at hearing this song, which made him lose sight of Andrea in the recollection of Benedetto, Madame Danglars was boasting to Monte-Cristo of her husband's strength of mind, who that very morning had lost three or four hundred thousand francs by a failure at Milan. The praise was well deserved, for had not the count heard it from the baroness, or by one of those means by which he knew everything, the baron's countenance would not have led him to suspect it.

"Hem!" thought Monte-Cristo, "he begins to conceal his losses; a month since he boasted of them."

Then aloud,—"Oh! madame, M. Danglars is so skillful, he will soon regain at the Bourse what he loses elsewhere."

"I see you are maintaining an erroneous idea, as well as many more," said Madame Danglars.

"What is it?" said Monte-Cristo.

"That M. Danglars speculates, whereas he never does so."

"Truly, madame, I recollect M. Debray told me —— apropos, what has become of him? I have seen nothing of him the last three or four days."

"Nor I," said Madame Danglars; "but you began a sentence, sir, and did not finish."

"Which?"

"M. Debray had told you——"

"Truly, he told me it was you who sacrificed to the demon of speculation."

"I was once very fond of it, but I am not so now."

"Then you are wrong, madame. Fortune is precarious; and if I were a woman, and fate had made me a banker's wife, whatever might be my confidence in my husband's good fortune, still, in speculation, you know, there is great risk. Well! I would secure for myself a fortune independent of him, even if I acquired it by placing my interest in hands unknown to him." Madame Danglars blushed, in spite of all her efforts.

"Stay," said Monte-Cristo, as though he had not observed her confusion, "I have heard of a lucky hit that was made yesterday on the Neapolitan bonds"

"I have none — nor have I ever possessed any, but really we have talked long enough of money, count, we are like two stockbrokers; have you heard how fate is persecuting the poor Villeforts?"

"What has happened?" said the count, apparently ignorant of all

"You know the Marquis de Saint-Méran died a few days after he had set out on his journey to Paris, and the marchioness a few days after her arrival?"

"Yes," said Monte-Cristo, "I have heard that; but, as *Claudius* said to *Hamlet*, 'it is a law of nature; their fathers died before them, and they mourned their loss; they will die before their children, who will, in their turn, grieve for them'"

"But that is not all"

"Not all!"

"No; they were going to marry their daughter ——"

"To M Franz d'Epinay Is it broken off?"

"Yesterday morning, it appears, Franz declined"

"Indeed! And is the reason known?"

"No"

"How extraordinary! And how does M de Villefort bear it?"

"As usual Like a philosopher."

Danglars returned at this moment alone

"Well!" said the baroness, "do you leave M. Cavalcanti with your daughter?"

"And Mademoiselle d'Armilly," said the banker; "do you consider her no one?" Then, turning to Monte-Cristo, he said, "Prince Cavalcanti is a charming young man, is he not? But is he really a prince?"

"I will not answer for it," said Monte-Cristo "His father was introduced to me as a marquis, so he ought to be a count, but I do not think he has much claim to that title."

"Why?" said the banker "If he is a prince, he is wrong not to maintain his rank; I do not like any one to deny his origin"

"Oh! you are a pure democrat," said Monte-Cristo, smiling

"But do you see to what you are exposing yourself? If, perchance, M. de Morcerf came, he would find M. Cavalcanti in that room, where he, the betrothed of Eugénie, has never been admitted"

"You may well say perchance," replied the banker; "for he comes so seldom, it would seem only chance that brings him"

"But should he come, and find that young man with your daughter, he might be displeased"

"He! you are mistaken; M. Albert would not do us the honor to be jealous; he does not like Eugénie sufficiently. Besides, I care not for his displeasure."

"Still, situated as we are ——"

"Yes, do you know how we are situated? At his mother's ball he danced once with Eugénie, and M. Cavalcanti three times, and he took no notice of it."

The valet announced M. le Vicomte Albert de Morcerf. The baroness rose hastily, and was going into the study, when Danglars stopped her.

"Stay!" said he.

She looked at him in amazement. Monte-Cristo appeared to be unconscious of what passed.

Albert entered, looking very handsome and in high spirits. He bowed politely to the baroness, familiarly to Danglars, and affectionately to Monte-Cristo. Then turning to the baroness,—"May I ask how Mademoiselle Danglars is?" said he.

"She is quite well," replied Danglars, quickly; "she is at the piano with M. Cavalcanti."

Albert preserved his calm and indifferent manner; he might feel perhaps annoyed, but he knew Monte-Cristo's eye was on him. "M. Cavalcanti has a fine tenor voice," said he, "and Mademoiselle Eugénie a splendid soprano; and then she plays on the piano like Thalberg. The concert must be a delightful one."

"They suit each other remarkably well," said Danglars.

Albert appeared not to notice this remark, which was, however, so rude that Madame Danglars blushed.

"I, too," said the young man, "am a musician — at least, my masters used to tell me so; but it is strange that my voice never would suit any other, and a soprano less than any."

Danglars smiled, and seemed to say, It is of no consequence. Then, hoping, doubtless, to effect his purpose, he said:

"The prince and my daughter were universally admired yesterday. You were not of the party, M. de Morcerf?"

"What prince?" asked Albert.

"Prince Cavalcanti," said Danglars, who persisted in giving the young man that title.

"Pardon me," said Albert, "I was not aware he was a prince. And Prince Cavalcanti sang with Mademoiselle Eugénie yesterday? It must have been charming, indeed. I regret not having heard them. But I was unable to accept your invitation, having promised to accompany my mother to a German concert given by the Countess of Château-Renaud."

Then after a rather awkward silence. "May I also be allowed," said de Morcerf, "to pay my respects to Mademoiselle Danglars?"

"Wait a moment," said the banker, stopping the young man; "do you hear that delightful cavatina? Ta, ta, ta, ti, ta, ti, ta; it is charming,

let them finish — one moment. Bravo! bravi! brava!" The banker was enthusiastic in his applause.

"Indeed," said Albert, "it is exquisite; it is impossible to understand the music of his country better than Prince Cavalcanti does. You said prince, did you not? But he can easily become one, if he is not already; it is no uncommon thing in Italy. But to return to the charming musicians — you should give us a treat, Danglars, without telling them there is a stranger. Ask them to sing one more song; it is so delightful to hear music in the distance, when the musicians are unrestrained by observation."

Danglars was quite annoyed by the young man's indifference. He took Monte-Cristo aside.

"What do you think of our lover?" said he.

"He appears cool! But, then, your word is given."

"Yes, doubtless, I have promised to give my daughter to a man who loves her, but not to one who does not. Even if Albert had Cavalcanti's fortune, he is so proud, I would not care to see him marry her."

"Oh!" said Monte-Cristo, "my fondness may blind me, but, I assure you, I consider Morcerf far preferable; and his father's position is good."

"Hem!" said Danglars.

"Why do you doubt?"

"The past — that obscurity on the past."

"But that does not affect the son. A month since you thought well of him; you will understand, I am in despair; I know nothing of young Cavalcanti, although you met at my house?"

"But I do."

"Have you made inquiry?"

"Yes; and I know him to be rich."

"What do you suppose him worth?"

"Fifty thousand per annum; and he is well educated."

"Hem?" said Monte-Cristo in his turn.

"He is a musician."

"So are all Italians."

"Come, count, you do not do that young man justice."

"Well, I acknowledge it annoys me, knowing your connection with the Morcerf family, to see him throw himself in the way." Danglars burst out laughing.

"What a Puritan you are!" said he; "that happens every day."

"But you cannot break it off thus; the Morcerfs are depending on this union."

"Indeed?"

"Positively."

"Then let them explain themselves; you should give the father a hint, you are so intimate with the family."

"I? — where the devil did you find out that?"

"At their ball; it was apparent enough. Why, did not the countess, the proud Mercédès, the disdainful Catalan, who will scarcely open her lips to her oldest acquaintances, take your arm, lead you into the garden into the private walks, and remain there for half an hour?"

"Baron, baron," cried Albert, "why do you not listen; for a man of your musical taste, what barbarism!"

"All right, all right, joke away," replied Danglars; then turning to Monte-Cristo,—

"But will you undertake to speak to the father?"

"Willingly, if you wish it."

"But let it be done explicitly and positively. If he demands my daughter, let him fix the day — declare his conditions: in short, let us either understand each other, or quarrel You understand — no more delay."

"Yes, sir, I will give my attention to the subject"

"I do not say I do it with pleasure, but I do expect him to speak out A banker must, you know, be a slave to his promise." And Danglars sighed as Cavalcanti had done half an hour before.

"Bravo!" cried Morcerf, as the scene closed. Danglars began to look suspiciously at Morcerf, when some one came and whispered a few words to him.

"I shall soon return," said the banker to Monte-Cristo; "wait for me. I shall, perhaps, have something to say to you."

The baroness took advantage of her husband's absence to push open the door of her daughter's study, and Andrea, who was sitting before the piano with Mademoiselle Eugénie, started up like a spring. Albert bowed to Mademoiselle Danglars with a smile, who, not appearing in the least disturbed, returned his bow with her usual coldness. Cavalcanti was evidently embarrassed; he bowed to Morcerf, who replied with the most impertinent look possible. Then Albert launched out in praise of Mademoiselle Danglars' voice, and on his regret that after what he had just heard, he had been unable to be present the previous evening

Cavalcanti being left alone, turned to Monte-Cristo.

"Come," said Madame Danglars, "leave music and compliments, and let us go and take tea"

"Come, Louise," said Mademoiselle Danglars to her friend

They passed into the next drawing-room, where tea was prepared. Just as they were beginning, in the English fashion, to leave the spoons in their cups, the door again opened, and Danglars entered, visibly agitated. Monte-Cristo observed it particularly, and by a look asked the banker for an explanation.

"I have just received my courier from Greece," said Danglars.

"Ah! ah!" said the count; "that was the reason of your running away from us"

"Yes"

"How is King Otho?" asked Albert, in the most sprightly tone.

Danglars cast another suspicious look toward him without answering, and Monte-Cristo turned away to conceal the expression of pity which passed over his features, but which was gone in a moment.

"We shall go together, shall we not?" said Albert to the count.

"If you like," replied the latter.

Albert could not understand the banker's look, and turning to Monte-Cristo, who understood it perfectly,—"Did you see," said he, "how he looked at me?"

"Yes," said the count; "but did you think there was anything particular in his look?"

"Indeed, I did; and what does he mean by his news from Greece?"

"How can I tell you?"

"Because I imagine you have correspondents in that country."

Monte-Cristo smiled significantly.

"Stop," said Albert, "here he comes. I shall compliment Mademoiselle Danglars on her cameo, while the father talks to you."

"If you compliment her at all, let it be on her voice, at least," said Monte-Cristo.

"No, every one would do that."

"My dear viscount, you are dreadfully impertinent."

Albert advanced toward Eugénie, smiling.

Meanwhile, Danglars, stooping to Monte-Cristo's ear,—"Your advice was excellent," said he; "there is a whole history connected with the names Fernand and Janina."

"Indeed!" said Monte-Cristo.

"Yes, I will tell you all; but take away the young man; I cannot endure his presence."

"He is going with me. Shall I send the father to you?"

"Immediately."

"Very well."

The count made a sign to Albert; they bowed to the ladies, and took their leave,—Albert perfectly indifferent to Mademoiselle Danglars's contempt, Monte-Cristo reiterating his advice to Madame Danglars on the prudence a banker's wife should exercise in providing for the future.

Cavalcanti remained master of the field.

CHAPTER LXXVII

HAYDÉE

SCARCELY had the count's horses cleared the angle of the boulevard, than Albert, turning toward the count, burst into a loud fit of laughter,—much too loud, in fact, not to give the idea of its being rather forced.

"Well!" said he, "I will ask you the same question which Charles IX. put to Catherine de Medicis, after the massacre of Saint Bartholomew: 'How have I played my little part?'"

"To what do you allude?" asked Monte-Cristo.

"To the installation of my rival at M. Danglars's!"

"What rival?"

"*Ma foi!* what rival? why, your protégé, M. Andrea Cavalcanti!"

"Ah, no joking, viscount, if you please; I do not patronize M. Andrea—at least, not as concerns M. Danglars."

"I should blame you for that, if the young man really needed your help; but, happily for me, he can dispense with it."

"What! do you think he is paying his addresses?"

"I am certain of it; watch his rolling eyes, listen to his loving sighs. He aspires to the hand of the proud Eugénie. Why, I have made a rhyme, on my word! Well, it was not my fault; never mind, I repeat he aspires to the hand of the proud Eugénie."

"What does that signify, so long as they favor your suit?"

"But it is not the case, my dear count; on the contrary, I am repulsed on all sides."

"What! on both sides!"

"It is so indeed; Mademoiselle Eugénie scarcely answers me, and Mademoiselle d'Armilly, her confidante, does not speak to me at all."

"But the father has the greatest regard possible for you," said Monte-Cristo.

"He? oh, no! he has plunged a thousand daggers into my heart; tragedy-weapons, I own, which, instead of wounding, sheathe their points in their own handles, but daggers which he nevertheless believed to be real and deadly."

"Jealousy indicates affection."

"True; but I am not jealous."

"He is."

"Of whom?—of Debray?"

"No, of you."

"Of me? I will engage to say that before a week is past the door will be closed against me."

"You are mistaken, my dear viscount."

"Prove it to me."

"Do you wish me to do so?"

"Yes."

"Well, I am charged with the commission of endeavoring to induce M. le Comte de Morcerf to make some definite arrangement with the baron."

"By whom are you charged?"

"By the baron himself."

"Oh!" said Albert, with all the cajolery of which he was capable, "you surely will not do that, my dear count."

"Certainly I shall, Albert, as I have promised to do it."

"Well," said Albert, with a sigh, "it seems you are determined to marry me."

"I am determined to try and be on good terms with everybody, at all events," said Monte-Cristo. "But apropos of Debray, how is it that I have not seen him lately at the baron's house?"

"There has been a misunderstanding."

"What, with the baroness?"

"No, with the baron."

"Has he perceived anything?"

"Ah! that is a good joke!"

"Do you think he suspects?" said Monte-Cristo, with a charming *naïveté*.

"Where have you come from, my dear count?" said Albert.

"From Congo, if you will."

"It must be farther off than even that."

"But what do I know of your Parisian husbands?"

"Oh! my dear count, husbands are pretty much the same everywhere; an individual of any country is a fair specimen of the race."

"But then, what can have led to the quarrel between Danglars and Debray? they seemed to understand each other so well!" said Monte-Cristo, with renewed energy.

"Ah! now you are trying to penetrate into the mysteries of Isis, in which I am not initiated. When M. Andrea Cavalcanti has become one of the family, you can ask him that question."

The carriage stopped.

"Here we are," said Monte-Cristo; "it is only half-past ten o'clock, come in."

"Certainly, I will."

"My carriage shall take you back."

"No, thank you; I gave orders for my *coupé* to follow me."

"There it is, then," said Monte-Cristo, as he stepped out of the carriage. They both went into the house; the drawing-room was lighted up—they entered it. "You will make tea for us, Baptistin," said the count. Baptistin left the room without waiting to answer, and in two seconds re-appeared, bringing a tray, ready prepared, and appearing to have sprung from the ground, like the repasts in fairy tales.

"Really, my dear count," said Morcerf, "what I admire in you is, not so much your riches, for perhaps there are people wealthier than you, nor is it your wit, for Beaumarchais might have possessed as much,—but it is your manner of being served, without any questions, in a moment, in a second; it is as if they guessed what you wanted by your manner of ringing, and made a point of keeping everything you want in constant readiness."

"What you say is perhaps true; they know my habits. For instance, you shall see; how do you wish to occupy yourself during tea-time?"

"Well, I should like to smoke."

Monte-Cristo took the gong and struck it once. In about the space of a second a private door opened, and Ali appeared, bringing two chibouks filled with excellent latakia.

"It is quite wonderful!" said Albert.

"Oh, no, it is as simple as possible," replied Monte-Cristo. "Ali knows I generally smoke whilst I am taking my tea or coffee; he has heard that I ordered tea; he knows that I brought you home with me; when I summoned him he guessed the reason, and, as he comes from a country where hospitality is especially manifested by the pipe, he brings two chibouks instead of one."

"Certainly you give a most common-place air to your explanation, but it is not the less true that you—— Ah! but what do I hear?" and Morcerf inclined his head toward the door, through which sounds seemed to issue resembling those of a guitar.

"*Ma foi!* my dear viscount, you are fated to hear music this evening; you have only escaped from the piano of Mademoiselle Danglars to be attacked by the guzla of Haydée."

"Haydée! what an adorable name! Are there, then, really women who bear the name of Haydée anywhere but in Byron's poems?"

"Certainly there are. Haydée is a very uncommon name in France, but it is common enough in Albania and Epirus; it is as if you said, for example, Chastity, Modesty, Innocence,—it is a kind of baptismal name, as you Parisians call it."

"Oh, that is charming!" said Albert; "how I should like to hear my countrywomen called Mademoiselle Goodness, Mademoiselle Silence, Mademoiselle Christian Charity! Only think, then, if Mademoiselle Danglars, instead of being called Claire Marie Eugénie, had been named Mademoiselle Chastity Modesty Innocence Danglars; what a fine effect that would have produced on the announcement of her marriage!"

"Silence!" said the count, "do not joke in so loud a tone; Haydée may hear you, perhaps."

"And you think she would be angry?"

"No, certainly not," said the count, with a haughty expression.

"She is very amiable, then, is she not?" said Albert.

"It is not to be called amiability, it is her duty; a slave does not dictate to a master."

"Come, you are joking yourself now; are there slaves nowadays?"

"Undoubtedly, as Haydée is mine."

"Really, count, you do nothing, and have nothing like other people. The slave of M. le Comte de Monte-Cristo! why, it is a rank of itself in France; and from the way in which you lavish money, it is a place that must be worth a hundred thousand francs a year."

"A hundred thousand francs! the poor girl originally possessed much more than that; she was born to treasures, to which those in the 'Thousand and One Nights' are trifles."

"She must be a princess, then?"

"You are right, and one of the greatest in her country, too."

"I thought so. But how did it happen that such a great princess became a slave?"

"How was it that Dionysius the Tyrant became a school-master? The fortune of war, my dear viscount,—the caprice of fortune."

"And is her name a secret?"

"For the world it is; but not for you, my dear viscount, who are one of my friends, and on whose silence I may rely, if I enjoin it; may I not do so?"

"Certainly! on my word of honor."

"You know the history of the Pacha of Janina!"

"Of Ali Tebelin! oh! yes! it was in his service that my father made his fortune."

Vasiliki.

"True, I had forgotten that."

"Well! what is Haydée to Ali Telebin?"

"Merely his daughter."

"What? the daughter of Ali Pacha?"

"And the beautiful Vasiliki."

"And your slave?"

"*Ma foi!* yes."

"But how did she become so?"

"Why, I bought her one day as I was passing through the market at Constantinople."

"Wonderful! With you, count, one does not live, but dream. Now, I am perhaps going to make an imprudent request, but ——"

"Say on."

"But, since you go out with Haydée, and sometimes even take her to the Opera ——"

"Well?"

"I think I may venture to ask you this favor."

"You may venture to ask me anything."

"Well, then, my dear count, present me to your princess."

"I will do so; but on two conditions."

"I accept them at once."

"The first is, that you will never tell any one that I have granted the interview."

"Very well," said Albert, extending his hand; "I swear I will not."

"The second is, that you will not tell her that your father ever served hers."

"I swear to that too!"

"Enough, viscount; you will remember those two vows, will you not? But I know you to be a man of honor."

The count again struck the gong. Ali re-appeared. "Tell Haydée," said he, "that I will take coffee with her, and give her to understand that I desire permission to present one of my friends to her."

Ali bowed and left the room.

"Now, understand me," said the count, "no direct questions, my dear Morcerf; if you wish to know anything, tell me, and I will ask her."

"Agreed."

Ali re-appeared for the third time, and drew back the tapestried hanging which concealed the door, to signify to his master and Albert that they were at liberty to pass on.

"Let us go in," said Monte-Cristo.

Albert passed his hand through his hair, and curled his mustache, and followed the count into the room, the latter having previously resumed his hat and gloves. Ali was stationed as a kind of advanced guard, and the door was kept by the three French *femmes-de-chambre*, commanded by Myrtho.

Haydée was awaiting her visitors in the first room, which was the drawing-room. Her large eyes were dilated with surprise, for it was the first time that any man, except Monte-Cristo, had entered. She was sitting on a sofa in an angle of the room, with her legs crossed, and had made for herself, as it were, a kind of nest in the rich Indian silks and embroideries. Near her was the instrument on which she had just been

playing; it was elegantly fashioned, and worthy of its mistress. On perceiving Monte-Cristo, she rose and welcomed him with a kind of smile peculiar to herself, expressive at once of filial affection and of love. Monte-Cristo advanced toward her and extended his hand, which she, as usual, raised to her lips.

Albert remained near the door, fascinated by the sight of such surpassing beauty, beheld, as it was, for the first time, and of which an inhabitant of more northern climes could form no idea.

"Whom do you bring?" asked the young girl, in Romaic, of Monte-Cristo; "is it a brother, a friend, a simple acquaintance, or an enemy?"

"A friend," said Monte-Cristo, in the same language.

"What is his name?"

"Viscount Albert; it is the same whom I rescued from the hands of the banditti at Rome."

"In what language would you like me to converse with him?"

Monte-Cristo turned to Albert. "Do you know modern Greek?" asked he.

"Alas! no," said Albert; "nor even ancient Greek, my dear count; never had Homer or Plato a poorer or more scornful scholar than myself."

"Then," said Haydée, proving by her remark that she had quite understood Monte-Cristo's question and Albert's answer, "then I will speak either in French or Italian, if my lord so wills it."

Monte-Cristo reflected one instant. "You will speak in Italian," said he.

Then, turning toward Albert,—"It is a pity you do not understand either ancient or modern Greek, both of which Haydée speaks so fluently; the poor child will be obliged to talk to you in Italian, which will give you but a very false idea of her powers of conversation."

The count made a sign to Haydée to address his visitor. "Sir, you are welcome as the friend of my lord and master," she said in excellent Tuscan, and with that soft Roman accent which makes the language of Dante as sonorous as that of Homer. "Ali, coffee and pipes." When he had left the room to execute the orders of his young mistress, she beckoned Albert to approach nearer to her. Monte-Cristo and Morcerf drew their seats toward a small table, on which were arranged music, drawings, and vases of flowers. Ali then entered, bringing coffee and chibouks; as to Baptistin, this portion of the building was interdicted to him. Albert refused the pipe which the Nubian offered him.

"Oh, take it—take it," said the count; "Haydée is almost as civilized as a Parisian; the smell of a Havana is disagreeable to her, but the tobacco of the East is a perfume, you know."

Ali left the room. The cups of coffee were prepared, with the addition of a sugar-bowl for Albert. Monte-Cristo and Haydée took the liquor in the Arabian manner,—that is to say, without sugar. Haydée took the Japan porcelain cup in her little slender fingers, and conveyed it to her mouth with all the innocent pleasure of a child when eating or drinking something that it likes. At this moment two women entered, bringing salvers filled with ices and sherbet, which they placed on two small tables appropriated to that purpose.

"My dear host, and you, signora," said Albert, in Italian, "excuse my apparent stupidity. I am quite bewildered, and it is natural that it should be so. Here I am in the heart of Paris, but a moment ago I heard the rumbling of the omnibuses and the tinkling of the bells of the lemonade-sellers, and now I am transported to the East; not such as I have seen it, but such as my dreams have painted it Oh! signora, if I could but speak Greek, your conversation, added to the fairy-scene which surrounds me, would furnish an evening that I could never forget."

"I speak sufficient Italian to converse with you, sir," said Haydée, quietly; "and if you like what is Eastern, I will do my best to make you find it here."

"On what subject shall I converse with her?" said Albert, in a low tone to Monte-Cristo.

"Just what you please, her country, her youthful reminiscences; or, if you like it better, you can talk of Rome, Naples, or Florence."

"Oh!" said Albert, "it is of no use to be in the company of a Greek if one converses just in the same style as with a Parisian; let me speak to her of the East."

"Do so, then, for of all themes that will be the most agreeable"

Albert turned toward Haydée "At what age did you leave Greece, signora?" asked he.

"When I was but five years old," replied Haydée.

"And have you any recollection of your country?"

"When I shut my eyes I see it all again. The mind has its eyes as well as the body; the former may forget; the latter always remembers."

"And how far back into the past do your recollections extend?"

"I could scarcely walk when my mother, who was called Vasiliki, which means royal," said the young girl, tossing her head proudly, "took me by the hand, and after putting in our purse all the money we possessed, we went out, both covered with veils, to solicit alms for the prisoners, saying, 'He who giveth to the poor lendeth to the Lord.' Then, when our purse was full, we returned to the palace, and without saying a word to my father, we sent all the money that had been given to us, as poor women, to the *hegonmenos* of the convent, where it was divided amongst the prisoners."

"And how old were you at that time?"

"I was three years old," said Haydée.

"Then you remember all which was passing around you when you were but three years old?" said Albert.

"All."

"Count," said Albert, in a low tone to Monte-Cristo, "do allow the signora to tell me something of her history. You prohibited my mentioning my father, but perhaps she will speak of him, and you have no idea how delighted I should be to hear our name pronounced by such beautiful lips."

Monte-Cristo turned to Haydée, and with an expression of countenance which commanded her to pay the most implicit attention to his words, he said in Greek, "Πατρὸς μὲν ἄτην μῆζε τὸ ὄνομα προδότου καὶ προδοσίαν εἰπὲ ἡμῖν,"—that is, "Tell us the fate of your father; but neither the name of the traitor nor the treason." Haydée sighed deeply, and a shade of sadness clouded her beautiful brow.

"What are you saying to her?" said Morcerf, in an undertone.

"I again reminded her that you were a friend, and that she need not conceal anything from you."

"Then," said Albert, "this pious pilgrimage in behalf of the prisoners was your first remembrance; what is the next?"

"Oh! then I remember sitting under the shade of some sycamore trees, on the borders of a lake, in the waters of which the trembling foliage was reflected as in a mirror. Under the oldest and thickest of these trees, reclining on cushions, sat my father; my mother was at his feet, and I, childlike, amused myself by playing with his long, white beard, which descended to his girdle, or with the diamond hilt of the cimeter attached to his girdle. Then, from time to time, there came to him an Albanian, who said something, to which I paid no attention, but which he always answered in the same tone of voice, either 'Kill,' or 'Pardon.'"

"It is very strange," said Albert, "to hear such words from the mouth of any but an actress on the stage; and one needs to be saying to one's self, 'This is no fiction,' in order to believe it. And how does France appear in your eyes, accustomed as they have been to gaze on such enchanted scenes?"

"I think it is a fine country," said Haydée, "but I see France as it really is, because I see it with the eyes of a woman; whereas my own country, which I saw with the eyes of a child, is enveloped in an atmosphere, luminous or otherwise, according as my remembrances of it are sad or joyous."

"So young," said Albert, falling into commonplace, "how you must have suffered!"

Haydée turned her eyes toward Monte-Cristo, who, making at the same time some imperceptible sign, murmured:

"Εἰπέ—speak."

"Nothing is so impressed on the mind as the memory of early childhood, and, with the exception of the two scenes I have described to you, all my earliest reminiscences are sad."

"Speak, speak, signora," said Albert, "I am listening with the most intense interest."

Haydée answered with a melancholy smile. "You wish me, then, to relate the history of my past sorrows?" said she.

"I beg you to do so," replied Albert.

"Well! I was but four years old, when one night I was suddenly awoke by my mother. We were in the palace of Janina; she snatched me from the cushions on which I was sleeping, and on opening my eyes I saw hers were filled with tears. She took me away without speaking. When I saw her weeping, I began to cry too. 'Silence, child!' said she. At other times, in spite of maternal endearments or threats, I had, with a child's caprice, been accustomed to continue to cry; but on this occasion there was an intonation of such extreme terror in my mother's voice, that I ceased at once. She bore me rapidly away. I saw then that we were descending a large staircase; around us all my mother's servants carrying trunks, bags, ornaments, jewels, purses of gold, were hurrying away in the greatest distraction. Behind the women came a guard of twenty men, armed with long guns and pistols, and dressed in the costume which the Greeks have assumed since they have again become a nation. You may imagine there was something startling and ominous," said Haydée, shaking her head, and turning pale at the mere remembrance of the scene, "in this long file of slaves and women only half-aroused from sleep, or at least, so they appeared to me, who was myself scarcely awake. Here and there, on the walls of the staircase, were reflected gigantic shadows, which trembled in the light of the pine-torches."

"'Quick!' said a voice at the end of the gallery. This voice made every one bow before it, like the wind passing over a field of corn. As for me, it made me tremble. This voice was that of my father. He marched the last, clothed in his splendid robes, and holding in his hand the carbine with which your emperor presented him, and leaning on his favorite Selim, he drove us all before him, as a shepherd would his straggling flock. My father," said Haydée, raising her head, "was that illustrious man known in Europe under the name of Ali Tebelin, pacha of Janina, and before whom Turkey trembled."

Albert, without knowing why, started on hearing these words pronounced with such a haughty and dignified accent; it appeared to him as if there was something supernaturally gloomy and terrible in the expression which gleamed from the brilliant eyes of Haydée at this moment; she appeared like a Pythoness evoking a specter, as she recalled to his mind the remembrance of the fearful death of this man, to the news of which all Europe had listened with horror.

"Soon," said Haydée, "we halted on our march, and found ourselves on the borders of a lake. My mother pressed me to her throbbing heart, and, at the distance of a few paces, I saw my father, who was glancing anxiously around. Four marble steps led down to the water's edge, and below them was a boat floating. From where we stood I could see, in the middle of the lake, a large black mass; it was the kiosk to which we were going. This kiosk appeared to me to be at a considerable distance, perhaps on account of the darkness. We stepped into the boat.

I remember well that the oars made no noise whatever in striking the water, and when I leaned over to ascertain the cause, I saw they were muffled with the sashes of our Palicares. Besides the rowers, the boat contained only the women, my father, mother, Selim, and myself. The

Palicares had remained on the shore of the lake; kneeling on the lowest of the marble steps, and making a rampart of the three others, in case of pursuit. Our bark flew like the wind. 'Why does the boat go so fast?' asked I of my mother.

"'Silence, child! Hush! we are flying.' I did not understand. Why should my father fly?—he, the all-powerful—he, before whom others were accustomed to fly—he, who had taken for his device—

'They hate me, then they fear me!'

"It was indeed a flight which my father was trying to effect. I have been told since that the garrison of the castle of Janina, fatigued with long service——"

Here Haydée cast a significant glance at Monte-Cristo, whose eyes had been riveted on her countenance during the whole course of her narrative. The young girl then continued slowly, like a person who is either inventing or suppressing some feature of the history which he is relating.

"You were saying, signora," said Albert, who was paying the most implicit attention to the recital, "that the garrison of Janina, fatigued with long service——"

"Had treated with the Seraskier Kourchid, who had been sent by the sultan to seize my father. It was then that Ali Tebelin took the resolution of retiring, after having sent to the sultan a French officer in whom he reposed great confidence, to the asylum which he had long before prepared for himself, and which he called *Kataphygion*, or the refuge."

"And this officer," asked Albert, "do you remember his name, signora?"

Monte-Cristo exchanged a rapid glance with the young girl, which was quite unperceived by Albert.

"No," said she, "I do not remember it just at this moment; but if it should occur to me presently, I will tell you."

Albert was on the point of pronouncing his father's name, when Monte-Cristo gently held up his finger in token of reproach; the young man recollected his vow, and was silent.

"It was toward this kiosk that we were rowing. A ground-floor, ornamented with arabesques, bathing its terraces in the water, and another floor, looking on the lake, was all which was visible to the eye. But beneath the ground-floor, stretching out into the island, was a large subterraneous cavern, to which my mother, myself, and the women were conducted. In this place were together 60,000 purses and 200 barrels; the purses contained 25,000,000 of money in gold, and the barrels were filled with 30,000 pounds of gun-powder.

"Near these barrels stood Selim, my father's favorite, whom I mentioned to you just now He was on watch day and night, with a lance in his hand, at the end of which was a lighted match, and he had orders to blow up all — kiosk, guards, women, gold, and Ali Tebelin himself — at the first signal given by my father. I remember well that the slaves, knowing this terrible deposit, passed days and nights in praying, crying, and groaning. As for me, I can never forget the pale complexion and black eye of the young soldier; and whenever the angel of death comes down to me, I am quite sure I shall recognize Selim. I cannot tell you how long we remained in this state; at that period I did not even know what time meant; sometimes, but very rarely, my father summoned me and my mother to the terrace of the palace; these were my hours of recreation, I, who never saw anything in the dismal cavern but the gloomy countenances of the slaves and the fiery lance of Selim.

"My father was endeavoring to pierce with his eager looks the remotest verge of the horizon, examining every black speck which appeared on the lake, whilst my mother, reclining by his side, rested her head on his shoulder, and I played at his feet, admiring everything I saw with that innocence of childhood which magnifies everything,— the heights of Pindus on the horizon, the castle of Janina rising white and angular from the blue waters of the lake, and the immense masses of black vegetation which, viewed in the distance, gave the idea of lichens clinging to the rocks, but were, in reality, gigantic fir-trees and myrtles

"One morning my father sent for us; we found the pacha calm, but paler than usual. 'Take courage, Vasiliki,' said he, 'to-day arrives the firman of the master, and my fate will be decided If my pardon be complete, we shall return triumphant to Janina; if the news be inauspicious, we must fly this night.'—'But supposing our enemy should not allow us to do so?' said my mother —'Oh! make yourself easy on that head,' said Ali, smiling, 'Selim and his flaming lance will settle that matter. They would be glad to see me dead, but they would not like themselves to die with me.'

"My mother only answered by sighs to these consolations, which she knew did not come from my father's heart. She prepared the iced water which he was constantly drinking, for, since his sojourn at the kiosk, he had been parched by a most violent fever, after which she perfumed his white beard and lighted his chibouk, from which he sat watching the smoke for hours as it was dissipated in air. Presently he made such a sudden movement that I was paralyzed with fear. Then, without taking his eyes from the object which had first attracted his attention, he asked for his telescope. My mother gave it to him, looking whiter than the marble against which she leaned. I saw my father's hand tremble. 'A boat!—two!—three!' murmured my father; —'four!' He then rose, seizing his arms and priming his pistols. 'Vasiliki,' said he to my mother, trembling perceptibly, 'the instant approaches which will decide everything. In the space of half an hour we shall know the sultan's answer. Go into the cavern with Haydée.'—'I will not quit you,' said Vasiliki; 'if you die, my lord, I will die with you.'—'Go to Selim!' cried my father.—'Adieu! my lord,' murmured my mother, determining quietly to wait the approach of death.—'Take away Vasiliki!' said my father to his Palicares.

"As for me, I had been forgotten; I ran toward him; he saw me hold out my arms to him, and he stooped down and pressed my forehead with his lips. Oh! that kiss! it was the last; it is still on my forehead. On descending, we distinguished through the lattice-work several boats which were gradually becoming more distinct. At first they were like black specks, they now looked like birds skimming the surface of the waves. During this time, in the kiosk, at the feet of my father, were seated twenty Palicares, concealed from view by an angle of the wall, and watching with eager eyes the arrival of the boats, and holding, ready, their long guns inlaid with mother-of-pearl and silver. Cartridges in great numbers were lying scattered on the floor; my father looked at his watch, and paced up and down in anguish. This was the scene which presented itself when I quitted my father after that last kiss.

"My mother and I traversed the passage to the tavern. Selim was still at his post, and smiled sadly on us. We fetched our cushions from the other end of the tavern, and sat down by Selim. In great dangers the devoted ones cling to each other; and, young as I was, I quite understood that some imminent danger was hanging over our heads.

Albert had often heard, not from his father, for he never spoke on the subject, but from strangers, the description of the last moments of the vizier of Janina; he had read different accounts of his death, but this history seemed to borrow new life from the voice and expression of the young girl; this living accent and melancholy expression at once charmed and horrified him.

As to Haydée, at these terrible reminiscences, she ceased speaking, her head leaning on her hand like a flower in a storm, and her eyes, gazing on vacancy, seemed still to see the green summit of Pindus, and the blue waters of the Lake of Janina, a magic mirror, reflecting the somber picture which she sketched. Monte-Cristo looked at her with an indescribable expression of interest and pity.

"Go on, my child!" said the count, in the Romaic language.

Haydée looked up abruptly, as if the sonorous tones of Monte-Cristo's voice had awakened her from a dream, and she resumed her narrative.

"It was about four o'clock in the afternoon; and although the day was brilliant out-of-doors, we were in the gloom of the cavern. One single light was burning there, and it appeared like a star set in a heaven of blackness; it was Selim's flaming lance. My mother was a Christian,

and she prayed. Selim repeated from time to time these sacred words: 'God is great!' However, my mother had still some hope. As she was coming down, she thought she recognized the French officer who had been sent to Constantinople, and in whom my father placed so much confidence, for he knew that all the soldiers of the French sultan were naturally noble and generous. She advanced some steps toward the staircase, and listened. 'They are approaching,' said she; 'perhaps they bring us peace and liberty!'

"'What do you fear, Vasiliki?' said Selim, in a voice at once so gentle and yet so proud; 'if they do not bring us peace we will give them death.' And he renewed the flame of his lance with an alacrity which reminded one of a Dionysius of old Crete. But I, who was only a little child, was terrified by this courage, which appeared to me both ferocious and senseless, and I recoiled from this frightful death amidst fire and flame.

"My mother experienced the same sensations, for I felt her tremble. 'Mamma, mamma,' said I, 'are we really to be killed?' And at the sound of my voice the slaves redoubled their cries and prayers.—'My child,' said Vasiliki, 'may God preserve you from ever wishing for that death which to-day you so much dread!' Then, whispering to Selim, she asked what were his master's orders. 'If he send me his poniard, it will signify that the sultan's intentions are not favorable, and I set fire to powder; if he send me his ring, the sultan pardons him, and I leave the magazine.'—'My friend,' said my mother, 'when your master's order arrives, if it is the poniard which he sends, instead of dispatching us by that death which we both dread, kill us with this same poniard.'—'Yes, Vasiliki,' replied Selim, tranquilly.

"Suddenly we heard loud cries; we listened: they were cries of joy; the name of the French officer who had been sent to Constantinople resounded on all sides amongst our Palicares; it was evident that he brought the answer of the sultan, and that it was favorable."

"And do you not remember the Frenchman's name?" said Morcerf, quite ready to aid the memory of the narrator. Monte-Cristo made a sign to him to be silent.

"I do not recollect it," said Haydée.

"The noise increased, steps were heard approaching; they were descending the steps to the cavern. Selim made ready his lance. Soon a figure appeared in the gray twilight, formed by the few rays of daylight which found their way in the entrance of the cavern. 'Who are you?' cried Selim. 'But whoever you may be, I charge you not to advance another step.'—'Glory to the Sultan!' said the figure. 'He grants a full pardon to the Vizier Ali; and not only gives him his life, but restores to him his fortune and his possessions.' My mother uttered a cry of joy, and clasped me to her bosom. 'Stop!' said Selim, seeing that she was about to go out; 'you see I have not yet received the ring.'—'True,' said my mother. And she fell on her knees, at the same time holding me up toward heaven, as if she desired, whilst praying to God in my behalf, to raise me actually to his presence."

And for the second time Haydée stopped, overcome by such violent emotion that the perspiration stood upon her pale brow, and her stifled voice seemed hardly able to find utterance, so parched and dry were her throat and lips.

Monte-Cristo poured a little iced water into a glass, and presented it to her, saying, with a mildness in which was also a shade of command,—"Courage." Haydée dried her eyes, and continued:

"By this time our eyes, habituated to the darkness, had recognized the messenger of the pacha,—it was a friend. Selim had also recognized him; but the brave young man only acknowledged one duty, which was to obey. 'In whose name do you come?' said he to him.—'I come in the name of our master, Ali Tebelin.'—'If you come from Ali himself,' said Selim, 'you know what you were charged to remit to me?'—'Yes,' said the messenger, 'and I bring you his ring.' At these words he raised his hand above his head, but it was too far off, and there was not light enough for Selim, where he was standing, to distinguish and recognize the object presented to his view. 'I do not see what you have in your hand,' said Selim.—'Approach, then,' said the messenger, 'or I will come nearer to you, if you prefer it.'—'I will agree to neither one nor the other,' replied the young soldier; 'place the object which I desire to see in that ray of light where you are, and retire whilst I examine it.'—'Be it so,' said the envoy; and he retired, after having first deposited the token agreed on in the place pointed out.

"Oh! how our hearts palpitated; for it did, indeed, seem to be a ring. But was it my father's ring? Selim, still holding in his hand the lighted match, walked toward the opening in the cavern, and aided by the ray of light, picked up the token.

"'It is well!' said he, kissing it; 'it is my master's ring!' And throwing the match on the ground, he trampled on it and extinguished it. The messenger uttered a cry of joy, and clapped his hands. At this signal four soldiers of the Seraskier Kourchid suddenly appeared, and Selim fell pierced by five blows. Each man had stabbed him separately; and, intoxicated by their crime, though still pale with fear, they rushed into the cavern looking to see if there was any fire, and rolling themselves on the bags of gold. At this moment my mother seized me in her arms, and bounding along turnings, known only to ourselves, she arrived at a private staircase of the kiosk, where was a scene of frightful tumult. The lower rooms were entirely filled with the tchodoars of Kourchid, that is to say, with our enemies. Just as my mother was on the point of pushing open a small door, we heard the voice of the pacha loud and threatening. My mother applied her eye to the crack between the boards; I luckily found a small opening, and looked in. 'What do you want?' said my father to some people who were holding a paper inscribed with characters of gold.—'What we want,' replied one of them, 'is to communicate to you the will of his highness. Do you see this firman?'—'I do,' said my father.—'Well, read it; he demands your head.'

"My father answered with a loud laugh, more frightful than any threat, and he had not ceased when two pistol-shots were discharged by his hands, and killed two men. The Palicares, who were lying around, sprang up and fired; and the room was filled with fire and smoke. At the same instant the firing began on the other side, and the balls penetrated the boards all round us. Oh! how noble, how grand, was the vizier, my father, in the midst of the balls, his cimeter in his hand, and his face black with powder! How his enemies fled before him! 'Selim! Selim!' cried he, 'guardian of the fire, do your duty!'—'Selim is dead!'

replied a voice, which seemed to come from the depths of the earth, 'and you are lost, Ali!' At the same moment an explosion was heard, and the floor of the room was shivered to atoms; the tchodoars were firing underneath; three or four Palicares fell with their bodies literally plowed with wounds.

"My father howled aloud; he plunged his fingers into the holes which the balls had made, and tore up one of the planks entire. But immediately through this opening twenty shots were fired, and the flame, rushing up like fire from the crater of a volcano, gained the tapestry, which it devoured. In the midst of all this frightful tumult and these terrific cries, two reports, fearfully distinct, followed by two shrieks more heart-rending than all, froze me with terror; these two shots had mortally wounded my father, and it was he who had given utterance to these frightful cries. However, he remained standing, clinging to a window. My mother tried to force the door, that she might go and die with him, but it was fastened on the inside. All around him were lying the Palicares, writhing in the death-throw, whilst two or three, who were only slightly wounded, sprang from the windows. At this crisis the whole flooring suddenly gave way; my father fell on one knee, and at the same moment twenty hands were thrust forth, armed with sabers, pistols, and poniards—twenty blows were instantaneously directed against one man, and my father disappeared in a whirlwind of fire kindled by these demons, as if hell itself were opening beneath his feet. I felt myself fall to the ground; it was my mother who had fainted."

Haydée's arms fell by her side, and she uttered a deep groan, at the same time looking toward the count, as if to ask if he were satisfied with her obedience to his commands.

Monte-Cristo rose and approached her; he took her hand, and said to her in Romaic:

"Calm yourself, my dear child, and take courage in remembering that there is a God who will punish traitors."

"It is a frightful story, count," said Albert, terrified at the paleness of Haydée's countenance, "and I reproach myself now for having been so cruelly thoughtless."

"Oh, it is nothing!" said Monte-Cristo. Then patting the young girl on the head, he continued:

"Haydée is very courageous; and she sometimes even finds consolation in the recital of her misfortunes."

"Because, my lord," said Haydée, eagerly, "my miseries recall to me your goodness."

Albert looked at her with curiosity, for she had not yet related what he most desired to know,—namely, how she had become the slave of the count. Haydée saw at a glance the same expression in the countenances of her two auditors; she continued:

"When my mother recovered her senses we were before the Seraskier. 'Kill me,' said she, 'but spare the honor of the widow of Ali.'—'It is not me to whom you must address yourself,' said Kourchid.—'To whom, then?'—'To your new master.'—'Who and where is he?'—'He is here.' And Kourchid pointed out one who had more than any contributed to the death of my father," said Haydée, in a tone of chastened anger.

"Then," said Albert, "you became the property of this man?"

"No," replied Haydée, "he did not dare to keep us, so we were sold to some slave-merchants who were going to Constantinople. We traversed Greece, and arrived half dead at the imperial gates. They were surrounded by a crowd of people, who opened a way for us to pass, when, suddenly, my mother, following with her eyes the looks of the crowd, uttered a piercing cry, and fell to the ground, pointing, as she did so, to a head over the gate. Above it were inscribed these words:

'This is the head of Ali Tebelin, Pacha of Janina.'

"I cried bitterly, and tried to raise my mother from the earth, but she was dead! I was taken to the slave-market, and was purchased by a rich Armenian. He caused me to be instructed, gave me masters, and when I was thirteen years of age he sold me to the Sultan Mahmoud."

"Of whom I bought her," said Monte-Cristo, "as I told you, Albert, with the emerald which formed a match to the one I had made into a box for the purpose of holding my pastilles of hashish."

"Oh! you are good! you are great! my lord!" said Haydée, kissing the count's hand, "and I am very fortunate in belonging to such a master."

Albert remained quite bewildered with all that he had seen and heard.

"Come! finish your cup of coffee," said Monte-Cristo; "the history is ended."

CHAPTER LXXVIII

NEWS FROM JANINA

FRANZ quitted the chamber of Noirtier so agitated and trembling that Valentine herself would have pitied him. Villefort had only just given utterance to a few incoherent sentences, and then retired to his study, where he received about two hours afterward the following letter:

"After the disclosure made this morning, M. Noirtier de Villefort cannot suppose any alliance possible between his family and that of M. Franz d'Epinay. M. d'Epinay is astonished that M. de Villefort, who appeared to be aware of the circumstances detailed this morning, should not have anticipated him in this announcement."

No one who had seen the magistrate at this moment would have supposed that he had anticipated the blow; it certainly never had occurred to him that his father would carry candor, or rather rudeness, so far as to relate such a history. In truth, Noirtier, who never cared for the opinion of his son, had never explained the affair to Villefort, so that he had always believed that the General de Quesnel, or the Baron d'Epinay, as he was styled, according as the speaker wished to use the title he had won for himself, or that conferred by others, fell the victim of assassination, and not that he was killed fairly in a duel. This harsh letter, from a young man generally so respectful, struck a mortal blow at the pride of Villefort.

Hardly had he read the letter, when his wife entered. The departure of Franz, when summoned by Noirtier, had so much astonished every one, that the position of Madame de Villefort, left alone with the notary and the witnesses, became every moment more embarrassing. Determined to bear it no longer, she left the room, saying she was going to see what had happened.

Villefort told her that an explanation had taken place between Noirtier, d'Epinay, and himself, and that the marriage of Valentine and

Franz was broken off. This was an awkward thing to have to report to those who were waiting. She, therefore, contented herself with saying that Noirtier having, at the commencement of the discussion, been attacked by a sort of apoplectic fit, the affair would necessarily be deferred for some days longer. This news, false as it was, followed so singularly in the train of the two similar misfortunes, that the auditors were astonished and retired without a remark.

During this time, Valentine, at once terrified and happy, after having embraced and thanked the feeble old man for thus breaking, with a single blow, the chain which she had considered as indissoluble, asked leave to retire to her own room, in order to recover her composure. Noirtier looked the permission which she solicited. But instead of going to her own room, Valentine, having once gained her liberty, entered the gallery, and opening a small door at the end of it, found herself at once in the garden.

In the midst of all the strange events which had crowded one on the other, an indefinable sentiment of dread had taken possession of Valentine's mind. She expected every moment that she should see Morrel appear, pale and trembling, to forbid the signing of the contract, like the Lord of Ravenswood in "The Bride of Lammermoor."

It was high time for her to make her appearance at the gate, for Maximilian had long awaited her coming. He had guessed what was going on when he saw Franz quit the cemetery with Villefort. He followed him, saw him enter, afterward go out, and then reenter with Albert and Château-Renaud. He had no longer any doubt, he therefore quickly hid himself in the inclosure, prepared for all events, and certain that Valentine would hasten to him the first moment she could. He was not mistaken; his eye, peering through the wooden partition, soon discovered the young girl, who, throwing aside all her usual precautions, walked at once to the gate. The first glance which Maximilian directed toward her entirely re-assured him, the first words she pronounced made his heart bound with delight.

"We are saved!" said Valentine.

"Saved!" repeated Morrel, not being able to conceive such intense happiness, "by whom?"

"By my grandfather. Oh, Morrel! pray love him well!"

Morrel swore to love him with all his soul; and at that moment he could safely promise to do so, for he was not content to love him merely as a friend or even as a father, he worshiped him as a god.

"But tell me, Valentine, how has it all been effected? what strange means has he used?"

Valentine was on the point of relating all, but she suddenly remembered that there was a terrible secret which concerned others as well as her grandfather, and she said:

"At some future time I will tell you all about it"

"But when will that be?"

"When I am your wife"

The conversation had now turned upon a topic that made Morrel ready to accede to anything. He was, therefore, satisfied with what he had just heard, and which was enough for one day. However, he would not leave without the promise of seeing Valentine again the next night. Valentine promised all that Morrel required of her, and certainly it was less difficult now for her to believe that she should marry Maximilian than it was an hour ago to assure herself that she should not marry Franz.

During the time occupied by the interview we have just detailed, Madame de Villefort had gone to visit Noirtier The old man looked at her with that stern and forbidding expression with which he was accustomed to receive her.

"Sir," said she, "it is superfluous for me to tell you that Valentine's marriage is broken off, since it was here that the rupture took place"

Noirtier's countenance remained immovable.

"But one thing I do not think you are aware of; that is, that I have always been opposed to this marriage, and that it was entered into entirely without my consent."

Noirtier regarded his daughter-in-law with the look of a man desiring an explanation.

"Now that this marriage, which I know you so much disliked, is done away with, I come to you on an errand which neither M. de Villefort nor Valentine could consistently undertake."

Noirtier's eyes demanded the nature of her mission

"I come to entreat you, sir," continued Madame de Villefort, "as the only one who has the right, inasmuch as I am the only one who will receive no benefit. I come to entreat you to restore, not your love, for that she has always possessed, but your fortune to your granddaughter"

There was a doubtful expression in Noirtier's eyes; he was evidently trying to discover the motive of this proceeding, and he could not succeed in doing so.

"May I hope, sir," said Madame de Villefort, "that your intentions accord with my request?"

Noirtier made a sign that they did.

"In that case, sir," rejoined Madame de Villefort, "I withdraw, grateful and happy." She then bowed to Noirtier and retired.

The next day Noirtier sent for the notary; the first will was torn up and a second made, in which he left the whole of his fortune to Valentine, on condition that she should never be separated from him. It was then generally reported that Mademoiselle de Villefort, the heiress of the Marquis and Marchioness de Saint-Méran, and restored to the good graces of her grandfather, would ultimately have an income of three hundred thousand livres.

Whilst the engagement was being broken at the house of Villefort, Morcerf had received the visit of Monte-Cristo, and to show his regard for Danglars, he assumed his dress uniform of lieutenant-general with all his orders, ordered his best horses, and drove to the Rue de la Chaussée d'Antin. Danglars was balancing his monthly accounts, and it was not the best time for finding him in good humor. At the first sight of his old friend, Danglars assumed his majestic air and settled himself in his easy-chair.

Morcerf, usually so formal, had assumed an affable and smiling manner, and feeling sure that the overture he was about to make would be well received, he did not adopt any manœuvres, but went at once straight to the point.

"Well, baron," said he, "here I am at last; some time has elapsed since our plans were formed, and they are not yet executed."

Morcerf paused at these words, to see the brow of Danglars cleared of the cloud which he attributed to his silence; but, on the contrary, to his great surprise it grew darker and more impassible.

"To what do you allude, M. le Comte?" said Danglars, as if he was trying in vain to guess at the meaning of the general's words.

"Ah!" said Morcerf; "I see you are a stickler for forms, my dear sir, and you remind me that the ceremonial rites should not be omitted. *Ma foi!* I beg your pardon, but as I have but one son, and it is the first time I have ever thought of marrying him, I am still serving my apprenticeship, you know: come, I will do my duty."

And Morcerf, with a forced smile, rose, and making a low bow to Danglars, said:

"M. le Baron, I have the honor of asking of you the hand of Mademoiselle Eugénie Danglars for my son, Viscount Albert de Morcerf."

But Danglars, instead of receiving this address in the favorable manner which Morcerf had expected, knit his brow, and without inviting the count, who was still standing, to take a seat, he said:

"M. le Comte, it will be necessary to reflect before I give you an answer."

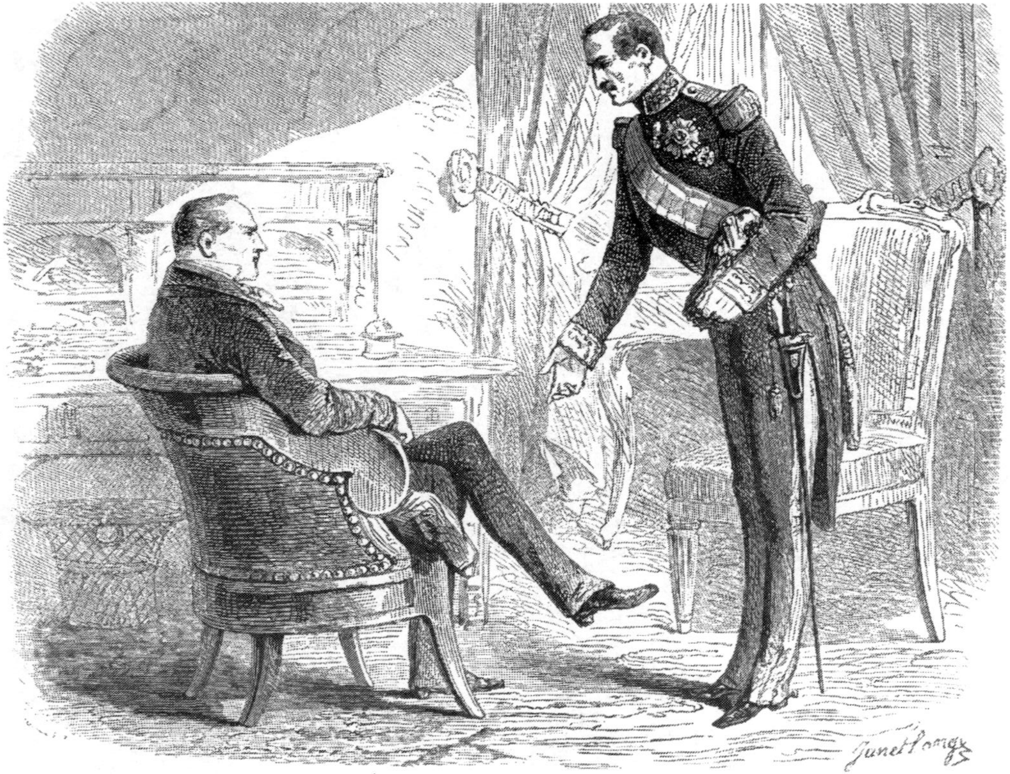

DANGLARS AND THE COUNT DE MORCERF.

"To reflect!" said Morcerf, more and more astonished, "have you not had enough time for reflection during the eight years since this marriage was first discussed?"

"M le Comte," said the banker, "things are constantly occurring to induce us to remodel what we have deemed arranged."

"I do not understand you, M. le Baron," said Morcerf.

"I mean to say, sir, that during the last fortnight unforeseen circumstances ——"

"Excuse me," said Morcerf, "but is it a play we are acting?"

"A play?"

"Yes; let us come more to the point."

"That is quite my desire."

"You have seen M. de Monte-Cristo, have you not?"

"I see him very often," said Danglars, drawing himself up; "he is a particular friend of mine."

"Well, in one of your late conversations with him, you said that I appeared to be forgetful and irresolute concerning this marriage, did you not?"

"I did say so."

"Well, here I am, proving at once that I am really neither the one nor the other, by summoning you to keep your promise."

Danglars did not answer.

"Have you so soon changed your mind," added Morcerf, "or have you only provoked my request that you may have the pleasure of seeing me humbled?"

Danglars, seeing that if he continued the conversation in the same tone in which he had begun it, the whole thing might turn out to his own disadvantage, turned to Morcerf, and said:

"M le Comte, you are right to be surprised at my reserve, and I assure you it costs me much to act in such a manner, but, believe me that imperative necessity enjoins it."

"These are all so many empty words, my dear sir," said Morcerf, "they might satisfy a new acquaintance, but the Count de Morcerf does not rank in that list, and when a man like him comes to another, recalls to him his plighted word, and this man fails to redeem the pledge, he has, at least, a right to exact from him a good reason for so doing"

Danglars was a coward, but did not wish to appear so; he was piqued at the tone which Morcerf had just assumed

"I am not without a good reason for my conduct," replied the banker.

"What do you mean to say?"

"I mean to say, that I have a good reason, but that it is difficult to explain"

"You must be aware, at all events, that I cannot be put off by your silence; but one thing at least is clear, which is, that you decline allying yourself with my family."

"No, sir," said Danglars; "I merely suspend my decision, that is all."

"And do you really flatter yourself that I shall yield to all your caprices, and quietly and humbly await the time of again being received into your good graces?"

"Then, M. le Comte, if you will not wait, we must look upon these projects as if they had never been entertained."

The count bit his lips till the blood almost started, to prevent the ebullition of anger which his proud and irritable temper scarcely allowed him to restrain; understanding, however, that in the present state of things the laugh would decidedly be against him, he turned from the door, toward which he had been directing his steps, and again confronted the banker. A cloud settled on his brow, evincing decided anxiety and uneasiness, instead of the expression of offended pride which had lately reigned there.

"My dear Danglars," said Morcerf, "we have been acquainted for many years, and consequently we ought to make some allowance for each other's failings. You owe me an explanation, and really it is but fair that I should know what unfortunate circumstance has deprived my son of your favor."

"It is no personal feeling toward the viscount, that is all I can say, sir," replied Danglars, who resumed his insolent manner as soon as he perceived that Morcerf was a little softened and calmed down.

"And toward whom do you bear this personal ill-feeling then?" said Morcerf, turning pale with anger. The expression of the count's face had not remained unperceived by the banker; he fixed on him a look of greater assurance than before, and said:

"You would thank me for not going further into particulars."

A trembling, caused by suppressed rage, shook the whole frame of the count, and making a violent effort over himself he said:

"I have a right to insist on your giving me an explanation. Is it Madame de Morcerf who has displeased you? is it my fortune which you find insufficient? is it because my opinions differ from yours?"

"Nothing of the kind, sir," replied Danglars; "if such had been the case, I only should have been to blame, inasmuch as I was aware of all these things when I made the engagement. No, do not seek any longer to discover the reason. Let us adopt the middle course, namely, delay, which implies neither a rupture nor an engagement. There is no hurry. My daughter is only seventeen years old, and your son twenty-one. Whilst we wait, time will be progressing, events will succeed each other, things which yesterday look obscure, appear but too clear to-morrow, and sometimes the lapse of a day, will destroy the most cruel calumnies."

"Calumnies, did you say, sir?" cried Morcerf, turning livid with rage. "Does any one dare to slander me?"

"M. le Comte, I told you that I considered it best to avoid all explanation."

"Then, sir, I am patiently to submit to your refusal?"

"Painful for me above all; yes, more painful to me than to you, for I had reckoned on the honor of your alliance, and the breaking off of a marriage-contract always injures the lady more than the gentleman."

"Enough, sir," said Morcerf, "we will speak no more on the subject."

And clenching his gloves with passion, he left the apartment. Danglars remarked that during the whole conversation Morcerf had never once dared to ask if it was on his own, Morcerf's, account that Danglars recalled his word.

That evening there was a long conference between several friends, and Cavalcanti, who had remained in the drawing-room with the ladies, was the last to leave the house of the banker.

The next morning, directly he awoke, Danglars asked for the newspapers; they were brought to him; he laid aside three or four, and at least fixed on *l'Impartial*: it was the paper of which Beauchamp was the chief editor. He hastily tore off the cover, opened the journal with nervous precipitation, passed contemptuously over the city column, and arriving at the miscellaneous intelligence, stopped, with a malicious smile, at a paragraph headed

Correspondence from Janina.

"Very good!" observed Danglars, after having read the paragraph, "here is a little article on Colonel Fernand, which, if I am not mistaken, will render the explanation which the Count de Morcerf required of me perfectly unnecessary."

At the same moment, that is, at nine o'clock in the morning, Albert de Morcerf, dressed in a black coat buttoned up to his chin, was walking with a quick step to Monte-Cristo's house in the Champs Elysées. When he presented himself at the gate the porter informed him that the count had gone out about half an hour previously.

"Did he take Baptistin with him?"

"No, M. le Vicomte."

"Call him then; I wish to speak to him."

The *concierge* went to seek the valet-de-chambre, and returned with him in an instant.

"My good friend," said Albert, "I beg pardon for my intrusion; but I was anxious to know from you if your master was really out."

"He is really out, sir," replied Baptistin.

"Out, even to me?"

"I know how happy my master always is to receive M. le Comte," said Baptistin; "and I should therefore never include him in any general order."

"You are right; and now I wish to see him on an affair of great importance; do you think it will be long before he comes in?"

"No, I think not; for he ordered his breakfast at ten o'clock."

"Well, I will go and take a turn in the Champs Elysées, and at ten o'clock I will return here; meanwhile, if M. le Comte should come in, will you beg him not to go out again without seeing me?"

"You may depend on my doing so, sir," said Baptistin.

Albert left the *fiacre* in which he had come standing at the door of the count, intending to take a turn on foot. As he was passing the Allée des Veuves, he thought he saw the count's horses standing at Gosset's shooting-gallery; he approached, and soon recognized the coachman.

"Is M. le Comte shooting in the gallery?" said Morcerf.

"Yes, sir," replied the coachman. Whilst he was speaking, Albert had heard the report of two or three pistol-shots. He entered, and on his way met the waiter.

"Excuse me, M. le Vicomte," said the lad; "but will you have the kindness to wait a moment?"

"What for, Philip?" asked Albert, who, being a constant visitor there, did not understand this opposition to his entrance.

"Because the person who is now in the gallery prefers being alone and never practices in the presence of any one."

"Not even before you, Philip? Then who loads his pistol?"

"His servant."

"A Nubian?"

"A Negro."

"It is he, then?"

"Do you know this gentleman?"

"Yes, and I am come to look for him; he is a friend of mine."

"Oh! that is quite another thing, then. I will go immediately and inform him of your arrival."

And Philip, urged by his own curiosity, entered the gallery; a second afterward Monte-Cristo appeared on the threshold.

"I ask your pardon, my dear count," said Albert, "for following you here; and I must first tell you that it was not the fault of your servants that I did so; I alone am to blame for this indiscretion. I went to your house, and they told me you were out, but that they expected you home at ten o'clock to breakfast. I was walking about in order to pass away the time till ten o'clock, when I caught sight of your carriage and horses."

"What you have just said induces me to hope that you intend breakfasting with me."

"No, thank you, I am not thinking of breakfast, just now; perhaps we may take that meal at a later hour and in worse company."

"What on earth are you talking of?"

"I am to fight to-day."

"What for?"

"For the sake of fighting!"

"Yes, I understand that, but what is the quarrel? People fight for all sorts of reasons, you know."

"I fight in the cause of honor."

"Ah! that is something serious."

"So serious, that I come to beg you to render me a service."

"What is it?"

"To be my second."

"That is a serious matter; let us speak of nothing till we get home. Ali, bring me some water."

The count turned up his sleeves, and passed into the little vestibule where the gentlemen were accustomed to wash their hands after shooting.

"Come in, M. le Vicomte," said Philip, in a low tone, "and I will show you something droll." Morcerf entered, and instead of the usual mark, he perceived some playing-cards fixed against the wall. At a distance Albert thought it was a complete suit, for he counted from the ace to the ten.

"Ah! ah!" said Albert, "I see you were preparing for a game of cards."

"No," said the count, "I was making a suit of cards."

"How?" said Albert.

"Those are really aces and twos which you see, but my balls have turned them into threes, fives, sevens, eights, nines, and tens."

Albert approached. In fact, the balls had actually pierced the cards in the exact places which the painted signs would otherwise have occupied, the lines and distances being as regularly kept as if they had been ruled with pencil.

In going up to the target, Morcerf picked up two or three swallows that had been rash enough to come within the range of the count's pistol.

"*Diable!*" said Morcerf.

"What would you have, my dear viscount?" said Monte-Cristo, wiping his hands on the towel which Ali had brought him; "I must occupy my leisure moments in some way or other. But come, I am at your service."

Both then entered Monte-Cristo's chariot, which in the course of a few minutes deposited them safely at No. 30. Monte-Cristo took Albert into his study, and pointing to a seat, placed another for himself.

"Now let us talk the matter over quietly," said the count.

"You see I am perfectly composed," said Albert.

"With whom are you going to fight?"

"With Beauchamp."

"Is he one of your friends?"

"Of course; it is always with friends that one fights."

"I suppose you have some cause of quarrel?"

"I have."

"What has he done to you?"

"There appeared in his journal last night—but wait, and read for yourself." And Albert handed over the paper to the count, who read as follows:

"A correspondent at Janina informs us of a fact of which until now we had remained in ignorance. The castle which formed the protection of the town was given up to the Turks by a French officer named Fernand, in whom the vizier, Ali Tebelin, had reposed the greatest confidence."

"Well!" said Monte-Cristo, "what do you see in that to annoy you?"

"What do I see in it?"

"Yes; how does it concern you if the castle of Janina was given up by a French officer?"

"It concerns me that my father, the Count de Morcerf, has the Christian name of Fernand!"

"Did your father serve Ali Pacha?"

"Yes; that is to say, he fought for the independence of the Greeks, and hence arises the calumny."

"Oh, my dear viscount, do talk reason!"

"I do not desire to do otherwise."

"Now, just tell me who the devil should know in France that the officer Fernand and the Count de Morcerf are the same person? and who cares now about Janina, which was taken in 1822 or 1823?"

"That just proves the perfidy: they have allowed all this time to elapse, and then, all of a sudden, rake up events which have been forgotten, to furnish scandal, to tarnish our high position. I inherit my father's name, and I do not choose that the shadow of doubt should darken it. I am going to send my seconds to Beauchamp, in whose journal this paragraph appears, and I shall insist on his retracting it."

"Beauchamp will never retract."

"Then we must fight."

"No, you will not, for he will tell you, that perhaps there were fifty officers in the Greek army bearing the same name."

"We will fight, nevertheless. I will efface that . . . My father . . such a brave soldier, a career so brilliant——"

"Oh, well, he will add, 'We are warranted in believing that this Fernand is not the Count de Morcerf, who also bears the same Christian name.'"

"I am determined not to be content with anything short of an entire retractation."

"And you intend to send your seconds?"

"Yes."

"You do wrong."

"Which means, I suppose, that you refuse the service which I asked of you?"

"You know my theory regarding duels, I told you my opinion on that subject, if you remember, when we were at Rome"

"Nevertheless, my dear count, I found you this morning engaged in an occupation little consistent with that opinion."

"Because, my dear fellow, you understand one must never be singular. If one's lot is cast amongst fools, it is necessary to study folly I shall, perhaps, find myself one day called out by some hare-brained scamp, who has no more real cause of quarrel with me than you have with Beauchamp; he may take me to task for some foolish trifle or other, he will send his seconds, or will insult me in some public place, and I suppose I am expected to kill him for all that"

"You admit that you would fight, then? Well, if so, why do you object to my doing so?"

"I do not say that you ought not to fight, I only say that a duel is a serious thing, and requires due reflection"

"Did he reflect before he insulted my father?"

"If he spoke hastily, and owns that he did so, you ought to be satisfied."

"Ah, my dear count, you are far too indulgent."

"And you far too exacting. Supposing, for instance, and do not be angry at what I am going to say——"

"Well!"

"Supposing the assertion to be really true?"

"A son ought not to submit to such a supposition regarding his father's honor"

"*Ma foi!* we live in times when there is much to which we must submit."

"That is precisely the fault of the age"

"And do you undertake to reform it?"

"Yes, as far as I am personally concerned"

"You are indeed rigid, my dear fellow!"

"Well, I own it."

"Are you quite impervious to good advice?"

"Not when it comes from a friend."

"And do you accord me that title?"

"Certainly I do"

"Well, then, before going to Beauchamp with your seconds, seek further information on the subject."

"From whom?"

"From Haydée"

"What! mix a woman up in the affair?—what can she do in it?"

"She can declare to you, for example, that your father had no hand whatever in the defeat and death of the vizier; or if by chance he had, indeed, the misfortune to——"

"I have already told you, my dear count, that I would not for one moment admit of such a supposition."

"You reject this means of information, then?"

"Most decidedly."

"Then, one last word of advice."

"Well! let it be the last."

"You do not wish to hear it, perhaps?"

"On the contrary, I request it."

"Do not send your seconds to Beauchamp—visit him alone."

"That would be contrary to all custom."

"Your case is not an ordinary one."

"And what is your reason for advising me to go alone?"

"Because then the affair will rest between you and Beauchamp."

"Explain yourself."

"I will do so. If Beauchamp be disposed to retract, you ought to give him the opportunity of doing it of his own free will; the satisfaction to you will be the same; if, on the contrary, he refuses to do so, it will then be quite time enough to admit two strangers into your secret."

"They will not be strangers, they will be friends."

"Ah, but the friends of to-day are the enemies of to-morrow; Beauchamp, for instance."

"So you recommend——"

"I recommend you to be prudent."

"Then you advise me to go alone to Beauchamp!"

"I do, and I will tell you why. When you wish to obtain some concession from a man's self-love, you must avoid the appearance of wishing to wound it"

"I believe you are right."

"I am glad of it"

"Then I will go alone."

"Go; but you would do better still by not going at all."

"That is impossible."

"Do so, then; it will be a wiser plan than the first which you proposed."

"But if, in spite of all my precautions, I am at last obliged to fight, will you not be my second?"

"My dear viscount," said Monte-Cristo, gravely, "you must have seen before to-day that at all times and in all places I have been at your disposal, but the service which you have just demanded of me is one which it is out of my power to render you."

"Why?"

"Perhaps you may know at some future period, and, in the mean time, I request your indulgence for my secret."

"Well, I will have Franz and Château-Renaud!"

"Do so, then, they will be the very men for it."

"But if I do fight, you will surely not object to giving me a lesson or two in shooting and fencing?"

"That, too, is impossible."

"What a singular being you are! — you will not interfere in anything."

"You are right — that is the principle on which I wish to act."

"We will say no more about it, then. Good-bye, count."

Morcerf took his hat, and left the room. He found his chariot at the door, and doing his utmost to restrain his anger, he drove at once to Beauchamp's house. Beauchamp was in his office. It was one of those gloomy, dusty-looking apartments, such as journalists' offices have always been. The servant announced Albert de Morcerf. Beauchamp repeated the name to himself, and then gave orders for him to be admitted. Albert entered.

Beauchamp uttered an exclamation of surprise on seeing his friend leap over and trample under foot all the newspapers which were strewed about the room.

"Here! here! my dear Albert!" said he, holding out his hand to the young man. "Are you out of your senses, or do you come peaceably to take breakfast with me? Try and find a seat — there is one by that geranium, which is the only thing in the room to remind me that there are other leaves in the world besides leaves of paper."

"Beauchamp," said Albert, "it is of your journal that I come to speak."

"Indeed! what do you wish to say about it?"

"I desire that a statement contained in it should be rectified."

"To what do you allude? But pray sit down."

"Thank you," said Albert, with a cold and formal bow.

"Will you now explain?"

"An announcement has been made which implicates the honor of a member of my family."

"What is it," said Beauchamp, much surprised, "surely you must be mistaken."

"It is an article headed 'Janina.'"

"'Janina?'"

"Yes; really you appear to be totally ignorant of the cause which brings me here."

"Such is really the case, I assure you, upon my honor! Baptiste, give me yesterday's paper," cried Beauchamp.

"Here, I have brought mine with me," replied Albert.

Beauchamp took the paper, and read the article to which Albert pointed, in an under-tone.

"You see it is a serious annoyance," said Morcerf, when Beauchamp had finished the perusal of the paragraph.

"Is the officer alluded to a relation of yours, then?" demanded the journalist.

"Yes," said Albert, blushing.

"Well, what do you wish me to do for you?" said Beauchamp, mildly.

"My dear Beauchamp, I wish you to contradict this statement." Beauchamp looked at Albert with a benevolent expression.

"Come," said he, "this matter will want a good deal of talking over; a retraction is always a serious thing, you know. Sit down and I will read it again."

Albert resumed his seat, and Beauchamp read, with more attention than at first, the lines denounced by his friend.

"Well," said Albert, in a determined tone, "you see that your paper has insulted a member of my family, and I insist on a retractation."

"You insist?"

"Yes, I insist."

"Permit me to remind you that you are not very diplomatic, my dear viscount."

"Nor do I wish to be," replied the young man rising. "I repeat that I am determined to have the announcement of yesterday contradicted. You have known me long enough," continued Albert, biting his lips convulsively, for he saw that Beauchamp's anger was beginning to rise,—"you have been my friend, and therefore sufficiently intimate with me to be aware that I am likely to maintain my resolution on this point."

"If I have been your friend, Morcerf, your present manner of speaking would almost lead me to forget that I ever bore that title. But wait a moment, do not let us get angry, or at least not yet. You are irritated and vexed—tell me how this Fernand is related to you?"

"He is merely my father," said Albert—"M. Fernand Mondego, Count de Morcerf, an old soldier, who has fought in twenty battles, and whose honorable scars they would denounce as badges of disgrace."

"Is it your father?" said Beauchamp; "that is quite another thing. Then I can well understand your indignation, my dear Albert. I will reperuse." And he read the paragraph for the third time, laying a stress on each word as he proceeded. "But the paper nowhere identifies this Fernand with your father."

"YOU WILL RETRACT THIS ASSERTION, WILL YOU NOT?"

"No; but the connection will be seen by others, and therefore I will have the article contradicted."

At the words *I will*, Beauchamp steadily raised his eyes to Albert's countenance, and then as gradually lowering them, he remained thoughtful for a few moments.

"You will retract this assertion, will you not, Beauchamp?" said Albert, with increased though stifled anger.

"Yes," replied Beauchamp.

"Immediately?" said Albert.

"When I am convinced the statement is false."

"What?"

"The thing is worth looking into, and I will take pains to investigate the matter thoroughly."

"But what is there to investigate, sir?" said Albert, enraged beyond measure at Beauchamp's last remark. "If you do not believe that it is my father, say so immediately; and if, on the contrary, you believe it to be him, state your reasons for doing so."

Beauchamp looked at Albert with the smile which was so peculiar to him, and which, in its numerous modifications, served to express every varied feeling of his mind.

"Sir," replied he, "if you came to me with the idea of demanding satisfaction, you should have gone at once to the point, and not have entertained me with the idle conversation to which I have been patiently listening for the last half-hour. Am I to put this construction on your visit?"

"Yes, if you will not consent to retract that infamous calumny."

"Wait a moment—no threats, if you please, M. Fernand Mondego, Vicomte de Morcerf; I never allow them from my enemies, and therefore shall not put up with them from my friends. You insist on my contradicting the article relating to General Fernand, an article in which, I assure you, on my word of honor, I have not taken the slightest share?"

"Yes, I insist on it!" said Albert, whose mind was beginning to get bewildered with the excitement of his feelings.

"And if I refuse, we fight?" said Beauchamp, in a calm tone.

"Yes," replied Albert, raising his voice.

"Well," said Beauchamp, "here is my answer, my dear sir. The article was not inserted by me—I was not even aware of it; but you have, by the step you have taken, called my attention to the paragraph in question, and it will remain until it shall be either contradicted or confirmed by some one who has a right to do so."

"Sir," said Albert, rising, "I will do myself the honor of sending my seconds to you, and you will be kind enough to arrange with them the place and the weapons."

"Certainly, my dear sir."

"And this evening, if you please, or to-morrow at the latest, we will meet."

"No, no! I will be on the ground at the proper time; but in my opinion (and I have a right to dictate the preliminaries, as it is I who have received the provocation)—in my opinion the time ought not to be yet. I know you fence well, and I only moderately; I know, too, that you are a good marksman—there we are about equal. I know that a duel between us two would be serious, because you are brave . . . . . and I am brave also. I do not, therefore, wish either to kill you or to be killed myself, without a cause. Now, I am going to put a question to you, and categorically, too. Do you insist on this retractation so far as to kill me if I do not make it, although I have repeated it more than once, and affirmed, on my honor, that I was ignorant of the thing with which you charge me, and although I still declare that it is impossible for any one but you to recognize the Count de Morcerf under the name of Fernand?"

"I maintain my original resolution."

"Very well, my dear sir; then I consent to cut throats with you. But I require three weeks' preparation; at the end of that time I shall come and say to you, 'The assertion is false, and I retract it,' or, 'The assertion is true,' when I shall immediately draw the sword from its sheath, or the pistols from the case, whichever you please."

"Three weeks!" cried Albert; "they will pass as slowly as three centuries when I am all the time suffering dishonor."

"Had you continued to remain on amicable terms with me, I should have said, 'Patience, my friend'; but you have constituted yourself my enemy, therefore I say, 'What does that signify to me, sir?'"

"Well, let it be three weeks, then," said Morcerf; "but remember, at the expiration of that time no delay or subterfuge will justify you in ——"

"M. Albert de Morcerf," said Beauchamp, rising in his turn, "I cannot throw you out of window for three weeks,—that is to say, for twenty-four days to come,—nor have you any right to split my skull open till that time has elapsed. To-day is the 29th of August; the 21st of September will, therefore, be the conclusion of the term agreed on, and till that time arrives,—and it is the advice of a gentleman which I am about to give you,—till then we will refrain from growling and barking like two dogs chained within sight of each other."

When he had concluded this speech, Beauchamp bowed coldly to Albert, turned his back upon him, and retired to his printing-office. Albert vented his anger on a pile of newspapers, which he scattered by switching them violently with his stick; after which he departed—

not, however, without walking back several times to the door of the printing-office.

Whilst Albert was lashing the front of his chariot in the same manner that he had done to the newspapers which were the innocent agents

of his discomfiture, as he was crossing the barrier he perceived Morrel, who was walking with a quick step and a bright eye. He was passing the Chinese Baths, and appeared to have come from the direction of the Porte Saint-Martin, and to be going toward the Magdalen.

"Ah," said Morcerf, "there goes a happy man!" And Albert was not mistaken in his opinion.

CHAPTER LXXIX

THE LEMONADE

MORREL was, in fact, very happy. Noirtier had just sent for him, and he was in such haste to know the reason of his doing so that he had not stopped to take a *fiacre*, placing infinitely more dependence on his own two legs than on the four legs of a cab-horse. He had, therefore, set off at a run from the Rue Mesley, and was hastening with rapid strides in the direction of the Faubourg Saint-Honoré.

Morrel advanced "at the double," and poor Barrois followed him as he best might; Morrel was only thirty-one, Barrois was sixty years of age; Morrel was in love, and Barrois was dying with heat. These two men, thus opposed in age and interests, resembled two sides of a triangle, parted at the base, but uniting at the apex. This point of union was Noirtier, and it was he who had just sent for Morrel, with the request that he would lose no time in coming to him — a command which Morrel obeyed to the letter, to the great discomfiture of Barrois. On arriving at the house, Morrel was not even out of breath, for love lends wings; but Barrois, who had long forgotten what it was to love, was exhausted.

The old servant introduced Morrel by a private entrance, closed the door of the study, and soon the rustling of a dress announced the arrival of Valentine. She looked marvelously beautiful in her deep mourning dress, and so fair was the dream that Morrel could almost have dispensed with the conversation of her grandfather.

But the easy-chair of the old man was heard rolling along the floor, and he soon made his appearance in the room. Noirtier acknowledged by a look of extreme kindness the thanks which Morrel lavished on him for his timely intervention on behalf of Valentine and himself — an intervention which had saved them from despair. Morrel then cast on

Valentine an interrogative look as to the new favor which he designed to bestow on him. She was sitting at a little distance from them, timidly awaiting the moment when she should be obliged to speak Noirtier, in his turn, fixed his eyes on her

"Am I to say what you told me?" asked Valentine. Noirtier made a sign that she was to do so.

"M. Morrel," said Valentine to the young man, who was regarding her with the most intense interest, "my grandfather, M. Noirtier, had a thousand things to say, which he told me three days ago; and now he has sent for you, that I may repeat them to you; I will repeat them, then; and since he has chosen me as his interpreter, I will be faithful to the trust, and will not alter a word of his intentions"

"Oh, I am listening with the greatest impatience," replied the young man; "speak, I beg of you."

Valentine cast down her eyes; this was a good omen for Morrel, for he knew that nothing but happiness could thus overcome Valentine

"My grandfather intends leaving this house," said she, "and Barrois is looking out for suitable apartments for him in another."

"But you, Mademoiselle de Villefort, you, who are necessary to M Noirtier's happiness——"

"Me?" interrupted Valentine, "I shall not leave my grandfather, that is an understood thing between us. My apartment will be close to his. Now, M de Villefort must either give his consent to this plan or his refusal; in the first case, I shall leave directly; and in the second, I shall await my majority, which will be completed in about ten months. Then I shall be free, I shall have an independent fortune, and——"

"And what?" demanded Morrel.

"And, with my grandfather's consent, I shall fulfill the promise which I have made you."

Valentine pronounced these few last words in such a low tone, that nothing but Morrel's intense interest in what she was saying could have enabled him to hear them

"Have I not explained your wishes, grandpapa?" said Valentine, addressing Noirtier

"Yes," looked the old man

"Once under my grandfather's roof, M Morrel can visit me in the presence of my good and worthy protector, if we still feel that the union we contemplated will be likely to insure our future comfort and happiness; in that case I shall expect M. Morrel to come and claim me at my own hands But, alas! I have heard it said that hearts inflamed by obstacles to their desire grow cold in time of security."

"Oh!" cried Morrel, almost tempted to throw himself on his knees before Noirtier as before God, and before Valentine as an angel, "what have I ever done in my life to merit such unbounded happiness?"

"Until that time," continued the young girl, in a calm and self-possessed tone of voice, "we will respect the usages of society, and ever the wishes of our relatives, so long as those wishes do not tend finally to separate us; in one word, and I repeat it, because it expresses everything — we will wait."

"And I swear to make all the sacrifices which this word imposes, sir," said Morrel, "not only with resignation, but with cheerfulness."

"Therefore," continued Valentine, looking playfully at Maximilian, "no more imprudence; do not compromise her who from this day regards herself as destined, honorably and happily, to bear your name?"

Morrel looked obedience to her commands. Noirtier regarded the lovers with a look of ineffable tenderness, whilst Barrois, who had remained in the room in the character of a man privileged to know everything that passed, smiled on the youthful couple as he wiped the perspiration from his bald forehead.

"How hot you look, my good Barrois!" said Valentine.

"Ah! I have been running very fast, mademoiselle; but I must do M. Morrel the justice to say that he ran still faster."

Noirtier directed their attention to a waiter, on which was placed a decanter containing lemonade and a glass. The decanter was nearly full, with the exception of a little, which had been already drunk by M. Noirtier.

"Come, Barrois," said the young girl, "take some of this lemonade; I see you are coveting a good draught of it."

"The fact is mademoiselle," said Barrois, "I am dying with thirst, and since you are so kind as to offer it me, I cannot say I should at all object to drinking your health in a glass of it."

"Take some, then, and come back immediately."

Barrois took away the waiter, and hardly was he outside the door, which, in his haste, he forgot to shut, then they saw him throw back his head and empty to the very dregs the glass which Valentine had filled. Valentine and Morrel were exchanging their adieux in the presence of Noirtier when a ring was heard at the door-bell. It was the signal of a visit. Valentine looked at her watch.

"It is past noon," said she, "and to-day is Saturday; I dare say it is the doctor, grandpapa."

Noirtier looked his conviction that she was right in her supposition.

"He will come in here, and M. Morrel had better go; do you think so, grandpapa?"

"Yes," signed the old man.

"Barrois!" cried Valentine, "Barrois!"

"I am coming, mademoiselle," replied he.

"Barrois will open the door for you," said Valentine, addressing Morrel. "And now remember one thing, Mr. Officer, that my grandfather commands you not to take any rash or ill-advised step which would be likely to compromise our happiness."

"I promised him to wait," replied Morrel; "and I will wait."

At this moment Barrois entered.

"Who rang?" asked Valentine.

"Doctor d'Avrigny," said Barrois, staggering as if he would fall.

"What is the matter, Barrois?" said Valentine. The old man did not answer, but looked at his master with wild staring eyes, whilst with his cramped hand he grasped a piece of furniture to enable him to stand upright.

"He is going to fall!" cried Morrel.

The trembling which had attacked Barrois gradually increased, the features of the face became quite altered, and the convulsive movement of the muscles indicated a most serious nervous attack. Noirtier, seeing Barrois in this pitiable condition, showed by his looks all the various emotions which can animate the heart of man. Barrois made some steps toward his master.

"Ah, sir!" said he, "tell me what is the matter with me. I am suffering — I cannot see. A thousand fiery darts are piercing my brain. Ah! don't touch me, pray don't."

By this time his haggard eyes were starting from their sockets; his head fell back, and the rest of the body began to stiffen.

Valentine uttered a cry of horror; Morrel took her in his arms, as if to defend her from some unknown danger.

"M. d'Avrigny! M. d'Avrigny" cried she, in a stifled voice. "Help! help!"

Barrois turned round and, with a great effort, stumbled a few steps, then fell at the feet of Noirtier, and resting his hand on the knee of the invalid, exclaimed:

"My master! my good master!"

At this moment Villefort, attracted by the noise, appeared on the threshold. Morrel relaxed his hold of Valentine, and retreating to a distant corner of the room, he remained half hidden behind a curtain. Pale as if he had been gazing on a serpent, he fixed his terrified eye on the agonized sufferer.

Noirtier, burning with impatience and terror, was in despair at his utter inability to help his old domestic, whom he regarded more in the light of a friend than a servant. One might trace the terrible conflict which was going on between the living, energetic mind, and the inanimate and helpless body, by the fearful swelling of the veins of his forehead and the contraction of the muscles round the eye.

Barrois, his features convulsed, his eyes suffused with blood, and his head thrown back, was lying at full length, beating the floor with his hands, whilst his legs were become so stiff that they looked as if they would break rather than bend. A slight appearance of foam was visible round the mouth, and he breathed painfully, and with extreme difficulty.

Villefort seemed stupified with astonishment, and remained gazing intently on the scene before him without uttering a word. He had not seen Morrel. After a moment of dumb contemplation, during which his face became pale, and his hair seemed to stand on end, he sprang toward the door, crying out:

"Doctor! doctor! come instantly, pray come!"

"Madame! madame!" cried Valentine, calling her step-mother, and running upstairs to meet her, "come quick, quick! and bring your bottle of smelling-salts with you."

"What is the matter?" said Madame de Villefort, in a harsh and constrained tone.

"Oh! come! come."

"But where is the doctor?" exclaimed Villefort; "where is he?"

Madame de Villefort now deliberately descended the staircase. In one hand she held her handkerchief, with which she appeared to be wiping her face, and in the other a bottle of English smelling-salts. Her first look on entering the room was at Noirtier, whose face, independent of the emotion which such a scene could not fail of producing, proclaimed him to be in possession of his usual health; her second glance was at the dying man. She turned pale, and her eye passed quickly from the servant, and rested on the master.

"In the name of heaven, madame," said Villefort, "where is the doctor? He was with you just now. You see this is a fit of apoplexy, and he might be saved if he could but be bled!"

"Has he eaten anything lately?" asked Madame de Villefort, eluding her husband's question.

"Madame," replied Valentine, "he has not even breakfasted. He has been running very fast on an errand with which my grandfather charged him, and when he returned he took nothing but a glass of lemonade."

"Ah!" said Madame de Villefort; "why did he not take wine? Lemonade was a very bad thing for him."

"Grandpapa's bottle of lemonade was standing just by his side; poor Barrois was very thirsty, and was thankful to drink anything he could find."

Madame de Villefort started. Noirtier looked at her with a glance of the most profound scrutiny.

"He has such a short neck," said she.

"Madame," said Villefort, "I ask where is M. d'Avrigny? In God's name, answer me!"

"He is with Edward, who is not quite well," replied Madame de Villefort, no longer being able to avoid answering.

Villefort rushed upstairs to fetch him himself.

"Take this," said Madame de Villefort, giving her smelling-bottle to Valentine. "They will, no doubt, bleed him, therefore I will retire, for I cannot endure the sight of blood." And she followed her husband upstairs.

Morrel now emerged from his hiding-place, where he had remained quite unperceived, so great had been the general confusion.

"Go away as quick as you can, Maximilian," said Valentine, "and stay till I send for you. Go."

Morrel looked toward Noirtier for permission to retire. The old man, who had preserved all his usual *sang-froid*, made a sign to him to do so. The young man pressed Valentine's hand to his lips, and then left the house by a back staircase.

At the same moment that he quitted the room, Villefort and the doctor entered by an opposite entrance. Barrois was now showing signs of returning consciousness; the crisis seemed past; a low moaning was heard, and he raised himself on one knee. D'Avrigny and Villefort laid him on a couch.

"What do you prescribe, doctor?" demanded Villefort.

"Give me some water and ether. You have some in the house, have you not?"

"Yes."

"Send for some oil of turpentine and tartar emetic."

Villefort immediately dispatched a messenger. "And now let every one retire."

"Must I go, too?" asked Valentine, timidly.

"Yes, mademoiselle, you especially," replied the doctor, abruptly.

Valentine looked at d'Avrigny with astonishment, kissed her grandfather on the forehead, and left the room. The doctor closed the door after her with a gloomy air.

"Look! look! doctor," said Villefort, "he is quite coming round again; I really do not think, after all, it is anything of consequence." D'Avrigny answered by a melancholy smile.

"How do you feel yourself, Barrois?" asked he.

"A little better, sir."

"Will you drink some of this ether and water?"

"I will try; but don't touch me."

"Why not?"

"Because I feel that if you were only to touch me with the tip of your finger the fit would return."

"Drink."

Barrois took the glass, and raising it to his purple lips, took about half of the liquid offered him.

"Where do you suffer?" asked the doctor.

"Everywhere; I feel a cramp over my whole body."

"Do you find any dazzling sensation before the eyes?"

"Yes."

"Any noise in the ears?"

"Frightful."

"When did you first feel that?"

"Just now."

"Suddenly?"

"Yes, like a clap of thunder."

"Did you feel nothing of it yesterday or the day before?"

"Nothing."

"No drowsiness?"

"None."

"What have you eaten to-day?"

"I have eaten nothing; I only drank a glass of my master's lemonade—that's all." And Barrois turned toward Noirtier, who, immovably fixed in his arm-chair, was contemplating this terrible scene without allowing a word or movement to escape him.

"Where is this lemonade?" asked the doctor, eagerly.

"Downstairs, in the decanter."

"Whereabouts downstairs?"

"In the kitchen."

"Shall I go and fetch it, doctor?" inquired Villefort.

"No, stay here and try to make Barrois drink the rest of this glass of ether and water. I will go myself and fetch the lemonade."

D'Avrigny bounded toward the door, flew down the back staircase, and almost knocked down Madame de Villefort in his haste, who was herself going down to the kitchen. D'Avrigny paid no attention to her; possessed with but one idea, he cleared the last four steps with a bound, and rushed into the kitchen, where he saw the decanter about three parts empty still standing on the waiter, where it had been left. He darted upon it as an eagle on its prey. Panting with loss of breath, he returned to the room he had just left. Madame de Villefort slowly ascended the steps which led to her room.

"Is this the decanter you spoke of?" asked d'Avrigny.

"Yes, doctor."

"Is this the same lemonade of which you partook?"

"I believe so."

"What did it taste like?"

"It had a bitter taste."

The doctor poured some drops of the lemonade into the palm of his hand, put his lips to it, and after having rinsed his mouth as a man does when he is tasting wine, he spat the liquor into the fire-place.

"It is no doubt the same," said he; "did you drink some, too, M. Noirtier?"

"Yes."

"And did you also discover a bitter taste?"

"Yes."

"Oh, doctor!" cried Barrois, "the fit is coming on again. Oh! have pity on me." The doctor flew to his patient.

"That emetic, Villefort; see if it is coming."

Villefort sprang into the passage, exclaiming, "The emetic! the emetic!—is it come yet?" No one answered. The most profound terror reigned throughout the house.

"If I had anything by means of which I could inflate the lungs," said d'Avrigny, looking around him, "perhaps I might prevent suffocation. But there is nothing which would do!—nothing!"

"Oh, sir," cried Barrois, "are you going to let me die without help? Oh! I am dying! Oh! save me!"

"A pen? a pen?" said the doctor. There was one lying on the table; he endeavored to introduce it into the mouth of the patient;

who, in the midst of his convulsions, was making vain attempts to vomit; but the jaws were so clenched that the pen could not pass them. This second attack was much more violent than the first, and he had slipped from the couch to the ground, where he was writhing in agony. The doctor left him in this paroxysm, knowing that he could do nothing to alleviate it, and going up to Noirtier. said abruptly:

"How do you find yourself?—well?"

"Yes."

"Light or heavy in the stomach?—light?"

"Yes."

"As you generally feel after the dose which I give you every Sunday?"

"Yes."

"Did Barrois make your lemonade?"

"Yes."

"Was it you who asked him to drink some of it?"

"No."

"Was it M. de Villefort?"

"No."

"Madame?"

"No."

"It was your granddaughter, then, was it not?"

"Yes."

A groan from Barrois, accompanied by a yawn which seemed to crack the very jawbones, attracted the attention of d'Avrigny; he left Noirtier, and returned to the sick man.

"Barrois," said the doctor, "can you speak?" Barrois muttered a few unintelligible words. "Try and make an effort to do so, my good man," said d'Avrigny. Barrois re-opened his blood-shot eyes.

"Who made the lemonade?"

"I did."

"Did you bring it to your master directly it was made?"

"No."

"You left it somewhere, then, in the mean time?"

"Yes; I left it in the pantry, because I was called away."

"Who brought it into this room, then?"

"Mademoiselle Valentine." D'Avrigny struck his forehead with his hand.

"Gracious Heaven!" exclaimed he.

"Doctor! doctor!" cried Barrois, who felt another fit coming.

"Will they never bring that emetic?" asked the doctor.

"Here is a glass with one already prepared," said Villefort, entering the room.

"Who prepared it?"

"The chemist who came here with me."

"Drink it," said the doctor to Barrois.

"Impossible, doctor, it is too late; my throat is closing up. I am choking! Oh! my heart! Ah! my head! Oh! what agony! Shall I suffer like this long?"

"No, no, friend," replied the doctor, "you will soon cease to suffer."

"Ah! I understand you," said the unhappy man. "My God, have mercy upon me!" And, uttering a fearful cry, Barrois fell back as if he had been struck by lightning.

D'Avrigny put his hand to his heart, and placed a glass before his lips.

"Well?" said Villefort.

"Go to the kitchen, and get me some syrup of violets."

Villefort went immediately.

"Do not be alarmed, M. Noirtier," said d'Avrigny, "I am going to take my patient into the next room to bleed him; this sort of attack is very frightful to witness."

And, taking Barrois under the arms, he dragged him into an adjoining room; but almost immediately, he returned to fetch the remainder of the lemonade. Noirtier closed his right eye.

"You want Valentine, do you not? I will tell them to send her to you."

Villefort returned, and d'Avrigny met him in the passage.

"Well, how is he now?" asked he.

"Come in here," said d'Avrigny; and he took him into the chamber where the sick man lay.

"Is he still in a fit?" said the *procureur du roi.*

"He is dead."

Villefort drew back a few steps, and, clasping his hands, exclaimed, with real amazement and sympathy, "Dead! and so soon, too!"

"Yes, it is very soon!" said the doctor, looking at the corpse before him; "but that ought not to astonish you; M. and Mme. de Saint-Méran died as soon. People die very suddenly in your house, M. de Villefort."

"What!" cried the magistrate, with an accent of horror and consternation, "are you still harping on that terrible idea?"

"Still, sir; and I shall always do so," replied d'Avrigny, "for it has never for one instant ceased to retain possession of my mind; and that you may be quite sure I am not mistaken this time, listen well to what I am going to say, M. de Villefort."

The magistrate trembled convulsively.

"There is a poison which destroys life almost without leaving any perceptible traces. I know it well; I have studied it in all its qualities and in the effects which it produces. I recognized the presence of this poison in the case of poor Barrois as well as in that of Madame de Saint-Méran. There is a way of detecting its presence. It restores the blue color of litmus-paper reddened by an acid, and it turns syrup of violets green. We have no litmus-paper, but, hark! here they come with the syrup of violets."

The doctor was right; steps were heard in the passage. M. d'Avrigny opened the door, and took from the hands of the femme-de-chambre a cup which contained two or three spoonfuls of the syrup; he then carefully closed the door.

"Look!" said he to the *procureur du roi*, whose heart beat so loudly that it might almost be heard; "here is in this cup some syrup of violets, and this decanter contains the remainder of the lemonade of which M. Noirtier and Barrois partook. If the lemonade be pure and inoffensive, the syrup will keep its color; if, on the contrary, the lemonade be poisonous, the syrup will become green. Look well at it!"

The doctor then slowly poured some drops of the lemonade from the decanter into the cup, and, in an instant, a kind of light cloudy sediment began to form at the bottom of the cup; this sediment first took a blue shade, then from the color of sapphire it passed to that of opal, and from opal to emerald. Arrived at this last hue, it changed no more. The result of the experiment left no doubt whatever on the mind.

"The unfortunate Barrois has been poisoned," said d'Avrigny, "and I will maintain this assertion before God and man."

Villefort said nothing, but he clasped his hands, opened his haggard eyes, and, overcome with his emotion, sank into a chair.

CHAPTER LXXX

THE ACCUSATION

D'AVRIGNY soon restored the magistrate to consciousness, who had looked like a second corpse in that chamber of death.

"Oh, death is in my house!" cried Villefort.

"Say, rather, crime!" replied the doctor.

"M. d'Avrigny," cried Villefort, "I cannot tell you all I feel at this moment,—terror, grief, madness."

"Yes," said d'Avrigny with an imposing calmness, "but I think it is now time to act. I think it is time to stop this torrent of mortality. I can no longer bear to be in possession of these secrets without the hope of seeing the victims and society generally revenged."

Villefort cast a gloomy look around him. "In my house!" murmured he, "in my house!"

"Come, magistrate," said d'Avrigny, "show yourself a man; as an interpreter of the law, do honor to your profession by sacrificing your selfish interests to it."

"You make me shudder, doctor! Do you talk of a sacrifice?"

"I do."

"Do you then suspect any one?"

"I suspect no one; death raps at your door—it enters—it goes, not blind, but with clear intelligence, from room to room. Well! I follow its course, I track its passage; I adopt the wisdom of the ancients, and feel my way, for my friendship for your family and my respect for you are as a twofold bandage over my eyes; well ——"

"Oh! speak, speak, doctor; I shall have courage."

"Well, sir, you have in your establishment, or in your family, perhaps, one of those frightful phenomena of which each century produces only one. Locusta and Agrippina, living at the same time, are an exception, and prove the determination of Providence to effect the entire ruin of the Roman empire, sullied by so many crimes. Brunehaut and Fredegonda are the results of the painful struggle of civilization in its infancy, when man was learning to control mind, were it even by an emissary

from the realms of darkness. All these women had been, or were, beautiful. The same flower of innocence had flourished, or was still flourishing on their brow, that is seen on the brow of the culprit in your house."

Villefort shrieked, clasped his hands, and looked at the doctor with a supplicating air. But the latter pursued without pity.

"'Seek whom the crime will profit,' says an axiom of jurisprudence."

"Doctor," cried Villefort, "alas, doctor! how often has man's justice been deceived by those fatal words. I know not why, but I feel that this crime ——"

"You acknowledge, then, the existence of the crime?"

"Yes, I see too plainly that it does exist. But it seems that it is intended to affect me personally. I fear an attack myself, after all these disasters."

"Oh, man!" murmured d'Avrigny, "the most selfish of all animals, the most personal of all creatures, who believes the earth turns, the sun shines, and death strikes for him alone,— an ant cursing God from the top of a blade of grass! And have those who have lost their lives lost nothing?— M. de Saint-Méran, Madame de Saint-Méran, M. Noirtier ——"

"How! M. Noirtier?"

"Yes; think you it was the poor servant's life was coveted? No, no! like Shakespeare's *Polonius*, he died for another. It was Noirtier the lemonade was intended for—it is Noirtier, in the logical order of events, who drank it; the other drank it only by accident; and although Barrois is dead, it was Noirtier whose death was wished for."

"But why did it not kill my father?"

"I told you one evening, in the garden, after Madame de Saint-Méran's death, because his system is accustomed to that very poison; and the dose was trifling for him, which would be fatal for another; because no one knows, not even the assassin, that, for the last twelve months, I have given M. Noirtier brucine for his paralytic affection; while the assassin is not ignorant, and has proved by experience that brucine is a violent poison."

"Pity, pity!" murmured Villefort, wringing his hands.

"Follow the culprit's steps; he first kills M. de Saint-Méran ——"

"Oh, doctor!"

"I would swear to it; what I heard of his symptoms agrees too well with what I have seen in the other cases." Villefort ceased to contend; he only groaned. "He first kills M. de Saint-Méran," repeated the doctor, "then Madame de Saint-Méran,—a double fortune to inherit." Villefort wiped the perspiration from his forehead. "Listen attentively."

"Alas!" stammered Villefort, "I do not lose a single word."

"M. Noirtier," resumed d'Avrigny, in the same pitiless tone,—"M. Noirtier had once made a will against you—against your family,—in favor of the poor, in fact; M. Noirtier is spared, because nothing is expected from him. But he has no sooner destroyed his first will and made a second, than, for fear he should make a third, he is struck down;

the will was made the day before yesterday, I believe; you see there has been no time lost."

"Oh, mercy, M. d'Avrigny!"

"No mercy, sir! The physician has a sacred mission on earth; and

to fulfill it he begins at the source of life, and goes down to the mysterious darkness of the tomb. When crime has been committed, and God, doubtless in anger, turns away his face, it is for the physician to bring the culprit to justice."

"Have mercy on my child, sir!" murmured Villefort.

"You see it is yourself who have first named her — you, her father."

"Have pity on Valentine! Listen! it is impossible. I would as willingly accuse myself! Valentine, whose heart is pure as a diamond, as innocent as a lily!"

"No pity, *M. le Procureur du Roi;* the crime is flagrant. Mademoiselle herself packed all the medicines which were sent to M. de Saint-Méran, and M. de Saint-Méran is dead. Mademoiselle de Villefort prepared all the cooling draughts which Madame de Saint-Méran took, and Madame de Saint-Meran is dead. Mademoiselle de Villefort took from the hands of Barrois, who was sent out, the lemonade which M. Noirtier has every morning, and he has escaped only by a miracle. Mademoiselle de Villefort is the culprit! She is the poisoner! *M. le Procureur du Roi,* I denounce Mademoiselle de Villefort; do your duty."

"Doctor, I resist no longer; I can no longer defend myself; I believe you; but, for pity's sake, spare my life, my honor!"

"M. de Villefort," replied the doctor, with increased vehemence, "there are occasions when I dispense with all foolish human circumspection. If your daughter had committed only one crime, and I saw her meditating another, I would say, 'Warn her, punish her, let her pass the remainder of her life in some cloister, in some convent, weeping and praying.' If she had committed two crimes, I would say, 'Here, M. de Villefort, is a poison that the poisoner is not acquainted with, one that has no known antidote, quick as thought, rapid as lightning, mortal as the thunderbolt; give her that poison, recommending her soul to God, and save your honor and your life, for it is yours she aims at; and I can picture her approaching your pillow with her hypocritical smiles and her sweet exhortations. Woe to you, M. de Villefort, if you do not strike first! This is what I would say had she only killed two persons; but she has seen three deaths,—has contemplated three murdered persons,—has knelt by three corpses! To the scaffold with the poisoner!—to the scaffold! Do you talk of your honor? Do what I tell you, and immortality awaits you!"

Villefort fell on his knees.

"Listen," said he; "I have not the strength of mind you have, or rather that which you would not have, if instead of my daughter Valentine your daughter Madeleine were concerned." The doctor turned pale. "Doctor, every son of woman is born to suffer and to die; I am content to suffer and to await death."

"Beware," said d'Avrigny; "it may come slowly; you will see it approach after having struck your father, your wife, perhaps your son."

Villefort, suffocating, pressed the doctor's arm.

"Listen!" cried he; "pity me,—help me! No, my daughter is not

guilty. If you drag us both before a tribunal I will still say, 'No, my daughter is not guilty;—there is no crime in my house.' I will not acknowledge a crime in my house; for when crime enters a dwelling, it is like death; it does not come alone. Listen!—What does it signify to you if I am murdered?—Are you my friend?—Are you a man?—Have you a heart?—No, you are a physician!—Well, I tell you I will not drag my daughter before a tribunal, and give her up to the executioner! The bare idea would kill me,—would drive me like a madman to dig my heart out with my finger-nails! And if you were mistaken, doctor!—if it were not my daughter!—If I should come one day, pale as a spectre, and say to you, 'Assassin! you have killed my child!' Hold! if that should happen, although I am a Christian, M. d'Avrigny, I should kill myself."

"Well," said the doctor, after a moment's silence; "I will wait."

Villefort looked at him as if he had doubted his words.

"Only," continued d'Avrigny, with a slow and solemn tone, "if any one falls ill in your house, if you feel yourself attacked, do not send for me, for I will come no more. I will consent to share this dreadful secret with you; but I will not allow shame and remorse to grow and increase in my conscience, as crime and misery will in your house."

"Then you abandon me, doctor?"

"Yes, for I can follow you no farther; and I only stop at the foot of the scaffold. Some further discovery will be made, which will bring this dreadful tragedy to a close. Adieu!"

"I entreat you, doctor!"

"All the horrors that disturb my thoughts make your house odious and fatal. Adieu, sir."

"One word,—one single word more, doctor! You go leaving me in all the horror of my situation, after increasing it by what you have revealed to me. But what will be reported of the sudden death of this poor old servant?"

"True," said d'Avrigny; "we will return."

The doctor went out first, followed by Villefort; the terrified servants were on the stairs and in the passage where the doctor would pass.

"Sir," said d'Avrigny to Villefort, so loud that all might hear, "poor Barrois has led too sedentary a life of late; accustomed formerly to ride on horseback, or in the carriage, to the four corners of Europe, the monotonous walk round that arm-chair has killed him: his blood has thickened; he was stout, had a short, thick neck, he was attacked with apoplexy, and I was called in too late. Apropos," added he, in a low tone, "take care to throw away that cup of syrup of violets in the ashes."

The doctor, without shaking hands with Villefort, without adding a word to what he had said, went out amid the tears and lamentations of the whole household. The same evening all Villefort's servants, who had assembled in the kitchen, and had a long consultation, came to tell Madame de Villefort they wished to leave. No entreaty, no proposition of increased wages, could induce them to remain; to every argument they replied, "We must go, for death is in this house."

They all left, in spite of prayers and entreaties, testifying their regret at leaving so good a master and mistress, and especially Mademoiselle Valentine, so good, so kind, and so gentle.

Villefort looked at Valentine as they said this. She was in tears; and, strange as it was, in spite of the emotions he felt at the sight of these tears, he looked also at Madame de Villefort, and it appeared to him as if a slight gloomy smile had passed over her thin lips, like those meteors which are seen passing inauspiciously between two clouds in a stormy sky.

CHAPTER LXXXI

THE ROOM OF THE RETIRED BAKER

THE evening of the day on which the Count de Morcerf had left Danglars' house with feelings of shame and anger, caused by the banker's coldness, Andrea Cavalcanti, with curled hair, mustaches in perfect order, and white gloves which fitted admirably, had entered the court-yard of the banker's house in La Chaussée d'Antin. He had not been more than ten minutes in the drawing-room before he drew Danglars aside into the recess of a bow-window; and, after an ingenious preamble, related to him all his anxieties since his noble father's departure. He had found, he said, in the banker's family, in which he had been received as a son, all the guarantees of happiness, which one ought to seek for in preference to the caprices of passion, and as regards passion itself, he had the felicity of meeting it in the lovely eyes of Mademoiselle Danglars.

Danglars listened with the most profound attention; he had expected this declaration the last two or three days; and when at last it came, his eyes glistened as much as they had lowered on listening to Morcerf. He would not, however, yield immediately to the young man's request, but made a few conscientious scruples.

"Are you not rather young, M. Andrea, to think of marrying?"

"I think not, sir," replied Cavalcanti; "in Italy the nobility generally marry young; life is so uncertain, we ought to secure happiness while it is within our reach."

"Well, sir," said Danglars, "in case your proposals, which do me honor, are accepted by my wife and daughter, by whom shall the preliminary arrangements be settled? So important a negotiation should, I think, be conducted by the respective fathers of the young people."

"Sir, my father is a man of great foresight and prudence. Imagining I might wish to settle in France, he left me at his departure, together with the papers constituting my identity, a letter promising, if he approved of my choice, one hundred and fifty thousand livres per annum from the day I was married. So far as I can judge, I suppose this to be a quarter of my father's revenue."

"I," said Danglars, "have always intended giving my daughter five hundred thousand francs as her dowry; she is, besides, my sole heiress."

"All would then be easily arranged if the baroness and her daughter are willing. We should command an annuity of one hundred and seventy-five thousand livres. Supposing, also, I should persuade the marquis to give me my capital, which is not likely, but still is possible, we would place these two or three millions in your hands, whose talent might make it realize ten per cent."

"I never give more than four per cent., and generally only three and a half; but, to my son-in-law I would give five, and we would share the profits."

"Very good, father-in-law," said Cavalcanti, yielding to his low-born nature, which would escape sometimes through the aristocratic gloss with which he sought to conceal it. Correcting himself immediately, he said, "Excuse me, sir; hope alone makes me almost mad,— what will not reality do?"

"But," said Danglars, who, on his part, did not perceive how soon the conversation, which was at first disinterested, was turning to a business transaction, "there is, doubtless, a part of your fortune your father could not refuse you?"

"Which?" asked the young man.

"That you inherit from your mother."

"Truly, from my mother, Leonora Corsinari."

"How much may it amount to?"

"Indeed, sir," said Andrea, "I assure you I have never given the subject a thought; but I suppose it must have been at least two millions."

Danglars felt as much overcome with joy as the miser who finds a lost treasure, or as the shipwrecked mariner who feels himself on the solid ground instead of in the abyss which he expected would swallow him up.

"Well, sir," said Andrea, bowing to the banker, respectfully, "may I hope?"

"You may not only hope," said Danglars, "but consider it a settled thing, if no obstacle arises on your part."

"I am, indeed, rejoiced," said Andrea.

"But," said Danglars, thoughtfully, "how is it that your patron, M. de Monte-Cristo, did not make this proposal for you?"

Andrea blushed imperceptibly.

"I have just left the count, sir," said he; "he is, doubtless, a delightful man, but inconceivably singular in his ideas; he esteems me highly; he even told me he had not the slightest doubt that my father would give me the capital instead of the interest of my property; he has promised to use his influence to obtain it for me; but he also declared that he never had taken upon himself the responsibility of making proposals for another, and he never would. I must, however, do him the justice to add that he assured me, if ever he had regretted the repugnance he felt to such a step, it was on this occasion, because he thought the projected union would be a happy and suitable one. Besides, if he will do nothing officially, he will answer any questions you propose to him. And now," continued he, with one of his most charming smiles, "having finished talking to the father-in-law, I must address myself to the banker."

"And what may you have to say to him?" said Danglars, laughing in his turn.

"That the day after to-morrow I shall have somewhere about four thousand francs to draw upon with your house; but the count, expecting my bachelor's revenue could not suffice for the increased expenses of the coming month, has offered me a draft for eighty thousand francs. It bears his signature, as you see, which is all-sufficient."

"Bring me a million such as that," said Danglars, "I shall be well pleased"—putting the draft in his pocket. "Fix your own hour for to-morrow, and my cashier shall call on you with a check for eighty thousand francs."

"At ten o'clock, then, if you please; I should like it early, as I am going into the country to-morrow."

"Very well, at ten o'clock; you are still at the Hôtel des Princes?"

"Yes."

The following morning, with the banker's usual punctuality, the eighty thousand francs were placed in the young man's hands, as he was on the point of starting, having left two hundred francs for Caderousse. He went out chiefly to avoid this dangerous enemy, and returned as late as possible in the evening.

But scarcely had he stepped out of his carriage, when the porter met him with a parcel in his hand.

"Sir," said he, "the man has been ——"

"What man?" said Andrea, carelessly, apparently forgetting him whom he but too well recollected.

"The man to whom your excellency pays that little annuity."

"Oh!" said Andrea, "my father's old servant. Well, you gave him the two hundred francs I had left for him?"

"Yes, your excellency." Andrea had expressed a wish to be thus addressed. "But," continued the porter, "he would not take them."

Andrea turned pale, but as it was dark no one noticed his paleness. "What, he would not take them?" said he, with slight emotion.

"No, he wished to speak to your excellency; I told him you were gone out, which, after some dispute, he believed, and gave me this letter, which he had brought with him already sealed."

"Give it me," said Andrea, and he read by the light of his carriage-lamp,—

"'You know where I live; I expect you to-morrow morning at nine o'clock.'"

Andrea examined it carefully, to ascertain if the letter had been opened, or if any indiscreet eyes had seen its contents, but it was so carefully folded, no one could have read it, and the seal was perfect.

"Very well," said he. "Poor man! he is a worthy creature." He left the porter to ponder on these words, not knowing which most to admire, the master or the servant.

"Take out the horses quickly, and come up to me," said Andrea to his groom. In two seconds the young man had reached his room and burned Caderousse's letter. The servant entered just as he had finished.

"You are about my height, Peter," said he.

"I have that honor, your excellency."

"You had a new livery yesterday?"

"Yes, sir."

"I have an engagement with a pretty little girl for this evening, and do not wish to be known; lend me your livery till to-morrow; I may sleep, perhaps, at an inn."

Peter obeyed. Five minutes after, Andrea left the hotel, completely disguised, took a cabriolet, and ordered the driver to take him to the Cheval Rouge, at Picpus. The next morning he left that inn as he had left the Hôtel des Princes, without being noticed, walked down the Faubourg Saint-Antoine, along the Boulevard to Rue Ménilmontant, and, stopping at the door of the third house on the left, looked for some one of whom to make inquiry in the porter's absence.

"For whom are you looking, my fine fellow?" asked the fruiteress on the opposite side.

"M. Pailletin, if you please, my good woman," replied Andrea.

"A retired baker?" asked the fruiteress.

"Exactly."

"He lives at the end of the yard, on the left, on the third story."

Andrea went as she directed him, and on the third floor he found a hare's paw, which, by the hasty ringing of the bell, it was evident he pulled with considerable ill-temper. A moment after, Caderousse's face appeared at the grating in the door.

"Ah! you are punctual," said he, as he unbolted the door.

"Confound you and your punctuality!" said Andrea, throwing himself into a chair in a manner which implied that he would rather have flung it at the head of his host.

"Come, come, my little fellow, don't be angry. See, I have thought about you — look at the good breakfast we are going to have; nothing but what you are fond of."

Andrea, indeed, inhaled the scent of something cooking, which was not unwelcome to him, hungry as he was; it was that mixture of fat and garlic peculiar to Provençal kitchens of an inferior order, added to that of dried fish, and above all, the pungent smell of musk and cloves. These odors escaped from two deep dishes, which were covered, and placed on a stove, and from a copper pan placed in an old iron pot. In

an adjoining room, Andrea saw also a tolerably clean table prepared for two, two bottles of wine sealed, the one with green, the other with yellow, a considerable portion of brandy in a decanter, and a measure of fruit in a cabbage-leaf, cleverly arranged on an earthenware plate.

"What do you think of it, my little fellow?" said Caderousse. "Ay!

that smells good! you know I used to be a good cook; do you recollect how you used to lick your fingers? You were among the first who tasted any of my dishes, and I think you relished them tolerably." While speaking, Caderousse went on peeling a fresh supply of onions.

"But," said Andrea, ill-temperedly, "*pardieu!* if you disturbed me only to breakfast with you, the devil take you!"

"My boy," said Caderousse, sententiously, "one can talk while eating. And then, you ungrateful being! you are not pleased to see an old friend? I am weeping with joy."

He was truly crying, but it would have been difficult to say whether joy or the onions produced the greatest effect on the lachrymal gland of the old inn-keeper of the Pont-du-Gard.

"Hold your tongue, hypocrite!" said Andrea; "you love me! You!"

"Yes, I do, or may the devil take me. I know it is a weakness," said Caderousse, "but it overpowers me."

"And yet it has not prevented your sending for me to play me some trick."

"Come!" said Caderousse, wiping his large knife on his apron, "if I did not like you, do you think I should endure the wretched life you lead me? Think for a moment: you have your servant's clothes on—you, therefore, keep a servant; I have none, and am obliged to prepare my own meals; you abuse my cookery because you dine at the table-d'hôte of the Hôtel des Princes, or the Café de Paris. Well! I, too, could keep a servant; I, too, could have a tilbury; I, too, could dine where I like; but why do I not? Because I would not annoy my little Benedetto. Come! just acknowledge that I could, eh!"

This address was accompanied by a look which was by no means difficult to understand.

"Well!" said Andrea, "admitting your love, why do you want me to breakfast with you?"

"That I may have the pleasure of seeing you, my little fellow."

"Of seeing me? what for? since we have made all our arrangements?"

"Eh! dear friend," said Caderousse, "are wills ever made without codicils? But first of all, you came to breakfast, did you not? Well! sit down, and let us begin with these sardines, and this fresh butter, which I have put on some vine-leaves, to please you, you rogue. Ah! yes; you look at my room, my four straw chairs, the plaster figures, three francs each. But what do you expect? this is not the Hôtel des Princes."

"Come! you are growing discontented, you are no longer happy; you, who only wished to appear a retired baker."

Caderousse sighed.

"Well! what have you to say? you have seen your dream realized."

"I can still say it is a dream; a retired baker, my poor Benedetto, is rich — he has an annuity."

"Well, you have an annuity."

"I have."

"Yes, since I bring you your two hundred francs."

Caderouse shrugged up his shoulders.

"It is humiliating," said he, "thus to receive money given grudgingly; an uncertain supply which may soon fail. You, see I am obliged to economize, in case your prosperity should cease. Well, my friend, fortune is inconstant, as said the chaplain of the —— regiment. I know your prosperity is great, rascal; you are to marry the daughter of Danglars."

"What! of Danglars?"

"Yes, to be sure! must I say Baron Danglars? I might as well say Count Benedetto. He was an old friend of mine, and if he had not so bad a memory, he ought to invite me to your wedding, seeing he came to mine. Yes, yes, to mine; forsooth! he was not so proud then; he was an under-clerk to the good M. Morrel. I have dined many times with him and the Count de Morcerf; so you see I have some high connections, and were I to cultivate them a little, we might meet in the same drawing-rooms."

"Come, your jealousy represents everything to you in the wrong light."

"That is all very fine, my Benedetto, but I know what I am saying. Perhaps I may one day put on my best coat, and presenting myself at the front door, introduce myself. Meanwhile let us sit down and eat."

Caderousse set the example, and attacked the breakfast with good appetite, praising each dish he set before his visitor. The latter seemed to have resigned himself; he drew the corks, and partook largely of the fish with the garlic and fat.

"Ah! comrade," said Caderousse, "you are getting on better terms with your old landlord!"

"Faith, yes," replied Andrea, whose hunger prevailed over every other feeling.

"So you like it, you rogue?"

"So much that I wonder how a man who can cook thus can complain of hard living."

"Do you see," said Caderousse, "all my happiness is marred by one thought?"

"What is that?"

"That I am dependent on another, I who have always gained my own livelihood honestly."

"Do not let that disturb you, I have enough for two."

"No, truly; you may believe me if you will; at the end of every month I am tormented by remorse."

"Good Caderousse!"

"So much so, that yesterday I would not take the two hundred francs."

"Yes, you wished to speak to me; but was it indeed remorse, tell me?"

"True remorse; and, besides, an idea had struck me."

Andrea shuddered; he always did so at Caderousse's ideas.

"It is miserable — do you see? — always to wait till the end of the month."

"Oh!" said Andrea, philosophically, determined to watch his companion narrowly, "does not life pass in waiting? Do I, for instance, do anything else? Well, I wait patiently, do I not?"

"Yes, because instead of expecting two hundred wretched francs, you expect five or six thousand, perhaps ten, perhaps even twelve; for you take care not to let any one know the utmost; down there, you always had little presents, and Christmas-boxes, which you tried to hide from your poor friend Caderousse. Fortunately he is a cunning fellow, that friend Caderousse."

"There you are beginning again to ramble, to talk again and again of the past! But what is the use of so much repetition?"

"Ah! you are only one-and-twenty, and can forget the past; I am fifty, and am obliged to recollect it. But let us return to business."

"Yes."

"I was going to say, if I were in your place ——"

"Well."

"I would realize ——"

"How would you realize?"

"I would ask for six months' in advance, under pretense of being able to purchase a farm, then with my six months' I would decamp."

"Well, well," said Andrea, "that is no bad thought."

"My dear friend," said Caderousse, "eat of my bread, and take my advice; you will be none the worse off, physically or morally."

"But," said Andrea, "why do you not act on the advice you give me? Why do you not realize a six months', a year's advance even, and retire to Brussels? Instead of living the retired baker, you might live as a bankrupt using his privileges; that would be very good."

"But how the devil would you have me retire on twelve hundred francs?"

"Ah! Caderousse," said Andrea, "how covetous you are! two months since you were dying with hunger."

"In eating the appetite grows," said Caderousse, grinning and showing his teeth, like a monkey laughing or a tiger growling. "And," added he, biting off, with those large white teeth, an enormous mouthful of bread, "I have formed a plan."

Caderousse's plans alarmed Andrea still more than his ideas: ideas were but the germ, the plan was reality.

"Let me see your plan; I dare say it is a pretty one."

"Why not? Who formed the plan by which we left the establishment of M.—M. What's-his-name, eh? was it not I? and it was no bad one I believe, since here we are!"

"I do not say," replied Andrea, "that you never make a good one; but let us see your plan."

"Well," pursued Caderousse, "can you, without expending one sou, put me in the way of getting fifteen thousand francs? No, fifteen thousand are not enough, I cannot again become an honest man with less than thirty thousand francs."

"No," replied Andrea, dryly, "no, I cannot."

"I do not think you understand me," replied Caderousse, calmly; "I said without your laying out a sou."

"Do you want me to commit a robbery, to spoil all my good fortune—and yours with mine—and both of us to be dragged down there again?"

"It would make very little difference to me," said Caderousse, "if I were re-taken; I am a poor creature to live alone, and sometimes pine for my old comrades; not like you, heartless creature, who would be glad never to see them again!"

Andrea did more than tremble this time, he turned pale.

"Come, Caderousse, no nonsense!" said he.

"Don't alarm yourself, my little Benedetto, but just point out to me some means of gaining those thirty thousand francs without your assistance; and I will contrive it."

"Well! I will see! I will look out!" said Andrea.

"Meanwhile you will raise my monthly allowance to five hundred francs, my little fellow? I have a fancy, and mean to get a housekeeper."

"Well! you shall have your five hundred francs," said Andrea; "but it is very hard for me, my poor Caderousse—you take advantage——"

"Bah!" said Caderousse, "when you have access to countless stores."

One would have said Andrea anticipated his companion's words, so did his eye flash like lightning; it was but for a moment.

"True," he replied, "and my protector is very kind."

"That dear protector," said Caderousse; "and how much does he give you monthly?"

"Five thousand francs."

"As many thousands as you give me hundreds! Truly, it is only bastards who are thus fortunate. Five thousand francs per month! what the devil can you do with all that?"

"Oh! it is no trouble to spend that; and I am like you,—I want a capital."

"A capital!—yes—I understand; every one would like a capital."

"Well! and I shall get one."

"Who will give it to you — your prince?"

"Yes, my prince. But unfortunately I must wait."

Brussels.

"You must wait for what?" asked Caderousse.

"For his death."

"The death of your prince?"

"Yes."

"How so?"

"Because he has made his will in my favor."

"Indeed?"

"On my honor."

"For how much?"

"For five hundred thousand."

"Only that! It's little enough!"

"But so it is."

"No, it cannot be!"

"Are you my friend, Caderousse?"

"Yes, in life or death."

"Well! I will tell you a secret."

"What is it?"

"But remember——"

"Ah! *pardieu!* mute as a carp."

"Well! I think——"

Andrea stopped and looked around.

"You think? Do not fear; *pardieu!* we are alone."

"I think I have discovered my father."

"Your true father?"

"Yes."

"Not old Cavalcanti?"

"No, for he is gone again; the true one, as you say."

"And that father is——"

"Well! Caderousse, it is Monte-Cristo."

"Bah!"

"Yes, you understand, that explains all. He cannot acknowledge me openly, it appears, but he does it through M. Cavalcanti, and gives him fifty thousand francs for it."

"Fifty thousand francs for being your father! I would have done it for half that, for twenty thousand, for fifteen thousand; why did you not think of me, ungrateful man?"

"Did I know anything about it, when it was all done when I was down there?"

"Ah! truly? And you say that by his will——"

"He leaves me five hundred thousand livres."

"Are you sure of it?"

"He showed it me; but that is not all—there is a codicil, as I said just now."

"Probably."

"And in that codicil he acknowledges me."

"Oh, what a good father! what an excellent father! what a very honest father!" said Caderousse, twirling a plate in the air between his two hands

"Now, say if I conceal anything from you?"

"No, and your confidence makes you honorable in my opinion; and your princely father, is he rich, very rich?"

"Yes, in truth, he does not himself know the amount of his fortune"

"Is it possible?"

"It is evident enough to me, who am always at his house The other day a banker's clerk brought him fifty thousand francs in a portfolio about the size of your plate, yesterday his banker brought him a hundred thousand francs in gold"

Caderousse was filled with wonder, the young man's words sounded to him like metal; and he thought he could hear the rushing of cascades of louis

"And you go into that house?" cried he, briskly.

"When I like"

Caderousse was thoughtful for a moment It was easy to perceive he was revolving some important idea in his mind. Then suddenly,—

"How I should like to see all that!" cried he, "how beautiful it must be!"

"It is, in fact, magnificent," said Andrea.

"And does he not live in the Champs Elysées?"

"Yes, No. 30."

"Ah!" said Caderousse, "No 30"

"Yes, a fine house standing alone, between a court-yard and a garden, you must know it"

"Possibly; but it is not the exterior I care for, it is the interior; what beautiful furniture there must be in it!"

"Have you ever seen the Tuileries?"

"No"

"Well, it surpasses that"

"It must be worth one's while to stoop, Andrea, when that good M Monte-Cristo lets fall his purse."

"It is not worth while to wait for that," said Andrea; "money is as plentiful in that house as fruit in an orchard."

"But you should take me there one day with you"

"How can I? On what plea?"

"You are right; but you have made my mouth water, I must absolutely see it; I shall find a way"

"No nonsense, Caderousse!"

"I will offer myself as frotteur."

"The rooms are all carpeted."

"Well, then, I must be contented to imagine it."

"That is the best plan, believe me."

"Try, at least, to give me an idea of what it is."

"How can I?"

"Nothing is easier. Is it large?"

"Middling."

"How is it arranged?"

"Faith, I should require pen, ink, and paper to make a plan."

"They are all here," said Caderousse, briskly. He fetched from an old secrétaire a sheet of white paper, and pen and ink. "Here," said Caderousse, "trace me all that on the paper, my boy."

Andrea took the pen with an imperceptible smile, and began:

"The house, as I said, is between the court and the garden; in this way, do you see?" Andrea traced the garden, the court, and the house.

"High walls?"

"Not more than eight or ten feet."

"That is not prudent," said Caderousse.

"In the court are orange-trees in pots, turf, and clumps of flowers."

"And no steel traps?"

"No."

"The stables?"

"Are on either side of the gate, which you see there." And Andrea continued his plan.

"Let us see the ground-floor," said Caderousse.

"On the ground-floor, dining-room, two drawing-rooms, billiard-room, staircase in the hall, and little back staircase."

"Windows?"

"Magnificent windows, so beautiful, so large, that I believe a man of your size could pass through each frame."

"Why, the devil! have they any stairs with such windows?"

"Luxury has everything."

"But shutters?"

"Yes, but they are never used. That Count of Monte-Cristo is an original, who loves to look at the sky even at night."

"And where do the servants sleep?"

"Oh! they have a house to themselves. Picture to yourself a pretty coach-house at the right-hand side, where the ladders are kept. Well! over that coach-house are the servants' rooms, with bells corresponding with the different apartments."

"Ah! the devil! bells!"

"What do you say?"

"Oh, nothing! I only say they cost a load of money to hang; and what is the use of them, I should like to know?"

ANDREA TRACING THE HOUSE.

"There used to be a dog let loose in the yard at night; but it has been taken to the house at Auteuil, to that you went to, you know."

"Yes."

"I was saying to him only yesterday, 'You are imprudent, M. le Comte; for when you go to Auteuil, and take your servants, the house is left unprotected.' — 'Well,' said he, 'what next?' — 'Well, next, some day you will be robbed.'"

"What did he answer?"

"He quietly said, 'What do I care if I am?'"

"Andrea, he has some secrétaire with a spring?"

"How do you know?"

"Yes, which catches the thief in a trap and plays a tune. I was told there was such at the last exhibition."

"He has simply a mahogany secrétaire, in which the key is always kept."

"And he is not robbed?"

"No; his servants are all devoted to him."

"There ought to be some money in that secrétaire?"

"There may be. No one knows what there is."

"And where is it?"

"On the first floor."

"Sketch me the plan of that floor, as you have done of the ground-floor, my boy."

"That is very simple." Andrea took the pen. "On the first story, do you see, there is the anteroom and drawing-room; to the right of the drawing-room, a library and a study; to the left, a bedroom and a dressing-room. The famous secrétaire is in the dressing-room."

"Is there a window in the dressing-room?"

"Two; one here and one there." Andrea sketched two windows in the room, which formed an angle on the plan, and appeared a smaller square added to the long square of the bedroom. Caderousse became thoughtful.

"Does he often go to Auteuil?" added he.

"Two or three times a week. To-morrow, for instance, he is going to spend the day and night there."

"Are you sure of it?"

"He has invited me to dine there."

"There is a life for you!" said Caderousse; "a town-house and a country-house."

"That is what it is to be rich."

"And shall you dine there?"

"Probably."

"When you dine there, do you sleep there?"

"If I like; I am at home there."

Caderousse looked at the young man, as if to get at the truth from the bottom of his heart. But Andrea drew a cigar-case from his pocket, took a Havana, quietly lit it, and began smoking.

"When do you want your five hundred francs?" said he to Caderousse.

"Now, if you have them." Andrea took five and twenty louis from his pocket.

"Yellow boys?" said Caderousse; "no, I thank you."

"Oh! you despise them."

"On the contrary, I esteem them; but will not have them."

"You will make a profit on them, idiot; gold is worth five sous premium."

"Exactly; and he who changes them will follow friend Caderousse, lay hands on him, and demand what farmers pay him their rent in gold. No nonsense, my good fellow; silver simply, round coins with the head of some monarch or other on them. Anybody may possess a five-franc piece."

"But do you suppose I carry five hundred francs about with me? I should want a porter."

"Well, leave them with your porter, he is to be trusted; I will call for them."

"To-day?"

"No, to-morrow; I shall not have time to-day."

"Well, to-morrow I will leave them when I go to Auteuil."

"May I depend on it?"

"Certainly."

"Because I shall secure my housekeeper on the strength of it."

"Secure her! But will that be all? Eh? And will you not torment me any more?"

"Never."

Caderousse had become so gloomy that Andrea feared he should be obliged to notice the change. He redoubled his gayety and carelessness.

"How sprightly you are!" said Caderousse; "one would say you were already in possession of your property."

"No, unfortunately; but when I do obtain it——"

"Well?"

"I shall remember old friends; I only tell you that."

"Yes, since you have such a good memory."

"What do you want? I thought you had ransomed me."

"I? What an idea! I, who am going to give you another piece of good advice."

"What is it?"

"To leave behind you the diamond you have on your finger. We shall both get in trouble. You will ruin both yourself and me by your folly."

"How so?" said Andrea.

"How? You put on a livery; you disguise yourself as a servant, and yet keep a diamond on your finger worth four or five thousand francs."

"You guess well."

"I know something of diamonds; I have had some."

"You do well to boast of it," said Andrea, who, without becoming angry, as Caderousse feared, at this new extortion, quietly resigned the ring. Caderousse looked so closely at it that Andrea well knew that he was examining if all the edges were perfect.

"It is a false diamond," said Caderousse.

"You are joking now," replied Andrea.

"Do not be angry; we can try it." Caderousse went to the window, touched the glass with it, and found it would cut.

"*Confiteor!*" said Caderousse, putting the diamond on his little finger; "I was mistaken; but those thieves of jewelers imitate so well that it is no longer worth while to rob a jeweler's shop — it is another branch of industry paralyzed."

"Have you finished now?" said Andrea,—"do you want anything more?—will you have my waistcoat or my certificate? Make free now you have begun."

"No; you are, after all, a good fellow; I will not detain you, and will try to cure myself of my ambition."

"But take care the same thing does not happen to you in selling the diamond you feared with the gold."

"I shall not sell it — do not fear."

"Not at least till the day after to-morrow," thought the young man.

"Happy rogue!" said Caderousse; "you are going to find your servants, your horses, your carriage, and your betrothed!"

"Yes," said Andrea.

"Well, I hope you will make a handsome wedding-present the day you marry Mademoiselle Danglars."

"I have already told you it is a fancy you have taken in your head."

"What fortune has she?"

"But I tell you ——"

"A million?"

Andrea shrugged up his shoulders.

"Let it be a million," said Caderousse; "you can never have so much as I wish you."

"Thank you," said the young man.

"Oh, I wish it you, with all my heart!" added Caderousse, with his hoarse laugh. "Stop, let me show you the way."

"It is not worth while."

"Yes, it is."

"Why?"

"Because there is a little secret, a precaution I thought it desirable to take, one of Huret and Fitchet's locks, revised and improved by Gaspard Caderousse; I will manufacture you a similar one when you are a capitalist."

"Thank you," said Andrea; "I will let you know a week beforehand."

They parted. Caderousse remained on the landing until he had not only seen Andrea go down the three stories, but also cross the court. Then he returned hastily, shut his door carefully, and began to study, like a clever architect, the plan Andrea had left him.

"Dear Benedetto," said he, "I think he will not be sorry to inherit his fortune, and he who hastens the day when he can touch his five hundred thousand will not be his worst friend."

CHAPTER LXXXII

THE BURGLARY

THE day following that on which the conversation we have related took place, the Count of Monte-Cristo set out for Auteuil, accompanied by Ali and several attendants, and also taking with him some horses he wished to try. He was induced to undertake this journey, of which the day before he had not even thought, and which had not either occurred to Andrea, by the arrival of Bertuccio from Normandy, with intelligence respecting the house and sloop. The house was ready, and the sloop, which had arrived a week before, lay at anchor in a small creek, with her crew of six men, who, after having observed all the requisite formalities, were ready again to put to sea.

The count praised Bertuccio's zeal, and ordered him to prepare for a speedy departure, as his stay in France would not be prolonged more than a month.

"Now," said he, "I may require to go in one night from Paris to Tréport; let eight fresh horses be in readiness on the road, which will enable me to go fifty leagues in ten hours."

"Your highness had already expressed that wish," said Bertuccio, "and the horses are ready. I have bought them, and stationed them myself at the most desirable posts, namely,—in villages, where no one generally stops."

"That's well," said Monte-Cristo. "I remain here a day or two; arrange accordingly."

As Bertuccio was leaving the room to give the requisite orders, Baptistin opened the door; he held a letter on a silver waiter.

"What do you do here?" asked the count, seeing him covered with dust; "I did not send for you, I think?"

Baptistin, without answering, approached the count, and presented the letter. "Important and urgent," said he.

The count opened the letter, and read:

"'M. de Monte-Cristo is warned that this night a man will enter his house in the Champs Elysées with the intention of carrying off some papers supposed to be in the secrétaire in the dressing-room. The count's well-known courage will render unnecessary the aid of the police, whose interference might seriously affect him who sends this advice. The count, either by an opening from the bedroom or by concealing himself in the dressing-room, would be able to defend his property himself. Many attendants or apparent precautions would prevent the villain from the attempt, and M. de Monte-Cristo would lose the opportunity of discovering an enemy whom chance has revealed to him who now sends this warning to the count,—a warning he might not be able to send another time, if this first attempt should fail and another be made '"

The count's first idea was that this was an artifice of a robber—a stupid trap to draw his attention from a minor danger in order to expose him to a greater. He was on the point of sending the letter to the commissaire de police, notwithstanding the advice of his anonymous friend, or, perhaps, *because* of that advice, when suddenly the idea occurred to him that it might be some personal enemy, whom he alone should recognize, and over whom, if such were the case, he alone could gain any advantage, as Fiesco had done over the Moor who would have killed him. We know the count's vigorous and daring mind, facing impossibilities with that energy which makes the great man.

From his past life, from his resolution to shrink from nothing, the count had acquired an inconceivable relish for the contests in which he had engaged, sometimes against nature, which is God, sometimes against the world, which may pass for the devil.

"They do not want my papers," said Monte-Cristo; "they want to kill me: they are no robbers, but assassins. I will not allow M. le Préfet de Police to interfere with my private affairs. I am rich enough, forsooth, to dispute his authority on this occasion."

The count recalled Baptistin, who had left the room after delivering the letter.

"Return to Paris," said he; "assemble the servants who remain there. I want all my household at Auteuil."

"But will no one remain in the house, my lord?" asked Baptistin.

"Yes, the porter."

"My lord will remember that the lodge is at a distance from the house."

"Well?"

"The house might be stripped without his hearing the least noise."

"By whom?"

"By thieves."

"You are a fool, M. Baptistin! Thieves might strip the house—it would annoy me less than to be disobeyed." Baptistin bowed.

"You understand me?" said the count. "Bring your comrades here,

The Invalides.

one and all; but let everything remain as usual, only close the shutters of the ground-floor."

"And those of the first floor?"

"You know they are never closed. Go!"

The count signified his intention of dining alone, and that no one but Ali should attend him. Having dined with his usual tranquillity and moderation, the count, making a signal to Ali to follow him, went out by the side-gate, and, on reaching the Bois de Boulogne, turned, apparently without design, toward Paris, and at twilight found himself opposite his house in the Champs Elysées. All was dark; one solitary, feeble light was burning in the porter's lodge, about forty paces distant from the house, as Baptistin had said.

Monte-Cristo leaned against a tree, and, with that eye which was so rarely deceived, searched the double avenue, examined the passers-by, and carefully looked down the neighboring streets, to see that no one was concealed. Ten minutes passed thus, and he was convinced no one was watching him. He hastened to the side-door with Ali, entered precipitately, and by the servants' staircase, of which he had the key, gained his bedroom without opening or disarranging a single curtain, without even the porter having the slightest suspicion that the house, which he supposed empty, contained its chief occupant.

Arrived in his bedroom, the count motioned to Ali to stop; then he passed into the dressing-room, which he examined: all was as usual—the precious secrétaire in its place, and the key in the secrétaire. He doubly locked it, took the key, returned to the bedroom door, removed the double staple of the bolt, and went in. Meanwhile Ali had procured the arms the count required,—namely, a short carbine, and a pair of double-barreled pistols, with which as sure an aim might be taken as with a single-barreled one. Thus armed, the count held the lives of five men in his hands. It was about half-past nine.

The count and Ali ate in haste a crust of bread and drank a glass of Spanish wine; then Monte-Cristo slipped aside one of the movable panels, which enabled him to see into the adjoining room. He had within his reach his pistols and carbine, and Ali, standing near him, held one of those small Arabian axes, whose form has not varied since the crusades. Through one of the windows of the bedroom, on a line with that in the dressing-room, the count could see into the street.

Two hours passed thus. It was intensely dark; still Ali, thanks to his wild nature, and the count, thanks, doubtless, to his long confinement, could distinguish in the darkness the slightest movement of the trees. The little light in the lodge had been long extinct. It might be expected that the attack, if indeed an attack was projected, would be made from the staircase of the ground-floor, and not from a window; in Monte-Cristo's idea, the villains sought his life, not his money. It would be his bedroom they would attack, and they must reach it by the back staircase, or by the window in the dressing-room.

The clock of the Invalides struck a quarter to twelve; the west wind bore on its moistened gusts the doleful vibration of the three strokes. As the last stroke died away, the count thought he heard a slight noise in the dressing-room; this first sound, or rather this first grinding, was

followed by a second; then a third; at the fourth, the count knew what to expect. A firm and well-practiced hand was engaged in cutting the four sides of a pane of glass with a diamond. The count felt his heart beat more rapidly.

Inured as men may be to danger, forewarned as they may be of peril, they understand, by the fluttering of the heart and the shuddering of the frame, the enormous difference between a dream and a reality, between the project and the execution. However, Monte-Cristo only made a sign to apprise Ali, who, understanding that danger was approaching from the other side, drew nearer to his master. Monte-Cristo was eager to ascertain the strength and number of his enemies.

The window whence the noise proceeded was opposite the opening by which the count could see into the dressing-room. He fixed his eyes on that window—he distinguished a shadow in the darkness; then one of the panes became quite opaque, as if a sheet of paper were stuck on the outside, then the square cracked without falling. Through the opening an arm was passed to find the fastening, then a second; the window turned on its hinges, and a man entered. He was alone.

"That's a daring rascal!" whispered the count.

At that moment Ali touched him slightly on the shoulder. He turned; Ali pointed to the window of the room in which they were, facing the street.

"Good!" said he, "there are two of them; one acts while the other watches." He made a sign to Ali not to lose sight of the man in the street, and returned to the one in the dressing-room.

The glass-cutter had entered, and was feeling his way, his arms stretched out before him. He appeared to be familiar with everything. There were two doors; he bolted them both.

When he drew near to that of the bedroom, Monte-Cristo expected he was coming in, and raised one of his pistols; but he simply heard the sound of the bolts sliding in their copper rings. It was only a precaution. The nocturnal visitor, ignorant of the count's having removed the staples, might now think himself at home, and pursue his purpose with full security.

Alone and uncontrolled, the man then drew from his pocket something which the count could not discern, placed it on a stand, then went straight to the secrétaire, felt the lock, and, contrary to his expectation, found that the key was missing. But the glass-cutter was a prudent man, who had provided for all emergencies. The count soon heard the rattling of a bunch of shapeless keys, such as the locksmith brings when called to force a lock, and which thieves call nightingales, doubtless from the music of their nightly song when they turn the precious lock.

"Ah, ah!" whispered Monte-Cristo, with a smile of disappointment, "he is only a thief!"

But the man in the dark could not find the right key. He reached the instrument he had placed on the stand, touched a spring, and immediately a pale light, just bright enough to render objects distinct, was reflected on the hands and countenance of the man.

"Why!" exclaimed Monte-Cristo, starting back, "it is——"

Ali raised his hatchet.

"Don't stir," whispered Monte-Cristo, "and put down your hatchet; we shall require no arms."

Then he added some words in a low tone, for the exclamation which surprise had drawn from the count, weak as it had been, had startled the man, who remained in the position of the old grinder.

It was an order which the count had given, for immediately Ali went noiselessly, and returned, bearing a black dress and a three-cornered hat. Meanwhile Monte-Cristo had rapidly taken off his greatcoat, waistcoat, and shirt, and one might distinguish by the glimmering through the open panel that he wore one of those pliant tunics of steel mail, of which the last in France, where daggers are no longer feared, was worn by King Louis XVI., who feared the dagger at his breast, and whose head was cleft with the axe. This tunic soon disappeared under a long cassock, as did his hair under a priest's wig; the three-cornered hat over this, effectually transformed the count into an abbé.

The man, hearing nothing more, had again raised himself, and, while Monte-Cristo was completing his disguise, had advanced straight to the secrétaire, whose lock was beginning to creak under his nightingale.

"Well done!" whispered the count, who depended on the secret spring, which was unknown to the picklock, clever as he might be,—"well done! you have a few minutes' work there."

And he advanced to the window. The man whom he had seen seated on a fence had got down, and was still pacing the street; but, strange as it appeared, he cared not for those who might pass from the avenue of the Champs Elysées or by the Faubourg Saint-Honoré; his attention was engrossed with what was passing at the count's, and his only aim appeared to be to discern every movement in the dressing-room.

Monte-Cristo suddenly struck his finger on his forehead, and a smile passed over his lips; then drawing near to Ali, he whispered:

"Remain here, concealed in the dark, and whatever noise you hear, whatever passes, only come in or show yourself if I call you."

Ali bowed in token of strict obedience. Monte-Cristo then drew a lighted taper from a closet, and when the thief was deeply engaged with his lock, silently opened the door, taking care that the light should shine directly on his face. The door opened so quietly that the thief heard no sound; but, to his astonishment, the room was in a moment light. He turned.

"Good-evening, dear M. Caderousse!" said Monte-Cristo; "what are you doing here at such an hour?"

"The Abbé Busóni!" exclaimed Caderousse; and not knowing how this strange apparition could have entered when he had bolted the doors, he let fall his bunch of keys, and remained motionless and stupefied. The count placed himself between Caderousse and the window, thus cutting off from the thief his only chance of retreat.

"The Abbé Busoni!" repeated Caderousse, fixing his haggard gaze on the count.

"Yes, doubtless, the Abbé Busoni himself!" replied Monte-Cristo. "And I am very glad you recognize me, dear M. Caderousse; it proves

"THE ABBÉ BUSONI!"

you have a good memory, for it must be about ten years since we last met."

This calmness of Busoni, combined with his irony and boldness, staggered Caderousse.

"The abbé, the abbé!" murmured he, clenching his fists, and his teeth chattering.

"So you would rob the Count of Monte-Cristo?" continued the false abbé.

"M. l'Abbé," murmured Caderousse, seeking to regain the window, which the count pitilessly intercepted,—"M. l'Abbé, I don't know—believe me—I take my oath——"

"A pane of glass out," continued the count, "a dark lantern, a bunch of false keys, a secrétaire half forced—it is tolerably evident——"

Caderousse was choking; he looked round for some corner to hide in—some way of escape.

"Come, come," continued the count, "I see you are still the same—an assassin."

"M. l'Abbé, since you know everything, you know it was not I—it was La Carconte; that was proved at the trial, since I was only condemned to the galleys."

"Is your time, then, expired, since I find you in a fair way to return there?"

"No, M. l'Abbé, I have been liberated by some one."

"That some one has done society a great kindness."

"Ah," said Caderousse, "I had promised——"

"And you are breaking your promise!" interrupted Monte-Cristo.

"Alas, yes!" said Caderousse, very uneasily.

"A bad relapse, that will lead you, if I mistake not, to the Place de Grève. So much the worse, so much the worse—*diavolo!* as they say in my country."

"M. l'Abbé, I am impelled——"

"Every criminal says the same thing."

"Poverty——"

"Pshaw!" said Busoni, disdainfully, "poverty may make a man beg, steal a loaf of bread at a baker's door, but not cause him to open a secrétaire in a house supposed to be inhabited. And when the jeweler Johannes had just paid you forty-five thousand francs for the diamond I had given you, and you killed him to get the diamond and the money, both, was that also poverty?"

"Pardon, M. l'Abbe!" said Caderousse; "you have saved my life once, save me again!"

"That is but poor encouragement."

"Are you alone, M. l'Abbé, or have you there soldiers ready to seize me?"

"I am alone," said the abbé, "and I will again have pity on you and will let you escape, at the risk of the fresh miseries my weakness may lead to, if you tell me the truth."

"Ah, M. l'Abbé," cried Caderousse, clasping his hands, and drawing nearer to Monte-Cristo, "I may indeed say you are my deliverer!"

"You mean to say you have been freed from confinement?"

"Yes, in truth, M. l'Abbé."

"Who was your liberator?"

"An Englishman."

"What was his name?"

"Lord Wilmore."

"I know him; I shall know if you lie."

"M. l'Abbé, I tell you the simple truth."

"Was this Englishman protecting you?"

"No, not me, but a young Corsican, my companion."

"What was this young Corsican's name?"

"Benedetto."

"Is that his Christian name?"

"He had no other; he was a foundling."

"Then this young man escaped with you?"

"He did."

"In what way?"

"We were working at Saint-Mandrier, near Toulon. Do you know Saint-Mandrier?"

"I do."

"In the hour of rest, between noon and one o'clock ——"

"Galley-slaves having a nap after dinner! We may well pity the poor fellow!" said the abbé.

"Nay," said Caderousse, "one can't always work — one is not a dog!"

"So much the better for the dogs!" said Monte-Cristo.

"While the rest slept, then, we went away a short distance; we severed our fetters with a file the Englishman had given us, and swam away."

"And what is become of this Benedetto?"

"I don't know."

"You ought to know."

"No, in truth; we parted at Hyères." And to give more weight to his protestation, Caderousse advanced another step toward the abbé, who remained motionless in his place, as calm as ever, and pursuing his interrogation.

"You lie!" said the Abbé Busoni, with a tone of irresistible authority.

"M. l'Abbé!"

"You lie! This man is still your friend, and you, perhaps, make use of him as your accomplice."

Hyères.

"Oh, Monsieur l'Abbé!"

"Since you left Toulon what have you lived on? Answer me!"

"On what I could get."

"You lie!" repeated the abbé, a third time, with a still more imperative tone. Caderousse, terrified, looked at the count. "You have lived on the money he has given you."

"True!" said Caderousse; "Benedetto has become the son of a great lord."

"How can he be the son of a great lord?"

"A natural son."

"And what is that great lord's name?"

"The Count of Monte-Cristo, the very same in whose house we are."

"Benedetto the count's son!" replied Monte-Cristo, astonished in his turn.

"Forsooth! I suppose so, since the count has found him a false father—since the count gives him four thousand francs a month, and leaves him five hundred thousand francs in his will."

"Ah! ah!" said the false abbé, who began to understand; "and what name does the young man bear meanwhile?"

"Andrea Cavalcanti."

"Is it, then, that young man whom my friend the Count of Monte-Cristo has received into his house, and who is going to marry Mademoiselle Danglars?"

"Exactly."

"And you suffer that, you wretch!—you, who know his life and his crime?"

"Why should I stand in a comrade's way?" said Caderousse.

"You are right; it is not you who should apprise M. Danglars, it is I."

"Do not do so, M. l'Abbé."

"Why not?"

"Because you would bring us to ruin."

"And you think that to save such villains as you I will become an abettor of their plot—an accomplice in their crimes?"

"M. l'Abbé," said Caderousse, drawing still nearer.

"I will expose all."

"To whom?"

"To M. Danglars."

"By Heaven!" cried Caderousse, drawing from his waistcoat an open knife, and striking the count in the breast, "you shall disclose nothing, M. l'Abbé!"

To Caderousse's great astonishment, the knife, instead of piercing the count's breast, flew back blunted. At the same moment the count seized with his left hand the assassin's wrist, and wrung it with such strength that the knife fell from his stiffened fingers, and Caderousse uttered a cry of pain. But the count, disregarding his cry, continued to wring the bandit's wrist, until, his arm being dislocated, he fell first on his knees, then flat on the floor.

The count then placed his foot on his head, saying, "I know not what restrains me from crushing thy skull, rascal!"

"Ah, mercy — mercy!" cried Caderousse.

The count withdrew his foot.

"Rise!" said he. Caderousse rose.

"What a wrist you have, M. l'Abbé!" said Caderousse, stroking his arm, all bruised by the fleshy pincers which had held it — "what a wrist! ——"

"Silence! God gives me strength to overcome a wild beast like you; in the name of that God I act — remember that, wretch! — and to spare thee at this moment is still serving him."

"Oh!" said Caderousse, groaning with pain.

"Take this pen and paper, and write what I dictate."

"I don't know how to write, M. l'Abbé."

"You lie! Take this pen, and write!"

Caderousse, awed by the superior power of the abbé, sat down and wrote:

"SIR:—The man whom you are receiving at your house, and to whom you intend to marry your daughter, is a felon who escaped with me from confinement at Toulon He was No. 59, and I No. 58. He was called Benedetto; but he is ignorant of his real name, having never known his parents."

"Sign it!" continued the count.

"But would you ruin me?"

"If I sought your ruin, fool, I should drag you to the first guard-house; besides, when that note is delivered, in all probability you will have no more to fear. Sign it, then!"

Caderousse signed it.

"The address, 'A Monsieur le Baron Danglars, banker, Rue de la Chaussée d'Antin.'"

Caderousse wrote the address. The abbé took the note.

"Now," said he, "that suffices—begone!"

"Which way?"

"The way you came."

"You wish me to get out at that window?"

"You got in very well."

"Oh! you have some design against me, M. l'Abbé."

"Idiot! what design can I have?"

"Why, then, not let me out by the door?"

"What would be the advantage of waking the porter?"

"M. l'Abbé, tell me, do you not wish me dead?"

"I wish what God wills."

"But swear that you will not strike me as I go down."

"Cowardly fool!"

"What do you intend doing with me?"

"I ask you what can I do? I have tried to make you a happy man, and you have turned out a murderer."

"M. l'Abbé," said Caderousse, "make one more attempt—try me once more!"

"I will," said the count. "Listen—you know if I may be relied on."

"Yes," said Caderousse.

"If you arrive safely at home——"

"What have I to fear, except from you?"

"If you reach your home safely, leave Paris, leave France; and wherever you may be, so long as you conduct yourself well, I will send you a small annuity; for, if you return home safely, then ——"

"Then?" asked Caderousse, shuddering.

"Then I shall believe God has forgiven you, and I will forgive you too."

"As true as I am a Christian," stammered Caderousse, "you will make me die of fright!"

"Now, begone!" said the count, pointing to the window.

Caderousse, scarcely yet relying on this promise, put his legs out of the window, and stood on the ladder.

"Now, go down," said the abbé, folding his arms. Understanding he had nothing more to fear from him, Caderousse began to go down. Then the count brought the taper to the window, that it might be seen in the Champs Elysées that a man was getting out of the window while another held a light.

"What are you doing, M. l'Abbé? Suppose a watchman should pass?" And he blew out the light. He then descended, but it was only when he felt his foot touch the ground that he was satisfied he was safe.

Monte-Cristo returned to his bedroom, and glancing rapidly from the garden to the street, he saw first Caderousse, who, after walking to the end of the garden, fixed his ladder against the wall at a different part from where he came in. The count then, looking over into the street, saw the man who appeared to be waiting run in the same direction, and place himself against the angle of the wall where Caderousse would come over. Caderousse climbed the ladder slowly, and looked over the coping to see if the street was quiet. No one could be seen or heard. The clock of the Invalides struck one. Then Caderousse sat astride the coping, and, drawing up his ladder, passed it over the wall; then began to descend, or rather to slide down by the two sides, which he did with an ease which proved how accustomed he was to the exercise. But, once started, he could not stop. In vain did he see a man start from the shadow when he was half-way down—in vain did he see an arm raised as he touched the ground.

Before he could defend himself that arm struck him so violently in the back that he let go the ladder, crying, "Help!" A second blow struck him almost immediately in the side, and he fell, calling, "Help! murder!" Then, as he rolled on the ground, his adversary seized him by the hair, and struck him a third blow in the chest.

This time Caderousse endeavored to call again, but he could only utter a groan, and he shuddered as the blood flowed from his three wounds. The assassin, finding he no longer cried, lifted his head up by the hair; his eyes were closed, and mouth distorted. The murderer, supposing him dead, let fall his head and disappeared.

Then Caderousse, feeling that he was leaving him, raised himself on elbow, and, with a dying voice, cried, with great effort:

"Murder! I am dying! Help, M. l'Abbé—help!"

This mournful appeal pierced the darkness. The door of the back-staircase opened, then the side-gate of the garden, and Ali and his master were on the spot with lights.

CHAPTER LXXXIII

THE HAND OF GOD

CADEROUSSE continued to call piteously, "M. l'Abbé, help! help!"

"What is the matter?" asked Monte-Cristo.

"Help!" cried Caderousse; "I am murdered!"

"We are here—take courage!"

"Ah, it's all over! You are come too late,—you are come to see me die. What blows! What blood!"

He fainted. Ali and his master conveyed the wounded man into a room. Monte-Cristo motioned to Ali to undress him, and he then examined his dreadful wounds.

"My God!" he exclaimed, "thy vengeance is sometimes delayed, but only that it may fall the more effectually." Ali looked at his master for further instructions. "Conduct here immediately the *procureur du roi*, M. de Villefort, who lives in the Faubourg Saint-Honoré. As you pass the lodge, wake the porter, and send him for a surgeon."

Ali obeyed, leaving the abbé alone with Caderousse, who had not yet revived.

When the wretched man again opened his eyes, the count looked at him with a mournful expression of pity, and his lips moved as if in prayer. "A surgeon, M. l'Abbé—a surgeon!" said Caderousse.

"I have sent for one," replied the abbé.

"I know he cannot save my life, but he may strengthen me to give my evidence."

"Against whom?"

"Against my murderer."

"Did you recognize him?"

"Yes—it was Benedetto."

"The young Corsican?"

"Himself."

"Your comrade?"

"Yes. After giving me the plan of this house, doubtless hoping I should kill the count and he thus become his heir, or that the count would kill me and I should be out of his way, he waylaid me, and has murdered me."

"I have also sent for the *procureur du roi.*"

"He will not come in time; I feel my life fast ebbing."

"Stop!" said Monte-Cristo. He left the room, and returned in five minutes with a phial. The dying man's eyes were all the time riveted on the door, through which he hoped succor would arrive.

"Hasten, M. l'Abbé!—hasten! I shall faint again!" Monte-Cristo approached, and dropped on his purple lips three or four drops of the contents of the phial. Caderousse drew a deep breath. Oh!" said he, "that is life to me; more, more!"

"Two drops more would kill you," replied the abbé.

"Oh, send for some one to whom I can denounce the wretch!"

"Shall I write your deposition? You can sign it."

"Yes, yes," said Caderousse; and his eyes glistened at the thought of this posthumous revenge. Monte-Cristo wrote:

"I die murdered by the Corsican Benedetto, my comrade in the galleys at Toulon, No. 59."

"Quick, quick!" said Caderousse, "or I shall be unable to sign it."

Monte-Cristo gave the pen to Caderousse, who collected all his strength, signed it, and fell back on the bed, saying:

"You will relate all the rest, M. l'Abbé; you will say he calls himself Andrea Cavalcanti. He lodges at the Hôtel des Princes. Oh, I am dying!" He again fainted. The abbé made him smell the contents of the phial, and he again opened his eyes. His desire for revenge had not forsaken him.

"Ah! you will tell all I have said; will you not, M. l'Abbé?"

"Yes, and much more."

"What more will you say?"

"I will say he had doubtless given you the plan of this house, in the hope the count would kill you. I will say, likewise, he had apprised the count by a note of your intention; and, the count being absent, I read the note, and sat up to await you."

"And he will be guillotined, will he not?" said Caderousse. "Promise me that, and I will die with that hope."

"I will say," continued the count, "that he followed and watched you the whole time, and when he saw you leave the house, ran to the angle of the wall to conceal himself."

"Did you see all that?"

"Remember my words: 'If you return home safely, I shall believe God has forgiven you, and I will forgive you also.'"

"And you did not warn me!" cried Caderousse, raising himself on

his elbows. "You knew I should be killed on leaving this house, and did not warn me!"

"No, for I saw God's justice placed in the hands of Benedetto, and should have thought it sacrilege to oppose the designs of Providence."

"God's justice! Speak not of it, M. l'Abbé. If God were just, you know many would be punished who now escape."

"Patience!" said the abbé, in a tone which made the dying man shudder — "have patience!"

Caderousse looked at him with amazement.

"Besides," said the abbé, "God is merciful to all, as he has been to you; he is first a father, then a judge."

"Do you, then, believe in God?" said Caderousse.

"Had I been so unhappy as not to believe in him until now," said Monte-Cristo, "I must believe on seeing you."

Caderousse raised his clenched hands toward heaven.

"Listen," said the abbé, extending his hand over the wounded man, as if to command him to believe; "this is what the God in whom, on your death-bed, you refuse to believe, has done for you; he gave you health, strength, regular employment, even friends—a life, in fact, which a man might enjoy with a calm conscience. Instead of improving these gifts, rarely granted so abundantly, this has been your course: you have given yourself up to sloth and drunkenness, and in a fit of intoxication ruined your best friend."

"Help!" cried Caderousse, "I require a surgeon, not a priest; perhaps I am not mortally wounded—I may not die; perhaps they can yet save my life."

"Your wounds are so far mortal, that without the three drops I gave you, you would now be dead. Listen, then."

"Ah!" murmured Caderousse, "what a strange priest you are! you drive the dying to despair, instead of consoling them."

"Listen," continued the abbé. "When you had betrayed your friend, God began not to strike, but to warn you; poverty overtook you; you had already passed half your life in coveting that which you might have honorably acquired, and already you contemplated crime under the excuse of want, when God worked a miracle in your behalf, sending you, by my hands, a fortune—brilliant, indeed, for you, who had never possessed any. But this unexpected, unhoped-for, unheard-of fortune sufficed you no longer when you once possessed it; you wished to double it; and how?—by a murder! You succeeded, and then God snatched it from you, and brought you to justice."

"It was not I who wished to kill the Jew," said Caderousse; "it was La Carconte."

"Yes," said Monte-Cristo, "and God, I cannot say in justice, for his justice would have slain you—but God, in his mercy, spared your life."

"*Pardieu!* to transport me for life; how merciful!"

"You thought it a mercy then, miserable wretch! The coward, who feared death, rejoiced at perpetual disgrace, for, like all galley-slaves, you said, 'I may escape from prison; I cannot from the grave.' And you said truly; the way was opened for you unexpectedly; an Englishman visited Toulon, who had vowed to rescue two men from infamy, and his choice fell on you and your companion; you received a second fortune, money and tranquillity were restored to you; and you, who had been condemned to a felon's life, might live as other men. Then, wretched creature! then you tempted God a third time. 'I have not enough,' you said, when you had more than you before possessed, and you committed a third crime, without reason, without excuse. God is wearied, he has punished you."

Caderousse was fast sinking. "Give me drink," said he: "I thirst — I burn!" Monte-Cristo gave him a glass of water. "And yet that villain, Benedetto, will escape!"

"No one, I tell you, will escape; Benedetto will be punished."

"Then, you, too, will be punished, for you did not do your duty as a priest — you should have prevented Benedetto from killing me."

"I?" said the count, with a smile which petrified the dying man, "when you had just broken your knife against the coat of mail which protected my breast! Yet, perhaps, if I had found you humble and penitent, I might have prevented Benedetto from killing you; but I found you proud and blood-thirsty, and I left you in the hands of God."

"I do not believe there is a God!" howled Caderousse; "you do not believe it: you lie — you lie!"

"Silence!" said the abbé; "you will force the last drop of blood from your veins. What! you do not believe in God when he is striking you dead? you will not believe in him, who requires but a prayer, a word, a tear, and he will forgive? God, who might have directed the assassin's dagger so as to end your career in a moment, has given you this quarter of an hour for repentance. Reflect, then, wretched man, and repent."

"No," said Caderousse, "no; I will not repent: there is no God, there is no Providence — all comes by chance."

"There is a Providence, there is a God," said Monte-Cristo, "of which you are a striking proof, as you lie in utter despair, denying him; while I stand before you, rich, happy, safe, and supplicating that God in whom you endeavor not to believe, while in your heart you still believe in him."

"But who are you, then?" asked Caderousse, fixing his dying eyes on the count.

"Look well at me!" said Monte-Cristo, putting the light near his face.

"Well! the abbé — the Abbé Busoni." Monte-Cristo took off the wig which disfigured him, and let fall his black hair, which added so much to the beauty of his pallid features.

"Oh!" said Caderousse, thunderstruck, "but for that black hair, I should say you were the Englishman, Lord Wilmore."

"I am neither the Abbé Busoni nor Lord Wilmore," said Monte-Cristo. "Think again; do you not recollect me?"

There was a magnetic tone in the count's words, which once more revived the exhausted powers of the miserable man.

"Yes, indeed," said he, "I think I have seen you and known you formerly."

"Yes, Caderousse, you have seen me, you knew me once."

"Who then are you? and why, if you knew me, do you let me die?"

"Because nothing can save you; your wounds are mortal. Had it been possible to save you, I should have considered it another proof of God's mercy, and I would again have endeavored to restore you, I swear by my father's tomb."

"By your father's tomb!" said Caderousse, supported by a supernatural power, and half-raising himself to see more distinctly the man who had just taken the oath which all men hold sacred; "who, then, are you?"

The count had watched the approach of death. He knew this was the last struggle, he approached the dying man, and leaning over him with a calm and melancholy look, he whispered:

"I am — I am ——"

And his almost closed lips uttered a name so low that the count himself appeared afraid to hear it. Caderousse, who had raised himself on his knees, and stretched out his arm, tried to draw back; then clasping his hands, and raising them with a desperate effort,—"Oh! my God! my God!" said he, "pardon me for having denied thee; thou dost exist; thou art indeed man's father in heaven and his judge on earth. My God, my Lord, I have long despised thee! Pardon me, my God; receive me, O my Lord!"

Caderousse sighed deeply, and fell back with a groan. The blood no longer flowed from his wounds. He was dead.

"*One!*" said the count, mysteriously, his eyes fixed on the corpse, disfigured by so awful a death.

Ten minutes afterward, the surgeon, and the *procureur du roi* arrived,—the one accompanied by the porter, the other by Ali, and were received by the Abbé Busoni, who was praying by the side of the corpse.

CHAPTER LXXXIV

BEAUCHAMP

THE daring attempt to rob the count was the topic of conversation throughout Paris for the next fortnight; the dying man had signed a deposition declaring Benedetto to be the assassin. The police had orders to make the strictest search for the murderer. Caderousse's knife, dark lantern, bunch of keys, and clothing, excepting the waistcoat, which could not be found, were deposited at the registry; the corpse was conveyed to La Morgue.

The count told every one this adventure had happened during his absence at Auteuil, and that he only knew what was related by the Abbé Busoni, who that evening, by mere chance, had requested to pass the night in his house, to examine some valuable books in his library

Bertuccio alone turned pale whenever Benedetto's name was mentioned in his presence; but there was no reason why any one should notice his doing so.

Villefort, being called on to verify the crime, was preparing the documents with the same ardor as he was accustomed to exercise in criminal cases, when called on to speak.

But three weeks had already passed, and the most diligent search had been unsuccessful; the attempted robbery and the murder of the robber by his comrade were almost forgotten in anticipation of the approaching marriage of Mademoiselle Danglars to the Count Andrea Cavalcanti. It was expected this wedding would shortly take place, as the young man was received at the banker's as the betrothed.

Letters had been dispatched to Cavalcanti, as the count's father, who highly approved of the union, regretted his inability to leave Parma at that time, and promised a wedding gift of a hundred and fifty thousand livres. It was agreed that the three millions should be intrusted to Danglars to improve; some persons, indeed, had tried to instill into the young man doubts of the solidity of his future father-in-law, who had of late sustained repeated losses, but with sublime disinterestedness and confidence the young man refused to listen, or to express a single doubt of the baron.

The baron, on his side, adored Count Andrea Cavalcanti; not so Mademoiselle Eugénie Danglars. With an instinctive hatred of matrimony, she suffered Andrea's attentions in order to get rid of Morcerf; but when Andrea urged his suit, she betrayed an entire dislike to him. The baron might possibly have perceived it, but attributing it to caprice, feigned ignorance.

The delay demanded by Beauchamp had nearly expired. Morcerf appreciated the advice of Monte-Cristo, to let things die away of their own accord; no one had taken up the remark about the general, and no one had recognized in the officer who betrayed the castle of Janina the noble count who sat in the House of Peers.

Albert, however, felt no less insulted; the few lines which had irritated him were certainly intended as an insult. Besides, the manner in which Beauchamp had closed the conference left a bitter recollection in his heart. He cherished the thought of the duel, hoping to conceal its true cause even from his seconds. Beauchamp had not been seen since the day he visited Albert; and those of whom the latter inquired always told him he was out on a journey which would detain him some days. Where he was no one knew. One morning Albert was awoke by his valet-de-chambre, who announced Beauchamp. Albert rubbed his eyes, ordered his servant to introduce him into the small smoking-room on the ground-floor, dressed himself quickly, and went down.

He found Beauchamp pacing the room; on perceiving him Beauchamp stopped.

"Your arrival here, without waiting my visit at your house to-day looks well, sir," said Albert. "Tell me, may I shake hands with you? saying, 'Beauchamp, acknowledge you have injured me, and retain my friendship,' or must I simply propose to you a choice of arms?"

"Albert," said Beauchamp, with a look of sorrow which stupefied the young man, "let us first sit down and talk."

"Rather, sir, before we sit down, I must demand your answer."

"Albert," said the journalist, "these are questions which it is difficult to answer."

"I will facilitate it by repeating the question, 'Will you, or will you not, retract?'"

"Morcerf, it is not enough to answer Yes or No to questions which concern the honor, the social interest, and the life of such a man as the Lieutenant-général Count de Morcerf, peer of France."

"What must then be done?"

"What I have done, Albert. I reasoned thus: Money, time, and fatigue are nothing compared with the reputation and interests of a whole family; probabilities will not suffice, only facts will justify a

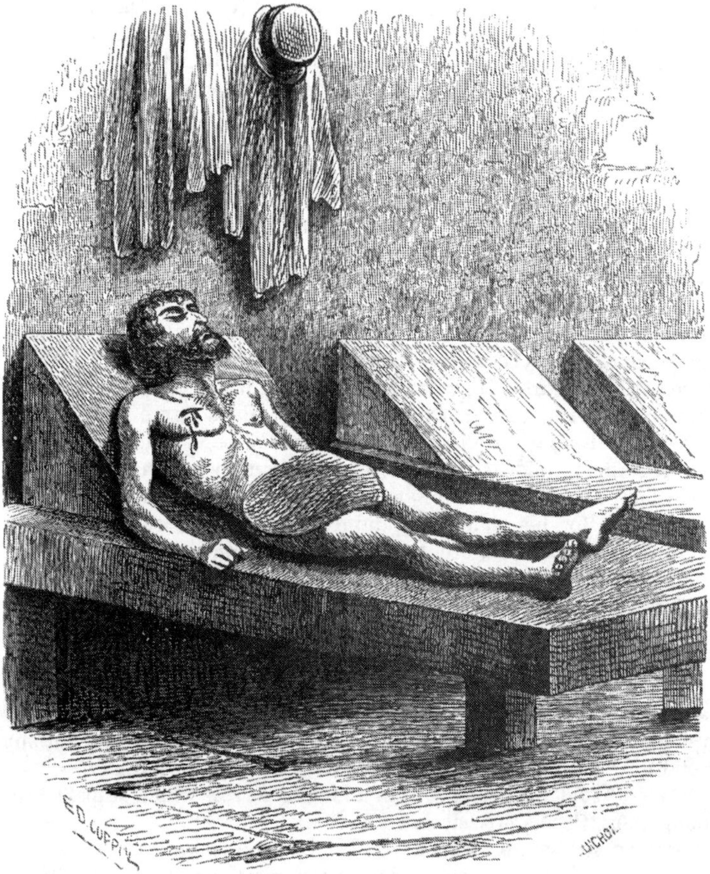

The Morgue.

deadly combat with a friend; if I strike with the sword or discharge the contents of a pistol at a man with whom, for three years, I have been on terms of intimacy, I must, at least, know why I do so; I must meet him with a heart at ease, and that quiet conscience which a man needs when his own arm must save his life."

"Well," asked Morcerf, impatiently, "what does all this mean?"

"It means that I have just returned from Janina."

"From Janina?"

"Yes."

"Impossible!"

"Here is my passport; examine the *visa*—Geneva, Milan, Venice, Trieste, Delvino, Janina. Will you believe the government of a republic, a kingdom, and an empire?" Albert cast his eyes on the passport, then raised them in astonishment to Beauchamp.

"You have been to Janina?" said he.

"Albert, had you been a stranger, a foreigner, a simple lord, like that Englishman who came to demand satisfaction three or four months since, and whom I killed to get rid of, I should not have taken this trouble; but I thought this mark of consideration due to you. I took a week to go, another to return, four days of quarantine, and forty-eight hours to stay there; that makes three weeks. I returned last night; and here I am."

"What circumlocution!—How long you are before you tell me what I most wish to know!"

"Because, in truth, Albert ——"

"You hesitate!"

"Yes,—I fear."

"You fear to acknowledge that your correspondent has deceived you? Oh! no self-love, Beauchamp. Acknowledge it, Beauchamp; your courage cannot be doubted."

"Not so," murmured the journalist; "on the contrary ——"

Albert turned frightfully pale; he endeavored to speak, but the words died on his lips.

"My friend," said Beauchamp, in the most affectionate tone, "I should gladly make an apology, but, alas! ——"

"But what?"

"The paragraph was correct, my friend."

"What! that French officer ——"

"Yes."

"Fernand?"

"Yes."

"The traitor who surrendered the castle of the man in whose service he was ——"

"Pardon me, my friend, that man was your father!"

Albert advanced furiously toward Beauchamp, but the latter restrained him more by a mild look than by his extended hand.

"My friend," said he, "here is a proof of it."

Albert opened the paper; it was an attestation of four notable inhabitants of Janina, proving that Colonel Fernand Mondego, in the service of Ali Tebelin, had surrendered the castle for two million crowns. The signatures were perfectly legal. Albert tottered and fell overpowered in

Venice.

a chair. It could no longer be doubted; the family name was fully given. After a moment's mournful silence, his heart overflowed, and he gave way to a flood of tears. Beauchamp, who had watched with sincere pity the young man's paroxysm of grief, approached him.

"Now, Albert," said he, "you understand me, do you not? I wished to see all, and to judge of everything for myself, hoping the explanation would be in your father's favor, and that I might do him justice. But, on the contrary, the particulars which are given prove that Fernand Mondego, raised by Ali Pacha to the rank of governor-general, is no other than Count Fernand de Morcerf; then, recollecting the honor you had done me, in admitting me to your friendship, I hastened to you."

Albert, still extended on the chair, covered his face with both hands, as if to prevent the light from reaching him.

"I hastened to you," continued Beauchamp, "to tell you, Albert, that in this changing age, the faults of a father cannot revert upon his children. Few have passed through this revolutionary period, in the midst of which we were born, without some stain of infamy or blood to soil the uniform of the soldier, the gown, or statesman. Now I have these proofs, Albert, and I am in your confidence, no human power can force me to a duel which your own conscience would reproach you with as criminal; but I come to offer you what you can no longer demand of me. Do you wish these proofs, these attestations, which I alone possess, to be destroyed? Do you wish this frightful secret to remain with us? Confided to me, it shall never escape my lips; say, Albert, my friend, do you wish it?"

Albert threw himself on Beauchamp's neck.

"Ah! noble fellow!" cried he.

"Take these," said Beauchamp, presenting the papers to Albert.

Albert seized them with a convulsive hand, tore them in pieces; and, trembling lest the least vestige should escape, and one day appear to confront him, he approached the wax-light, always kept burning for cigars, and consumed every fragment.

"Dear, excellent friend!" murmured Albert, still burning the papers.

"Let all be forgotten as a sorrowful dream," said Beauchamp; "let it vanish as the last sparks from the blackened paper, and disappear as the smoke from those silent ashes."

"Yes, yes," said Albert, "and may there remain only the eternal friendship which I promised to my deliverer, which shall be transmitted to our children's children, and shall always remind me that I owe my life and the honor of my name to you; for had this been known, oh! Beauchamp, I should have destroyed myself; or,—no, my poor mother! I could not have killed her by the same blow,—I should have fled from my country."

"Dear Albert," said Beauchamp. But this sudden and factitious joy soon forsook the young man, and was succeeded by still greater grief.

"Well," said Beauchamp, "what still oppresses you, my friend?"

"I am broken-hearted," said Albert. "Listen, Beauchamp! I cannot thus, in a moment, relinquish the respect, the confidence, and pride with which a father's untarnished name inspires a son. Oh! Beauchamp, Beauchamp! how shall I now approach mine? Shall I draw back my forehead from his embrace, or withhold my hand from his? I am the most wretched of men. Ah! my mother, my poor mother!" said Albert,

gazing through his tears at his mother's portrait; "if you know this, how much must you suffer?"

"Come," said Beauchamp, taking both his hands, "take courage, my friend."

"But how came that first note inserted in your journal? Some unknown enemy,—an invisible foe has done this."

"The more must you fortify yourself, Albert. Let no trace of emotion be visible on your countenance; bear your grief as the cloud bears within it ruin and death; a fatal secret, known only when the storm bursts. Go, my friend, reserve your strength for the moment when the crash shall come."

"You think, then, all is not over yet?" said Albert, horror-stricken.

"I think nothing, my friend; but all things are possible. Apropos ——"

"What?" said Albert, seeing Beauchamp hesitated.

"Are you going to marry Mademoiselle Danglars?"

"Why do you ask me now?"

"Because the rupture or the fulfillment of this engagement is connected with the person of whom we are speaking."

"How?" said Albert, whose brow reddened; "you think M. Danglars ——"

"I ask you only how your engagement stands? Pray put no construction on my words I do not mean they should convey, and give them no undue weight."

"No," said Albert, "the engagement is broken off."

"Well!" said Beauchamp. Then, seeing the young man was about to relapse into melancholy,—"Let us go out, Albert," said he; "a ride in the Bois in the phaeton, or on horseback, will refresh you; we will then return to breakfast, and you shall attend to your affairs, and I to mine."

"Willingly," said Albert; "but let us walk; I think a little exertion would do me good."

The two friends walked out along the boulevard. When they arrived at the Madeleine:—

"Since we are out," said Beauchamp, "let us call on M. de Monte-Cristo; he is admirably adapted to revive one's spirits, because he never interrogates; and, in my opinion, those who ask no questions are the best comforters."

"Gladly," said Albert; "let us call, I like him."

CHAPTER LXXXV

THE JOURNEY

MONTE-CRISTO uttered a joyful exclamation on seeing the young people together. "Ah! ah!" said he, "I hope all is over, explained and settled."

"Yes," said Beauchamp; "the absurd reports have died away, and should they be renewed, I would be the first to oppose them; so let us speak no more of it."

"Albert will tell you," replied the count, "that I gave him the same advice. Look," added he, "I am finishing the most execrable morning's work."

"What is it?" said Albert; "arranging your papers, apparently."

"My papers, thank God, no! my papers are all in capital order, because I have none; but M. Cavalcanti's."

"M. Cavalcanti's?" asked Beauchamp.

"Yes; do you not know that this is a young man whom the count is introducing?" said Morcerf.

"Let us not misunderstand each other," replied Monte-Cristo; "I introduce no one, and certainly not M. Cavalcanti."

"And who," said Albert, with a forced smile, "is to marry Mademoiselle Danglars instead of me, which grieves me cruelly."

"What! Cavalcanti is going to marry Mademoiselle Danglars?" asked Beauchamp.

"Certainly! do you come from the end of the world?" said Monte-Cristo; "you, a journalist, the spouse of Fame! it is the talk of all Paris."

"And you, count, have made this match?" asked Beauchamp.

"I? Silence, Monsieur the newsmonger, do not spread that report. I make a match! No, you do not know me; I have done all in my power to oppose it."

"Ah! I understand," said Beauchamp, "on our friend Albert's account."

"On my account?" said the young man; "oh, no, indeed! the count will do me the justice to assert that I have, on the contrary, always entreated him to break off my engagement, and happily it is ended. The count pretends I have not him to thank; well, like the ancients, I will raise an altar *Deo ignoto.*"

"Listen," said Monte-Cristo; "I have had little to do with it, for I am at variance both with the father-in-law and the young man; there is only Mademoiselle Eugénie, who appears but little charmed with the thoughts of matrimony, and who, seeing how little I was disposed to persuade her to renounce her dear liberty, retains any affection for me. Oh, yes, in spite of all I could say. I do not know the young man; he is said to be of good family and rich, but in my eyes such stories are mere gossip. I have repeated this to M. Danglars till I am tired, but he is fascinated with his friend from Lucca. I have even informed him of a circumstance I consider very serious; the young man was changed at nurse, either stolen by gypsies, or lost by his tutor, I scarcely know which. But I do know his father lost sight of him for more than ten years; what he did during these ten years, God only knows. Well, all that was useless. They have commissioned me to write to the major to demand his papers; and here they are. I send them on, but will have nothing more to do with the matter."

"And what does Mademoiselle d'Armilly say to you for robbing her of her pupil?"

"Forsooth! I know not; but I understand she is going to Italy. Madame Danglars asked me for letters of recommendation for the *impresari;* I gave her a few lines for the director of the Del Valle Theater, who is under some obligation to me. But what is the matter, Albert? you look dull; are you, after all, unconsciously in love with Mademoiselle Eugénie?"

"I am not aware of it," said Albert, smiling sorrowfully. Beauchamp turned to look at some paintings.

"But," continued Monte-Cristo, "you are not in your usual spirits?"

"I have a dreadful headache," said Albert.

"Well! my dear viscount," said Monte-Cristo, "I have an infallible remedy to propose to you."

"What is that?" asked the young man.

"A change."

"Indeed!" said Albert.

"Yes; and as I am just now excessively annoyed, I shall go from home. Shall we go together?"

"You annoyed, count?" said Beauchamp; "and by what?"

"*Pardieu!* you think very lightly of it; I should like to see you with an indictment preparing in your house."

"What indictment?"

"The one M. de Villefort is preparing against my amiable assassin — some brigand escaped from the galleys apparently."

"True," said Beauchamp; "I saw it in the paper. Who is this Caderousse?"

"Some provincial, it appears. M. de Villefort heard of him at Marseilles, and M. Danglars recollects having seen him. Consequently, *M. le Procureur* is very active in the affair, and the prefect of police very much interested; and, thanks to that interest, for which I am very grateful, they send me all the robbers of Paris and the neighborhood, under pretense of their being Caderousse's murderers; so that in three months, if this continue, every robber and assassin in France will have the plan of my house at his fingers' ends. Therefore, I am resolved to desert them and to go to some remote corner of the earth, and shall be happy if you will accompany me, viscount."

"Willingly."

"Then it is settled?"

"Yes; but where?"

"I have told you, where the air is pure, where every sound soothes, where one is sure to be humbled, however proud may be his nature. I love that humiliation, I, who am master of the universe, as was Augustus."

"But where are you really going?"

"To sea, viscount; to the sea—I am a sailor. I was rocked when an infant in the arms of old Ocean, and on the bosom of the beautiful Amphitrite; I have sported with the green mantle of the one and the azure robe of the other; I love the sea as a mistress, and pine if I do not often see her."

"Let us go, count."

"To the sea?"

"Yes."

"You accept my proposal?"

"I do."

"Well, viscount, there will be in my court-yard this evening a good traveling britska, with four post-horses, in which one may rest as in a bed. M. Beauchamp, it holds four very well; will you accompany us?"

"Thank you, I have just returned from the sea."

"What! you have been to the sea?"

"Yes; I have just made a little excursion to the Borromées Islands."

"What of that? come with us," said Albert.

"No, dear Morcerf; you know I only refuse when the thing is impossible. Besides, it is important," added he, in a low tone, "that I should remain in Paris just now to watch the letter-box of the paper."

"Ah! you are a good and an excellent friend," said Albert; "yes, you are right; watch, watch, Beauchamp, and try to discover the enemy who made this disclosure."

Albert and Beauchamp parted; the last pressure of their hands expressed what their tongues could not before a stranger.

"Beauchamp is a worthy fellow," said Monte-Cristo, when the journalist was gone; "is he not, Albert?"

"Yes, and a sincere friend; I love him devotedly. But now we are alone, although it is immaterial to me, where are we going?"

"Into Normandy, if you like."

"Delightful; shall we be quite retired? have no society, no neighbors?"

"Our companions will be riding-horses, dogs to hunt with, and a fishing-boat."

"Exactly what I wish for; I will apprise my mother of my intention, and return to you."

"But shall you be allowed to go into Normandy?"

"I may go where I please."

"Yes, I am aware you may go alone, since I once met you in Italy—but to accompany the mysterious Monte-Cristo?"

"You forget, count, that I have often told you of the deep interest my mother takes in you."

"'Woman is fickle,' said Francis I.; 'woman is like a wave of the sea,' said Shakspere; both the great king and the poet ought to have known Woman well."

"My mother is not Woman, but a woman."

"Pardon me, if, as a foreigner, I do not perfectly comprehend the subtle distinctions of your language."

"I mean, my mother clings to her sentiments; when once entertained they are entertained forever."

"Ah, indeed!" said Monte-Cristo, sighing, "and you think she does me the honor of entertaining for me any sentiment except that of perfect indifference."

"I repeat it, you must really be a very strange and superior man, for my mother is so absorbed by the interest you have excited, that when I am with her, she speaks of no one else."

"And does she try to make you dislike a Manfred like me?"

"On the contrary, she often says, 'Morcerf, I believe the count to be a noble fellow; try to gain his esteem.'"

"Indeed!" said Monte-Cristo, sighing.

"You see, then," said Albert, "that instead of opposing, she will encourage me."

"Adieu, then, until five o'clock; be punctual, and we shall arrive at twelve or one."

"At Tréport?"

"Yes; or in the neighborhood."

"But can we travel forty-eight leagues in eight hours?"

"Easily," said Monte-Cristo.

"You are certainly a prodigy; you will soon not only surpass the railway, which would not be very difficult in France, but even the telegraph."

"Meanwhile, viscount, since we cannot perform the journey in less than seven or eight hours, do not keep me waiting."

"Do not fear; I have nothing now to do but to prepare."

Monte-Cristo smiled as he nodded to Albert, then remained a moment absorbed in deep meditation. But passing his hand across his forehead as if to dispel his reverie, he rang the bell twice, and Bertuccio entered.

"Bertuccio," said he, "I intend going this evening to Normandy, instead of to-morrow or the next day; you will have sufficient time before five o'clock; dispatch a messenger to apprise the grooms at the first station. M. de Morcerf will accompany me."

Bertuccio obeyed, dispatched a courier to Pontoise to say the traveling-carriage would arrive at six o'clock. From Pontoise another express was sent to the next stage, and in six hours all the horses stationed on the road were ready.

Before his departure the count went to Haydée's apartments, told her his intention, and resigned everything to her care.

Albert was punctual. The journey soon became interesting from its rapidity, of which Morcerf had formed no previous idea.

"Truly," said Monte-Cristo, "with your post-horses going at the rate of two leagues an hour, and that absurd law that one traveler shall not pass another without permission, so that an invalid or ill-tempered traveler may detain those who are well and active, it is impossible to move; I escape this annoyance by traveling with my own postilion and horses; do I not, Ali?"

The count put his head out of the window and uttered a cry of encouragement, and the horses appeared to fly. The carriage rolled with a thundering noise over the pavement, and every one turned to notice the dazzling meteor. Ali, smiling, repeated the cry, grasped the reins with a firm hand, and urged on his horses, whose beautiful manes floated in the breeze. This child of the desert was in his element; and with his black face and sparkling eyes, appeared in a cloud of dust that he raised like the genius of the simoom and the god of the hurricane

"I never knew till now the delight of speed," said Morcerf, and the last cloud disappeared from his brow; "but where the devil do you get such horses? are they made to order?"

"Precisely," said the count; "six years since I bought a horse in Hungary remarkable for its swiftness. I bought him for I know not what sum, it is Bertuccio who pays The thirty-two that we shall use to-night are its progeny, they are all entirely black, with the exception of a star upon the forehead"

"That is perfectly admirable; but what do you do, count, with all these horses?"

"You see, I travel with them"

"But you are not always traveling"

"When I no longer require them, Bertuccio will sell them, and he expects to realize thirty or forty thousand francs by the sale."

"But no monarch in Europe will be wealthy enough to purchase them."

"Then he will sell them to some Eastern vizier, who will empty his coffers to purchase them, and refill them by applying the bastinado to his subjects."

"Count, may I suggest one idea to you?"

"Certainly."

"It is that, next to you, Bertuccio must be the richest gentleman in Europe"

"You are mistaken, viscount; I am sure he has not a franc in his pockets, if you turned them inside out."

"Then he must be a wonder. My dear count, if you tell me many more marvelous things, I warn you I shall not believe them."

"There is nothing marvelous in my case M Albert figures out common sense; that is all Now listen to this dilemma. Why does a steward rob his master?"

"Because, I suppose, it is his nature to do so, he robs for the love of robbing"

"You are mistaken, it is because he has a wife and family, and ambitious desires for himself and them Also because he is not sure of always retaining his situation, and wishes to provide for the future. Now, M. Bertuccio is alone in the world; he uses my property without accounting for the use he makes of it, he is sure never to leave my service."

"Why?"

"Because I should never get a better"

"Probabilities are deceptive."

"But I deal in certainties; he is the best servant over whom you have the power of life and death."

"Do you possess that right over Bertuccio?"

"Yes."

There are words which close a conversation as if with an iron door; such was the count's "yes."

The whole journey was performed with equal rapidity; the thirty-two horses, dispersed at seven stages, arrived in eight hours. In the middle of the night they arrived at the gate of a beautiful park. The porter was in attendance; he had been apprised by the groom of the last stage of the count's approach. It was half-past two in the morning when Morcerf was conducted to his apartments, where a bath and supper were prepared. The servant who had traveled at the back of the carriage waited on him; Baptistin, who rode in front, attended the count.

Albert bathed, took his supper, and went to bed. All night he was lulled by the melancholy noise of the swell of the sea. On rising, he went to his window, which opened on a terrace, having the sea, that is, immensity in front, and at the back a pretty park bounded by a small forest. In a creek lay a little sloop, with a narrow hull and high masts, bearing on its flag the Monte-Cristo arms, which were a mountain *or*, on a sea *azure*, with a cross *gules* in chief which might be an allusion to his name that recalled Calvary, the mount rendered by our Lord's passion more precious than gold, and to the degrading cross which his blood had rendered holy; or it might be some personal remembrance of suffering and regeneration buried in the night of this mysterious personage's past life.

Around the schooner lay a number of small fishing-boats belonging to the fishermen of the neighboring village, as humble subjects awaiting orders from their queen. There, as in every spot where Monte-Cristo stopped, if but for two days, all was organized for comfort; life at once became easy.

Albert found in his anteroom two guns, with all the accoutrements for hunting; a higher room, on the ground-floor, containing all the ingenious instruments which the English — great fishers, because they are patient and lazy — have not yet induced the conservative fishers of France to adopt. The day passed in pursuing those exercises in which Monte-Cristo excelled; they killed a dozen pheasants in the park, as many trout in the stream, dined in a turret overlooking the ocean, and took tea in the library.

Toward the evening of the third day, Albert, completely tired with the exercise, which appeared sport to Monte-Cristo, was sleeping in an arm-chair near the window, while the count was designing with his architect the plan of a conservatory in his house, when the sound of a

horse dashing over the pebbles on the high road made Albert raise his head. He looked out of the window, and was disagreeably surprised to see his own valet-de-chambre, whom he had not brought, that he might not inconvenience Monte-Cristo.

"Florentin here!" cried he, starting up; "is my mother ill?" And he hastened to the door.

Monte-Cristo watched him; he saw him approach the valet, who drew a small sealed parcel from his pocket, containing a newspaper and a letter.

"From whom is this?" said he, eagerly.

"From M. Beauchamp," replied Florentin.

"Did he send you?"

"Yes, sir; he sent for me to his house, gave me money for my journey, procured a horse, and made me promise not to stop till I had rejoined you; I have come in fifteen hours."

Albert opened the letter with fear, uttered a shriek on reading the first line, and seized the paper. His sight was dimmed, his legs sank under him, and he would have fallen had not Florentin supported him.

"Poor young man!" said Monte-Cristo, with a low voice; "it is then true that the sin of the father shall fall on the children to the third and fourth generation."

Meanwhile Albert had revived, and continuing to read, he threw back his hair, saying:

"Florentin, is your horse fit to return immediately?"

"It is a poor, lame post-horse."

"In what state was the house when you left?"

"All was quiet; but on returning from M. Beauchamp's, I found madame in tears; she had sent for me to know when you would return. I told her my orders from M. Beauchamp; she first extended her arms to prevent me, but after a moment's reflection,—'Go,' said she, 'Florentin, and fetch him.'"

"Yes, my mother," said Albert, "I will return, and woe to the infamous wretch! But first I must go ——"

He returned, completely changed, to the room where he had left Monte-Cristo. He was no longer the same man; five minutes had sufficed to change Albert completely. He had gone out as usual, but returned with a trembling voice, a feverish look, an eye glittering under blue-veined lids, and a tottering step, like a drunkard's.

"Count," said he, "I thank you for your hospitality, which I would gladly have enjoyed longer, but I must return to Paris."

"What has happened?"

"A great misfortune, more important to me than life. No questions, but a horse."

"My stables are at your command, viscount; but you will kill yourself by riding on horseback; take a post-chaise or a carriage."

"No, it would delay me, and I require that fatigue you fear; it will do me good."

Albert reeled as if shot with a cannon-ball, and fell on a chair near the door. Monte-Cristo saw not this second weakness, he was at the window, calling:

"Ali, a horse for M. Morcerf! quick, he is in a hurry!"

These words restored Albert; he darted from the room, followed by the count.

"Thank you!" cried he, throwing himself on his horse.

"Return as soon as you can, Florentin. Must I use any pass-word to procure a horse?"

"Only dismount; another will be immediately saddled."

Albert hesitated a moment. "You may think my departure strange and foolish," said the young man; "you know not how a paragraph in a newspaper may exasperate. Read that," said he, "when I am gone, that you may not be witness of my anger."

While the count picked up the paper Albert put spurs to his horse, which, astonished that his rider should deem such a stimulus necessary, started with the rapidity of an arrow. The count watched him with a feeling of compassion, and when he had completely disappeared, read as follows:

"The French officer in the service of Ali, Pacha of Janina, alluded to three weeks since in the *Impartial*, who not only surrendered the castle of Janina, but sold his benefactor to the Turks, styled himself truly at that time Fernand, as our honorable brother states; but he has since added to his Christian name a title of nobility and a family name. He now calls himself the Count of Morcerf, and ranks among the peers."

Thus this terrible secret, which Beauchamp had so generously destroyed, appeared again as an armed phantom; and another paper, cruelly informed, had published, two days after Albert's departure for Normandy, the few lines which had almost distracted the unfortunate young man.

CHAPTER LXXXVI

THE TRIAL

AT eight o'clock in the morning Albert had arrived, like a lightning-flash, at Beauchamp's door. The valet-de-chambre had received orders to introduce him into his master's room, who was just then bathing.

"Here I am, Albert said."

"Well, my poor friend," replied Beauchamp, "I expected you."

"Here I am! I need not say I think you are too faithful and too kind to have spoken to any one of that painful circumstance. Your having sent for me is another proof of your affection. So, without losing time, tell me, have you any idea whence this blow proceeds?"

"I will say a couple of words about that, immediately."

"Yes! but first tell me all the particulars of this shameful plot."

Beauchamp proceeded to relate to the young man, overwhelmed with shame and grief, the following facts: Two days previously, the article had appeared in another paper besides the *Impartial*, and, what was more serious, one that was well known as a Government paper. Beauchamp was breakfasting when he read the passage: he sent immediately for a cabriolet, and hastened to the publisher's office. Although professing diametrically opposite principles from those of the editor of the accusing paper, Beauchamp, as it sometimes, we may say often, happens, was his intimate friend. The editor was reading, with apparent delight, a leading article in his paper on beet-root sugar, probably a composition of his own.

"Ah! *pardieu!*" said Beauchamp, "with the paper in your hand, my friend, I need not tell you the cause of my visit."

"Are you, perchance, concerned in the sugar question?" asked the editor of the ministerial paper.

"No," replied Beauchamp, "I have not considered the question; a totally different subject interests me."

"What is it?"

"The article relative to Morcerf."

"Indeed! Is it not a curious affair?"

"So curious, that I think you are running a great risk of a prosecution for defamation of character."

"Not at all; we have received with the information all the requisite proofs, and we are quite sure M. de Morcerf will keep quiet; besides, it is rendering a service to one's country to denounce those wretches who are unworthy of the honor it bestows on them."

Beauchamp remained thunder-struck.

"Who, then, has so correctly informed you?" asked he; "for my paper, which had announced the subject, has been obliged to stop for want of proof, and yet we are more interested than you in exposing M. de Morcerf, as he is a peer of France, and we are of the opposition."

"Oh! that is very simple; we have not sought to scandalize; this news was brought to us. A man arrived, yesterday, from Janina, bringing the formidable bundle; and as we hesitated to publish the accusatory article, he told us it should be inserted in some other paper. You know, Beauchamp, the value of a bit of important news. We could not let it slip. Now the stroke is made; it is terrible, and will echo through Europe."

Beauchamp understood that nothing remained but to submit, and left the office to dispatch a courier to Morcerf. But what he had been unable to write to Albert, as the events took place after the messenger's departure, was, that the same day, a great agitation was manifest in the House of Peers among the usually calm groups of the noble assembly. Every one had arrived almost before the usual hour, and was conversing on the melancholy event which was to attract the attention of the public toward one of their most illustrious members. Some were reading, in low tones, the article; others making comments and recalling circumstances which substantiated the charges still more.

The Count de Morcerf was no favorite with his colleagues. Like all upstarts, he had had recourse to a great deal of haughtiness to maintain his position. The true nobility laughed at him, the talented repudiated him, and the honorable instinctively despised him. The count was in the terrible position of an expiatory victim; the finger of God once pointed at him, every one was prepared to raise the hue and cry after him

The Count de Morcerf alone knew nothing. He did not take in the paper containing the defamatory news, and had passed the morning in writing letters and in trying a horse. He arrived at his usual hour, with a proud look and insolent demeanor; he alighted, passed through the corridors, and entered the house without observing the hesitation of the door-keepers or the coolness of his colleagues.

Business had already commenced half an hour when he entered. Every one held the accusing paper, but, as usual, no one liked to take upon himself the responsibility of the attack. At length an honorable peer, Morcerf's acknowledged enemy, ascended the tribune with that solemnity which announced the expected moment had arrived. There was an imposing silence; Morcerf alone knew not why such profound attention was given to an orator who was not always listened to with so much complacency.

The count did not notice the introduction, in which the speaker announced that his communication would be of that vital importance that it demanded the undivided attention of the House; but, at the words Janina and Colonel Fernand, he turned so awfully pale that every member shuddered and fixed his eyes upon him. Moral wounds have this peculiarity,—they conceal themselves, but never close; always painful, always ready to bleed when touched, they remain fresh and open in the heart.

The article having been read during this painful silence, it was only then disturbed by a universal shudder, and immediately restored when the orator resumed. He stated his scruples and the difficulties of the case: it was the honor of M. de Morcerf, and that of the whole House, he proposed to defend, by provoking a debate on those personal questions always so warmly agitated. He concluded by calling for an examination, speedy enough to confound the calumnious report before it had time to spread, and to restore M. de Morcerf to the position he had long held in public opinion.

Morcerf was so completely overwhelmed by this enormous and unexpected calamity that he could scarcely stammer a few words as he looked round on the assembly. This timidity, which might proceed from the astonishment of innocence as well as the shame of guilt, conciliated some in his favor; for men who are truly generous are always ready to compassionate when the misfortune of their enemy surpasses the limits of their hatred. The president put the question to the vote, and it was decided that the examination should take place. The count was asked what time he required to prepare his defense. Morcerf's courage had revived when he found himself alive after this horrible blow.

"My lords," answered he, "it is not by time that one repels attacks like that made on me by enemies unknown to me, and, doubtless, hidden in obscurity; it is immediately, and by a thunderbolt, I must repel the flash of lightning which, for a moment, startled me. Oh! that I could, instead of taking up this defense, shed my last drop of blood to prove to my noble colleagues that I am their equal in worth."

These words made a favorable impression on behalf of the accused.

"I demand, then, that the examination shall take place as soon as possible, and I will furnish the house with all necessary information."

"What day do you fix?" asked the president.

"To-day I am at your service," replied the count.

The president rang the bell. "Does the House approve that the examination should take place to-day?"

COUNT DE MORCERF ENTERS THE CHAMBER.

"Yes!" was the unanimous answer

A committee of twelve members was chosen to examine the proofs brought forward by Morcerf. The examination would commence at eight o'clock that evening in the committee-room, and, if it were necessary to postpone it, it would be resumed each evening at the same hour Morcerf asked leave to retire; he had to collect the documents he had long been preparing against this storm, which his sagacity had foreseen.

Beauchamp related to the young man all the facts we have just narrated; his story, however, had over ours all the advantage of the animation of living things over the coldness of dead things.

Albert listened, trembling now with hope, then with anger, and then again with shame, for, from Beauchamp's revelations, he knew his father was guilty, and he asked himself how, since he was guilty, he could prove his innocence Beauchamp hesitated to continue his narrative.

"What next?" asked Albert.

"What next? My friend, you impose a painful task on me. Must you know all?"

"Absolutely, and rather from your lips than another's"

"Prepare your courage, then, for never will you have required it more."

Albert passed his hand over his forehead, as if to try his strength, as a man, who is preparing to defend his life, proves his shield and bends his sword. He thought himself strong enough, for he mistook fever for energy. "Proceed," said he.

"The evening arrived: all Paris was in expectation. Many said your father had only to show himself to confound the charge, many others said he would not appear, while some asserted they had seen him start for Brussels, and others went to the police-office to inquire if he had taken out a passport. I used all my influence with one of the committee, a young peer of my acquaintance, to get introduced into a sort of gallery He called for me at seven o'clock, and, before any one had arrived, asked one of the door-keepers to place me in a box I was concealed by a column, and in complete obscurity, I could hope to hear and see the whole of the terrible scene which was about to take place. At eight o'clock all were in their places, and M. de Morcerf entered at the last stroke He held some papers in his hand; his countenance was calm Contrary to his usual custom, his manner was unaffected, his dress particularly quiet, and, after the habit of old soldiers, buttoned completely up to the chin His presence produced a good effect. His committee was far from being ill-disposed; several of the members came forward to shake hands with him."

Albert felt his heart bursting at these particulars, but gratitude mingled with his sorrow; he would gladly have embraced those who had given his father this proof of esteem at a moment when his honor was so powerfully attacked.

"At this moment one of the door-keepers brought in a letter for the president. 'You are at liberty to speak, M. de Morcerf,' said the president, as he unsealed the letter; and the count began his defense, I assure you, Albert, in a most eloquent and skillful manner. He produced documents, proving that the Vizier of Janina had, to the last moment, honored him with his entire confidence, since he had intrusted him with a negotiation of life and death with the sultan. He produced the ring, his mark of authority, with which Ali Pacha generally sealed his letters, and which the latter had given to him that he might, on his return at any hour of the day or night, were he even in his harem, gain access to him. Unfortunately, the negotiation failed, and when he returned to defend his benefactor, he was dead. 'But,' said the count, 'so great was Ali Pacha's confidence, that on his death-bed, he confided his favorite mistress and her daughter to my care.'"

Albert started on hearing these words; the history of Haydée recurred to him, and he remembered what she had said of that message and the ring, and the manner in which she had been sold and made a slave.

"And what effect did this discourse produce?" anxiously inquired Albert.

"I acknowledge it affected me, and, indeed, all the committee also," said Beauchamp.

"Meanwhile, the president carelessly opened the letter which had been brought to him; but the first lines aroused his attention. He read them again and again, and fixing his eyes on M. de Morcerf: 'M. le Comte,' said he, 'you have said the Vizier of Janina had confided his wife and daughter to your care?'—'Yes, sir,' replied Morcerf, 'but in that, like all the rest, misfortune pursued me; on my return, Vasiliki and her daughter Haydée had disappeared.'—'Did you know them?'—'My intimacy with the pacha and his unlimited confidence had gained me an introduction to them, and I had seen them above twenty times.'—'Have you any idea what is become of them?'—'Yes, sir; I heard they had fallen victims to their sorrow, and, perhaps, to their poverty. I was not rich; my life was in constant danger; I could not seek them, to my great regret.' The president frowned imperceptibly. 'Gentlemen,' said he, 'you have heard M. le Comte de Morcerf's defense. Can you, M. le Comte, produce any witnesses to the truth of what you have asserted?'—'Alas! no, sir,' replied the count, 'all those who surrounded the vizier, or who knew me at his court, are either dead or scattered, alone, I believe, of all my countrymen, I survived that dreadful war: I have only the letters of Ali Tebelin, which I have placed before you; the ring, a token of his good-will, which is here; and, lastly, the most convincing proof I can offer, namely, after an anonymous attack, the absence of all witnesses against my veracity and the purity of my military life.'

"A murmur of approbation ran through the assembly, and at this moment, Albert, had nothing more transpired, your father's cause had been gained It only remained to put it to the vote, when the president resumed: 'Gentlemen, and you, M. le Comte, you will not be displeased, I presume, to listen to one who calls himself a very important witness, and who has just presented himself He is, doubtless, come to prove the perfect innocence of our colleague. Here is a letter I have just received on the subject, shall it be read, or shall it be passed over? and shall we not regard this incident?' M de Morcerf turned pale, and clinched his hands on the papers he held The committee decided to hear the letter; the count was thoughtful and silent. The president read:

"'Mr. President,—I can furnish the committee of inquiry into the conduct of the Lieutenant-General Count de Morcerf in Epirus and in Macedonia with important particulars.'

"The president paused, and the count turned pale. The president looked at his auditors interrogatively. 'Proceed,' was heard on all sides The president resumed:

"'I was on the spot at the death of Ali Pacha; I was present during his last moments; I know what is become of Vasiliki and Haydée; I am at the command of the committee, and even claim the honor of being heard. I shall be in the lobby when this note is delivered to you'

"'And who is this witness, or rather this enemy?' asked the count, in a tone in which there was a visible alteration. 'We shall know, sir,' replied the president. 'Is the committee willing to hear this witness?' 'Yes, yes,' said they all at once.

"The door-keeper was called 'Is there any one in the lobby?' said the president.—'Yes, sir.'—'Who is it?'—'A woman accompanied by a servant' Every one looked at his neighbor. 'Introduce her,' said the president Five minutes after, the door-keeper again appeared: all eyes were fixed on the door, and I," said Beauchamp, "shared the general expectation and anxiety. Behind the door-keeper walked a woman enveloped in a large veil, which completely concealed her. It was evident, from the figure which her veil betrayed and the perfumes she had about her, that she was young and elegant, but that was all. The president requested her to throw aside her veil, and it was then seen she was dressed in the Grecian costume, and was remarkably beautiful."

"Ah!" said Albert, "it was she."

"Who?"

"Haydée."

"Who told you that?"

"Alas! I guess it. But go on, Beauchamp. You see I am calm and strong. And yet we must be drawing near the disclosure."

"M. de Morcerf," continued Beauchamp, "looked at this woman with surprise and terror. Her lips were about to pass his sentence of life or death. To all the committee the adventure was so extraordinary and curious, that the interest they had felt for the count's safety became now quite a secondary matter. The president himself advanced to place a seat for the young lady; but she indicated that she would remain standing. As for the count, he had fallen on his chair; it was evident his legs refused to support him.

"'Madame,' said the president, 'you have engaged to furnish the committee with some important particulars respecting the affair at Janina, and you have stated that you were an eye-witness of the events.'—'I was, indeed!' said the stranger, with a tone of sweet melancholy, and with the sonorous voice peculiar to the East.

"'But allow me to say you must have been very young then.'—'I was four years old; but as those events deeply concerned me, not a single particular has escaped my memory.'—'In what manner could those events concern you? and who are you, that they should have made so deep an impression on you?'—'On them depended my father's life,' replied she. 'I am Haydée, the daughter of Ali Tebelin, Pacha of Janina, and of Vasiliki, his beloved wife.'

"The blush of mingled pride and modesty which suddenly suffused the cheeks of the young female, the brilliance of her eye, and her highly important communication, produced an inexpressible effect on the assembly. As for the count, he could not have been more overwhelmed if a thunderbolt had fallen at his feet and opened before him an immense gulf.

"'Madame,' replied the president, bowing with profound respect, 'allow me to ask one question, it shall be the last: Can you prove the authenticity of what you have now stated?'

"'I can, sir,' said Haydée, drawing from under her veil a satin satchel highly perfumed; 'for here is the register of my birth, signed by my father and his principal officers; and that of my baptism, my father having consented to my being brought up in my mother's faith; this letter has been sealed by the grand primate of Macedonia and Epirus, and lastly, (and perhaps the most important), the record of the sale of my person and that of my mother to the Armenian merchant El-Kobbir, by the French officer, who, in his infamous bargain with the Porte, had reserved as his part of the booty, the wife and daughter of his bene-

factor, whom he sold for the sum of four hundred thousand francs.' A greenish paleness spread over the count's cheeks, and his eyes became blood-shot, at these terrible imputations, which were listened to by the assembly with an ill-foreboding silence.

"Haydée, still calm, but whose calmness was more dreadful than the anger of another would have been, handed to the president the record of her sale, registered in Arabic. It had been supposed some of these papers might be registered in the Arabic, Romaic, or Turkish language, and the interpreter of the House was in attendance. One of the noble peers, who was familiar with the Arabic language, having studied it during the sublime Egyptian campaign, followed with his eye as the translator read aloud:

"'I, El-Kobbir, a slave-merchant, and furnisher of the harem of his highness, acknowledge having received for transmission to the Sublime Emperor, from the French lord, Count of Monte-Cristo, an emerald valued at eight hundred thousand francs, as the ransom of a young Christian slave of eleven years of age, named Haydée, the acknowledged daughter of the late Lord Ali Tebelin, Pacha of Janina, and of Vasiliki, his favorite; she having been sold to me seven years previously, with her mother, who had died on arriving at Constantinople, by a French colonel in the service of the Vizier Ali Tebelin, named Fernand Mondego. The above-mentioned purchase was made on his highness's account, whose mandate I had, for the sum of four hundred thousand francs.

"'Given at Constantinople, by authority of his highness, in the year 1247 of the Hegira. Signed, EL-KOBBIR.

"'That this record should have all due authority, it shall bear the imperial seal, which the vendor is bound to have affixed to it.'

"Near the merchant's signature there was, indeed, the seal of the Sublime Emperor. A dreadful silence succeeded the reading of this paper; the count could only look, and his gaze, fixed as if unconsciously on Haydée, seemed one of fire and blood. 'Madame,' said the president, 'can we not examine the Count of Monte-Cristo, who is now, I believe, in Paris?'

"'Sir,' said Haydée, 'the Count of Monte-Cristo, my other father, has been in Normandy the last three days.'

"'Who, then, has counseled you to take this step, one for which the court is deeply indebted to you, and which is perfectly natural, considering your birth and your misfortunes?'—'Sir,' replied Haydée, 'I have been led to take this step from a feeling of respect and grief. Although a Christian, may God forgive me! I have always sought to revenge my illustrious father. Since I set my foot in France, and knew the traitor lived in Paris, I have watched carefully. I live retired in the house of my noble protector, but I do it from choice; I love retirement and silence, because I can live with my thoughts and recollections of past days. But M. le Comte de Monte-Cristo surrounds me with every paternal care, and I am ignorant of nothing which passes in the world. I hear its distant echoes; I see all the newspapers, every periodical, as well as every new melody; and by thus watching the course of the life of others, I learned what had passed this morning in the House of Peers, and what was to take place this evening; then I wrote.'

"'Then,' remarked the president, 'the Count of Monte-Cristo knows nothing of your present proceedings?'—'He is quite unaware of them;

Constantinople.

and I have but one fear, which is, that he should disapprove of what I have done. But it is a glorious day for me,' continued the young girl, raising her ardent gaze to heaven, 'that on which I find at last an opportunity of avenging my father!'

"The count had not uttered one word the whole of this time. His colleagues looked at him, and doubtless pitied his blighted prospects, which sank under the perfumed breath of a woman. His misery was depicted by sinister lines on his countenance. 'M. de Morcerf,' said the president, 'do you recognize this lady as the daughter of Ali Tebelin, Pacha of Janina?'—'No,' said Morcerf, attempting to rise; 'it is a base plot, contrived by my enemies.' Haydée, whose eyes had been fixed upon the door, as if expecting some one, turned hastily, and, seeing the count standing, shrieked, 'You do not know me?' said she. 'Well, I fortunately recognize you! You are Fernand Mondego, the French officer, who led the troops of my noble father! It is you who surrendered the Castle of Janina! It is you who, sent by him to Constantinople, to treat with the emperor for the life or death of your benefactor, brought back a false mandate, granting full pardon! It is you who, with that mandate, obtained the pacha's ring, which gave you authority over Selim, the fire-keeper! It is you who stabbed Selim! It is you who sold us, my mother and me, to the merchant El-Kobbir. Assassin! assassin! assassin! you have still on your brow your master's blood! Look, gentlemen, all!'

"These words had been pronounced with such enthusiasm of truth, that every eye was fixed on the count's forehead, and he himself passed his hand across it, as if he felt Ali's blood still moist upon it. 'You positively recognize M. de Morcerf as the officer, Fernand Mondego?'—'Indeed I do!' cried Haydée. 'Oh, my mother! it was you who told me, "You were free, you had a beloved father, you were destined to be almost a queen. Look well at that man; it is he who raised your father's head on the point of a spear; it is he who sold us; it is he who forsook us! Look well at his right hand, on which he has a large wound; if you forgot his features, you would know him by that hand, into which fell, one by one, the golden pieces of the merchant El-Kobbir!" I know him! Ah! let him say now if he does not recognize me!' Each word fell like a dagger on Morcerf, and deprived him of a portion of his energy; as she uttered the last, he hid hastily in his bosom his hand, which had indeed been mutilated by a wound, and fell back on his chair, overwhelmed by wretchedness and despair. This scene completely changed the opinion of the assembly respecting the accused count.

"'M. le Comte de Morcerf,' said the president, 'do not allow yourself to be depressed; answer. The justice of the court is supreme and impartial as that of God; it will not suffer you to be trampled on by your enemies without giving you an opportunity of defending yourself. Shall further inquiries be made? Shall two members of the House be sent to Janina? Speak!' Morcerf did not reply. Then all the members looked at each other with terror. They knew the count's energetic and violent temper; it must be, indeed, a dreadful blow which would deprive him of courage to defend himself. They expected this silence,

resembling a sleep, would be followed by an awakening like a thunderbolt. 'Well,' asked the president, 'what is your decision?'

"'I have no reply to make,' said the count in a low tone.

"'Has the daughter of Ali Tebelin spoken the truth?' said the president. 'Is she, then, the terrible witness to whose charge you dare not plead "Not guilty?" Have you really committed the crimes of which you are accused?' The count looked around him with an expression which might have softened tigers, but which could not disarm his judges. Then he raised his eyes toward the ceiling, but withdrew them immediately, as if he feared the roof would open and reveal to his distressed view that second tribunal called heaven, and that other judge named God. Then, with a hasty movement, he tore open his coat, which seemed to stifle him, and flew from the room like a madman; his footstep was heard one moment in the corridor, then the rattling of his carriage-wheels as he was driven rapidly away. 'Gentlemen,' said the president, when silence was restored, 'is M. le Comte de Morcerf convicted of felony, and degrading conduct, treason and——?'—'Yes,' replied all the members of the committee of inquiry with a unanimous voice.

"Haydée had remained until the close of the meeting. She heard the count's sentence pronounced without betraying an expression of joy or pity; then drawing her veil over her face, she bowed majestically to the councillors, and left with that dignified step which Virgil attributes to his goddesses

CHAPTER LXXXVII

THE CHALLENGE

"THEN," continued Beauchamp, "I took advantage of the silence and the darkness to leave the house without being seen. The door-keeper who had introduced me conducted me through the corridors to a private entrance opening into la Rue de Vaugirard. I left with mingled feelings of sorrow and delight. Excuse me, Albert, sorrow on your account, and delight with that noble girl, thus pursuing paternal vengeance. Yes, Albert, from whatever source the blow may have proceeded—it may be from an enemy, but that enemy is only the agent of Providence."

Albert held his head between his hands; he raised his face, red with shame and bathed in tears, and seizing Beauchamp's arm:—

"My friend," said he, "my life is ended. I cannot calmly say with you, 'Providence has struck the blow'; but I must discover who pursues me with this hatred, and when I have found him I will kill him, or he will kill me. I rely on your friendship to assist me, Beauchamp, if contempt has not banished it from your heart."

"Contempt, my friend! how does this misfortune affect you? No, happily that unjust prejudice is forgotten which made the son responsible for the father's actions. Review your life, Albert: although it is only just beginning, was a summer's day ever brighter than your dawn? No, Albert, take my advice. You are young and rich: leave Paris; all is soon forgotten in the great Babylon of excited life and changing taste. You will return after three or four years with a Russian princess for a bride, and no one will think more of what occurred yesterday and still less of what happened sixteen years ago."

"Thank you, my dear Beauchamp—thank you for the excellent feeling which prompts your advice; but it cannot be thus. I have told you my wish, or, if it must be so, I will say determination. You understand that, interested as I am in this affair, I cannot see it in the same light as you do. What appears to you to emanate from a celestial source, seems to me to proceed from one far less pure. Providence appears to me to have no share in this affair; and happily so, for instead of the invisible, impalpable agent of celestial rewards and punishments, I shall find one both palpable and visible, on whom I shall revenge myself, I assure you, for all I have suffered during the last month. Now, I repeat, Beauchamp, I wish to return to human and material existence; and if you are still the friend you profess to be, help me to discover the hand that struck the blow."

"Be it so," said Beauchamp; "if you must have me descend to earth, I submit; and if you will seek your enemy, I will assist you, and I will engage to find him, my honor being almost as deeply interested as yours."

"Well, then, you understand, Beauchamp, that we begin our research immediately. Each moment's delay is an eternity for me. The calumniator is not yet punished, and he may hope he will not be; but, on my honor, if he thinks so, he deceives himself."

"Well, listen, Morcerf."

"Ah, Beauchamp, I see you know something already: you will restore me to life."

"I do not say there is any truth in what I am going to tell you; but it is, at least, as a light in a dark night: by following it we may, perhaps, discover something more certain."

"Tell me; satisfy my impatience."

"Well, I will tell you what I did not like to mention on my return from Janina."

"Say on."

"I went, of course, to the chief banker of the town to make inquiries. At the first word, before I had even mentioned your father's name:—

"'Ah,' said he, 'I guess what brings you here.'—'How, and why?'—'Because a fortnight since I was questioned on the same subject.'—'By whom?—'By a banker of Paris, my correspondent.'—'Whose name is ——'—'Danglars.'"

"He!" cried Albert; "yes, it is indeed he who has so long pursued my father with jealous hatred. He, the man who would be popular, cannot forgive the Count de Morcerf for being created a peer; and this marriage, broken off without a reason being assigned—yes, it is all from the same cause."

"Inquire, Albert, but do not be angry without reason; inquire, and if it is true ——"

"Oh, yes, if it is true," cried the young man, "he shall pay me all I have suffered."

"Beware, Morcerf, he is already an old man."

"I will respect his age as he has respected the honor of my family; if my father had offended him, why did he not attack him personally? Oh, no, he was afraid to encounter him face to face."

"I do not condemn you, Albert; I only restrain you. Act prudently."

"Oh, do not fear, besides, you will accompany me. Beauchamp, solemn transactions should be sanctioned by a witness. Before this day closes, if M. Danglars is guilty, he shall cease to live, or I will die. *Pardieu!* Beauchamp, mine shall be a splendid funeral!"

"When such resolutions are made, Albert, they should be promptly executed. Do you wish to go to M. Danglars? Let us go immediately."

They sent for a cab. On entering the banker's mansion, they perceived the phaeton and servant of M. Andrea Cavalcanti.

"Ah! *parbleu!* that's good," said Albert, with a gloomy tone. "If M. Danglars will not fight with me, I will kill his son-in-law; Cavalcanti will certainly fight."

The servant announced the young man, but the banker, recollecting what had transpired the day before, did not wish him admitted. It was, however, too late; Albert had followed the footman, and, hearing the order given, forced the door open, and, followed by Beauchamp, found himself in the banker's cabinet.

"Sir," cried the latter, "am I no longer at liberty to receive whom I choose in my house? You appear to forget yourself sadly."

"No, sir," said Albert, coldly; "there are circumstances in which one cannot, except through cowardice—I offer you that refuge—refuse to admit certain persons at least."

"What is your errand, then, with me, sir?"

"I mean," said Albert, approaching, without apparently noticing Cavalcanti, who stood with his back toward the fireplace,—"I mean to propose a meeting in some retired corner, where no one will interrupt us for ten minutes, that will be sufficient, where two men having met, one of them will remain on the ground."

Danglars turned pale; Cavalcanti moved a step forward, and Albert turned toward him.

"And you, too," said he, "come, if you like, M. le Comte, you have a claim, being almost one of the family, and I will give as many rendezvous of that kind as I can find persons willing to accept them."

Cavalcanti looked at Danglars with a stupefied air; and the latter, making an effort, rose and advanced between the two young people.

Albert's attack on Andrea had placed him on a different footing, and he hoped this visit had another cause than that he had at first supposed.

"Indeed, sir," said he to Albert, "if you are come to quarrel with this gentleman, because I have preferred him to you, I shall resign the case to the *procureur du roi*."

"You mistake, sir," said Morcerf, with a gloomy smile; "I am not alluding in the least to a marriage, and I only addressed myself to M. Cavalcanti because he appeared disposed to interfere between us. In one respect you are right, for I am ready to quarrel with every one to-day; but you have the first claim, M. Danglars."

"Sir," replied Danglars, pale with anger and fear, "I warn you, when I have the misfortune to meet with a mad dog, I kill it; and far from thinking myself guilty of a crime, I believe I do society a kindness. Now, if you are mad, and try to bite me, I will kill you without pity. Is it my fault that your father has dishonored himself?"

"Yes; miserable wretch!" cried Morcerf, "it is your fault."

Danglars retreated a few steps. "My fault!" said he; "you must be mad! What do I know of the Grecian history? Have I traveled in that country? Did I advise your father to sell the Castle of Janina—to betray——"

"Silence!" said Albert, with a thundering voice. "No; it is not you who have directly made this exposure and brought this sorrow on us, but you have hypocritically provoked it."

"I?"

"Yes; you! How came it known?"

"I suppose you read it in the paper in the account from Janina."

"Who wrote to Janina?"

"To Janina?"

"Yes. Who wrote for particulars concerning my father?"

"I imagine any one may write to Janina."

"But one person only wrote!"

"One only?"

"Yes, and that was you."

"I, doubtless, wrote. It appears to me that when about to marry your daughter to a young man, it is right to make some inquiries respecting his family; it is not only a right but a duty."

"You wrote, sir, knowing what answer you would receive."

"I, indeed! I assure you," cried Danglars, with a confidence and security proceeding less from fear than from the interest he really felt for the unhappy young man, "I solemnly declare to you, that I should never have thought of writing to Janina, had I known anything of Ali Pacha's misfortunes."

MORCERF DEMANDS AN EXPLANATION FROM DANGLARS.

"Who, then, urged you to write? Tell me."

"*Pardieu!* it was the most simple thing in the world. I was speaking of your father's past history. I said the origin of his fortune remained obscure. The person to whom I addressed my scruples asked me where your father had acquired his property? I answered, 'In Greece.'—'Then write to Janina.'"

"And who thus advised you?"

"No other than your friend, Monte-Cristo."

"The Count of Monte-Cristo told you to write to Janina?"

"Yes; and I wrote, and will show you my correspondence, if you like."

Albert and Beauchamp looked at each other.

"Sir," said Beauchamp, who had not yet spoken, "you appear to accuse the count, who is absent from Paris at this moment, and cannot justify himself."

"I accuse no one, sir," said Danglars, "I relate, and I will repeat before the count what I have said to you."

"Does the count know what answer you received?"

"Yes; I showed it to him."

"Did he know my father's Christian name was Fernand, and his family name Mondego?"

"Yes; I had told him that long since, and I did nothing more than any other would have done in my circumstances, and perhaps less. When, the day after the arrival of this answer, your father came, by the advice of Monte-Cristo, to ask my daughter's hand for you, I decidedly refused him, but without any explanation or exposure. In short, why should I have any more to do with the affair? How did the honor or disgrace of M. de Morcerf affect me? It neither bulled nor beared the market."

Albert felt the color mounting to his brow; there was no doubt upon the subject, Danglars defended himself with the baseness, but, at the same time, with the assurance of a man who speaks the truth, at least in part, if not wholly—not for conscience' sake, but through fear. Besides, what was Morcerf seeking? It was not whether Danglars or Monte-Cristo was more or less guilty; it was a man who would answer for the offense, whether trifling or serious; it was a man who would fight, and it was evident Danglars would not fight.

In addition to this, everything forgotten or unperceived before, presented itself now to his recollection. Monte-Cristo knew everything, as he had bought the daughter of Ali Pacha; and, knowing everything, he had advised Danglars to write to Janina. The answer known, he had yielded to Albert's wish to be introduced to Haydée, and allowed the conversation to turn on the death of Ali, and had not opposed Haydée's recital (but having, doubtless, warned the young girl, in the few Romaic words he spoke to her, not to discover Morcerf's father). Besides, had he not begged of Morcerf not to mention his father's name before Haydée? Lastly, he had taken Albert to Normandy when he knew the final blow approached. There could be no doubt that all had been calculated and previously arranged; Monte-Cristo then was in league with his father's enemies. Albert took Beauchamp aside, and communicated these ideas to him.

"You are right," said the latter; "M. Danglars has only been a secondary agent in this affair; and it is of M. de Monte-Cristo that you must demand an explanation."

Albert turned.

"Sir," said he to Danglars, "understand that I do not take a final leave of you; I must ascertain if your insinuations are just, and am going now to inquire of the Count of Monte-Cristo."

He bowed to the banker, and went out with Beauchamp, without appearing to notice Cavalcanti. Danglars accompanied him to the door, where he again assured Albert no motive of personal hatred influenced him against the Count de Morcerf.

CHAPTER LXXXVIII

THE INSULT

AT the banker's door Beauchamp stopped Morcerf.

"Listen," said he; "but just now I told you it was of M. de Monte-Cristo you must demand an explanation."

"Yes; and we are going to his house."

"Reflect, Morcerf, one moment before you go."

"On what shall I reflect?"

"On the importance of the step you are taking."

"Is it more serious than going to M. Danglars?"

"Yes; M. Danglars is a money-lover, and those who love money, you know, think too much of what they risk to be easily induced to fight a duel. The other is, on the contrary, to all appearance, a true nobleman; but do you not fear to find in him the bravo?"

"I only fear one thing—namely, to find a man who will not fight."

"Do not be alarmed," said Beauchamp, "he will meet you. My only fear is that he will be too strong for you."

"My friend," said Morcerf, with a sweet smile, "that is what I wish; the happiest thing that could occur to me would be to die in my father's stead; that would save us all."

"Your mother would die of grief."

"My poor mother!" said Albert, passing his hand across his eyes, "I know she would; but better so than die of shame."

"Are you quite decided, Albert?"

"Yes; let us go."

"But do you think we shall find the count at home?"

"He intended returning some hours after me, and doubtless he is now at home."

They ordered the driver to take them to No. 30 Champs Elysées. Beauchamp wished to go in alone; but Albert observed, as this was an unusual circumstance, he might be allowed to deviate from the etiquette of duels. The cause which the young man espoused was one so sacred, that Beauchamp had only to comply with all his wishes; he yielded, and contented himself with following Morcerf. Albert bounded from the porter's lodge to the steps. He was received by Baptistin. The count had, indeed, just arrived, but he was bathing, and had forbidden that any one should be admitted.

"But after his bath?" asked Morcerf.

"My master will go to dinner."

"And after dinner?"

"He will sleep an hour."

"Then?"

"He is going to the Opera."

"Are you sure of it?" asked Albert.

"Quite, sir; my master has ordered his horses at eight o'clock precisely."

"Very good," replied Albert; "that is all I wished to know."

Then, turning toward Beauchamp, "If you have anything to attend to, Beauchamp, do it directly; if you have any appointment for this evening, defer it till to-morrow. I depend on you to accompany me to the Opera; and, if you can, bring Château-Renaud with you."

Beauchamp availed himself of Albert's permission, and left him, promising to call for him at a quarter before eight. On his return home, Albert expressed his wish to Franz, Debray, and Morrel, to see them at the Opera that evening. Then he went to see his mother, who, since the events of the day before, had refused to see any one, and had kept her room. He found her in bed, overwhelmed with grief at this public humiliation.

The sight of Albert produced the effect which might naturally be expected on Mercédès; she pressed her son's hand, and sobbed aloud; but her tears relieved her. Albert stood one moment speechless by the side of his mother's bed. It was evident, from his pale face and knit brows, that his resolution to revenge himself was growing weaker.

"My dear mother," said he, "do you know if M. de Morcerf has any enemy?"

Mercédès started; she noticed that the young man did not say my father.

"My son," she said, "persons in the count's situation have many secret enemies. Those who are known are not the most dangerous."

"I know it, and appeal to your penetration. You are of so superior a mind, nothing escapes you."

"Why do you say so?"

"Because, for instance, you noticed, on the evening of the ball we gave, M. de Monte-Cristo would eat nothing in our house."

Mercédès raised herself on her feverish arm.

"M. de Monte-Cristo!" she exclaimed; "and how is he connected with the question you have asked me?"

"You know, my mother, M. de Monte-Cristo is almost an Oriental, and it is customary with them to secure full liberty of revenge by not eating or drinking in the house of their enemies."

"Do you say M. de Monte-Cristo is our enemy?" replied Mercédès, becoming paler than the sheet which covered her. "Who told you so?

Why, you are mad, Albert! M. de Monte-Cristo has only shown us kindness. M. de Monte-Cristo saved your life; you, yourself, presented him to us. Oh! I entreat you, my son, if you had entertained such an idea, dispel it; and my counsel to you—even more, my prayer, is, retain his friendship."

"My mother," replied the young man, "you have special reasons for telling me to conciliate that man."

"I!" said Mercédès, blushing as rapidly as she had turned pale, and again becoming paler than ever.

"Yes, doubtless; and it is not because he can never do us any harm?"

Mercédès shuddered, and, fixing on her son a scrutinizing gaze, "You speak strangely," said she to Albert, "and you appear to have some singular prejudices. What has the count done? Three days since you were with him in Normandy; only three days since we looked on him as our best friend."

An ironical smile passed over Albert's lips. Mercédès saw it, and, with her double instinct of a woman and a mother, she guessed all, but, prudent and strong-minded, she concealed both her sorrows and her fears. Albert was silent; an instant after, the countess resumed:

"You came to inquire after my health; I will candidly acknowledge I am not well. You should install yourself here and cheer my solitude. I do not wish to be left alone."

"My mother," said the young man, "you know how gladly I would obey your wish; but an urgent and important affair obliges me to leave you the whole evening"

"Well!" replied Mercédès, sighing; "go, Albert, I will not make you a slave to your filial piety."

Albert pretended he did not hear, bowed to his mother, and quitted her. Scarcely had he shut her door, than Mercédès called a confidential servant, and ordered him to follow Albert wherever he should go that evening, and to come and tell her immediately what he observed. Then she rang for her lady's maid, and, weak as she was, she dressed, in order to be ready for whatever might happen. The footman's mission was an easy one. Albert went to his room, and dressed with unusual care. At ten minutes to eight Beauchamp arrived; he had seen Château-Renaud, who had promised to be in the orchestra-stalls before the curtain was raised. Both got into Albert's *coupé*, who, having no reason to conceal where he was going, called aloud, "To the Opera." In his impatience, he arrived before the commencement of the performance.

Château-Renaud was at his post; apprised by Beauchamp of the circumstances, he required no explanation from Albert. The conduct of this son, seeking to avenge his father, was so natural, that Château-Renaud did not seek to dissuade him, and was content with renewing his assurances of devotedness to Albert. Debray was not yet come, but Albert knew he seldom lost a scene at the Opera.

Albert wandered about the theater until the curtain was drawn up. He hoped to meet with Monte-Cristo either in the lobby or on the stairs.

Opera House.

The bell summoned him to his seat, and he entered the stalls with Château-Renaud and Beauchamp. But his eyes scarcely quitted the box between the columns, which remained obstinately closed during the whole of the first act. At last, as Albert was looking at his watch, about the hundredth time, at the commencement of the second act the door opened, and Monte-Cristo, dressed in black, entered, and, leaning over the front of the box, looked round the pit. Morrel followed him, and looked also for his sister and brother-in-law; he soon discovered them in another box, and kissed his hand to them.

The count, in his survey of the pit, encountered a pale face and threatening eyes, which evidently sought to gain his attention. He recognized Albert, but thought it better not to notice him, as he looked so angry and discomposed. Without communicating his thoughts to his companion, he sat down, drew out his opera-glass, and looked another way. Although apparently not noticing Albert, he did not, however, lose sight of him; and when the curtain fell at the end of the second act, he saw him leave the orchestra with his two friends. Then his head was seen passing at the back of the boxes, and the count knew the approaching storm was intended to fall on him. He was at the moment conversing cheerfully with Morrel, but he was well prepared for what might happen.

The door opened, and Monte-Cristo, turning round, saw Albert, pale and trembling, followed by Beauchamp and Château-Renaud.

"Well," cried he, with that benevolent politeness which distinguished his salutation from the common civilities of the world, "my cavalier has attained his object. Good-evening, M. de Morcerf."

The countenance of this man, who possessed such extraordinary control over his feelings, expressed the most perfect cordiality. Morrel only then recollected the letter he had received from the viscount, in which, without assigning any reason, he begged him to go to the Opera, but he understood that something terrible was brooding.

"We are not come here, sir, to exchange hypocritical expressions of politeness, or false professions of friendship," said Albert, "but to demand an explanation, count."

The trembling voice of the young man was scarcely audible.

"An explanation at the Opera?" said the count, with that calm tone and penetrating eye which characterizes the man who knows his cause is good. "Little acquainted as I am with the habits of Parisians, I should not have thought this the place for such a demand."

"Still, if people will shut themselves up," said Albert, "and cannot be seen because they are bathing, dining, or asleep, we must avail ourselves of the opportunity whenever they are to be seen."

"I am not difficult of access, sir; for yesterday, if my memory does not deceive me, you were at my house."

"Yesterday I was at your house, sir," said the young man; "because then I knew not who you were."

In pronouncing these words Albert had raised his voice so as to be heard by those in the adjoining boxes and in the lobby Thus the attention of many was attracted by this altercation

"Where are you come from, sir?" said Monte-Cristo "You do not appear to be in the possession of your senses."

"Provided I understand your perfidy, sir, and succeed in making you understand that I will be revenged, I shall be reasonable enough," said Albert, furiously.

"I do not understand you, sir," replied Monte-Cristo; "and, if I did, your tone is too high. I am at home here, and I alone have a right to raise my voice above another's. Leave the box, sir!"

Monte-Cristo pointed toward the door with the most commanding dignity.

"Ah! I shall know how to make you leave your home!" replied Albert, clasping in his convulsed grasp the glove which Monte-Cristo did not lose sight of.

"Well, well!" said Monte-Cristo, quietly, "I see you wish to quarrel with me: but I would give you one counsel, and do not forget it. it is a bad habit to make a display of a challenge. Display is not becoming to every one, M de Morcerf"

At this name a murmur of astonishment passed round the group of spectators of this scene. They had talked of no one but Morcerf the whole day. Albert understood the allusion in a moment, and was about to throw his glove at the count, when Morrel seized his hand, while Beauchamp and Château-Renaud, fearing the scene would surpass the limits of a challenge, held him back, but Monte-Cristo, without rising, and leaning forward in his chair, merely extended his hand, and taking the damp, crushed glove from the hand of the young man:—

"Sir," said he, in a solemn tone, "I consider your glove thrown, and will return it to you round a bullet Now, leave me, or I will summon my servants to throw you out at the door"

Wild, almost unconscious, and with eyes inflamed, Albert stepped back, and Morrel closed the door.

Monte-Cristo took up his glass again as if nothing had happened; he certainly must have had a heart of brass and face of marble Morrel whispered, "What have you done to him?"

"I? Nothing—at least personally," said Monte-Cristo

"But there must be some cause for this strange scene"

"The Count de Morcerf's adventure exasperates the young man."

"Have you anything to do with it?"

"It was by Haydée the house was informed of his father's treason."

"Indeed!" said Morrel. "I had been told, but would not credit it, that the Grecian slave I have seen with you here in this very box was the daughter of Ali Pacha."

"It is, notwithstanding, true."

"Then," said Morrel, "I understand it all, and this scene was premeditated."

"How so?"

"Yes. Albert wrote to request me to come to the Opera, doubtless that I might be a witness to the insult he meant to offer you."

"Probably," said Monte-Cristo, with his imperturbable tranquillity.

"But what will you do with him?"

"With whom?"

"With Albert."

"What will I do with Albert? As certainly, Maximilian, as I now press your hand, I will kill him before ten o'clock to morrow morning." Morrel, in his turn, took Monte-Cristo's hand in both of his, and he shuddered to feel how cold and steady it was.

"Ah! count," said he, "his father loves him so much!"

"Do not speak to me of that!" said Monte-Cristo, with the first movement of anger he had betrayed; "I will make him suffer."

Morrel, amazed, let fall Monte-Cristo's hand. "Count! count!" said he.

"Dear Maximilian," interrupted the count, "listen how adorably Duprez is singing that line,—

'O Mathilde' idole de mon âme!'

I was the first to discover Duprez at Naples, and the first to applaud him 'Bravo! bravo!'"

Morrel saw it was useless to say more, and refrained. The curtain, which had been drawn up during the scene with Albert, again fell, and a rap was heard at the door.

"Come in!" said Monte-Cristo, without his voice betraying the least emotion; and immediately Beauchamp appeared. "Good-evening, M. Beauchamp," said Monte-Cristo, as if this was the first time he had seen the journalist that evening; "take a seat."

Beauchamp bowed, and, sitting down, "Sir," said he, "I just now accompanied M. de Morcerf, as you saw."

"And that means," replied Monte-Cristo, laughing, "that you had, probably, just dined together. I am happy to see, M. Beauchamp, you are more sober than he was."

"Sir," said M. Beauchamp, "Albert was wrong, I acknowledge, to betray so much anger, and I come, on my own account, to apologize for him. And having done so, on my own account only, you understand, M. le Comte, I would add that I believe you too gentlemanly to refuse giving him some explanation concerning your connection with Janina Then I will add two words about the young Greek girl."

Monte-Cristo motioned him to be silent. "Come," said he, laughing, "there are all my hopes about to be destroyed"

"How so?" asked Beauchamp.

"Doubtless you wish to make me appear a very eccentric character; I am, in your opinion, a Lara, a Manfred, a Lord Ruthven · then, just as I am arriving at the climax, you defeat your own end, and seek to make a commonplace man of me. You bring me down to your own level, and demand explanations! Indeed, M Beauchamp, it is quite laughable."

"Yet," replied Beauchamp, haughtily, "there are occasions when probity commands —— "

"M Beauchamp," interposed this strange man, "the Count of Monte-Cristo bows to none but the Count of Monte-Cristo himself. Say no more, I entreat you I do what I please, M Beauchamp, and it is always well done."

"Sir," replied the young man, "honest men are not to be paid with such coin. I require honorable guarantees"

"I am, sir, a living guarantee," replied Monte-Cristo, motionless, but with a threatening look; "we have both blood in our veins which we wish to shed — that is our mutual guarantee. Tell the viscount so, and that to-morrow, before ten o'clock, I shall see what color his is."

"Then I have only to make arrangements for the duel," said Beauchamp

"It is quite immaterial to me," said Monte-Cristo, "and it was very unnecessary to disturb me at the Opera for such a trifle. In France people fight with the sword or pistol, in the colonies with the carbine, in Arabia with the dagger. Tell your client that, although I am the insulted party, in order to carry out my eccentricity, I leave him the choice of arms, and will accept without discussion, without dispute, anything, even combat by drawing lots, which is always stupid, but with me different from other people, as I am sure to gain"

"Sure to gain!" repeated Beauchamp, looking with amazement at the count.

"Certainly," said Monte-Cristo, slightly shrugging up his shoulders, "otherwise I would not fight with M. de Morcerf. I shall kill him — I cannot help it. Only by a single line this evening at my house let me know the arms and the hour; I do not like to be kept waiting."

"Pistols, then, at eight o'clock, in the Bois de Vincennes," said Beauchamp, quite disconcerted, not knowing if he was dealing with an arrogant braggadocio or a supernatural being.

"Very well, sir," said Monte-Cristo. "Now all that is settled; do let me see the performance, and tell your friend Albert not to come any more this evening; he will hurt himself with all his ill-chosen barbarisms; let him go home and go to sleep."

Beauchamp left the box, perfectly amazed.

"Now," said Monte-Cristo, turning toward Morrel, "I may depend upon you, may I not?"

"Certainly," said Morrel, "I am at your service, count; still —"

"What?"

"It is desirable I should know the real cause."

"That is to say, you would rather not?"

"No."

"The young man himself is acting blindfolded, and knows not the true cause, which is known only to God and to me; but I give you my word, Morrel, that God who does know it will be on our side."

"Enough," said Morrel, "who is your second witness?"

"I know no one in Paris, Morrel, on whom I could confer that honor besides you and your brother Emmanuel. Do you think Emmanuel would oblige me?"

"I will answer for him, count."

"Well, that is all I require. To-morrow morning, at seven o'clock, you will be with me, will you not?"

"We will."

"Hush! the curtain is rising. Listen! I never lose a note of this opera if I can avoid it; it is wonderful music, that of 'William Tell.'"

"EDMOND, YOU WILL NOT KILL MY SON?"

CHAPTER LXXXIX

THE NIGHT

MONSIEUR DE MONTE-CRISTO waited, according to his usual custom, until Duprez had sung his famous "Suivez-moi;" then he rose, and went out. Morrel took leave of him at the door, renewing his promise to be with him the next morning at seven o'clock, and to bring Emmanuel with him. Then he stepped into his *coupé*, calm and smiling, and was at home in five minutes. No one who knew the count could mistake his expression, when, on entering, he said:

"Ali, bring me my pistols with the ivory stock."

Ali brought the box to his master, who examined his arms with a solicitude very natural to a man who is about to intrust his life to a little powder and shot. These were peculiar pistols, which Monte-Cristo had had made to shoot at a target in his room. A cap was sufficient to drive out the ball, and from the adjoining room no one would have suspected the count was, as sportsmen would say, keeping his hand in.

He was just taking one in his hand and looking for the point to aim at, on a little iron plate, which served him as a target, when his cabinet-door opened, and Baptistin entered. Before he had spoken a word the count perceived in the next room a woman, veiled, who had followed closely after Baptistin, and now, seeing the count with a pistol in his hand and swords on the table, rushed in. Baptistin looked at his master, who made a sign to him, and he went out, closing the door after him.

"Who are you, madame?" said the count to the veiled lady.

The stranger cast one look around her, to be certain they were quite alone, then bending, as if she would have knelt, and joining her hands, she said, with an accent of despair:

"Edmond, you will not kill my son?"

The count retreated a step, uttered a slight exclamation, and let fall the pistol he held.

"What name did you pronounce then, Madame de Morcerf?" said he.

"Yours," cried she, throwing back her veil,—"yours, which I alone, perhaps, have not forgotten. Edmond, it is not Madame de Morcerf who is coming to you, it is Mercédès."

"Mercédès is dead, madame," said Monte-Cristo; "I know no one now of that name."

"Mercédès lives, sir, and she remembers, for she alone recognized you when she saw you, and even before she saw you, by your voice, Edmond,—by the simple sound of your voice, and from that moment she has followed your steps, watched you, feared you, and she needs not to inquire what hand has dealt the blow which now strikes M. de Morcerf."

"Fernand, do you mean?" replied Monte-Cristo, with bitter irony; "since we are recalling names, let us remember them all." Monte-Cristo had pronounced the name of Fernand with such an expression of hatred that Mercédès felt a thrill of horror run through every vein.

"You see, Edmond, I am not mistaken, and have cause to say, 'spare my son!'"

"And who told you, madame, I have any hostile intentions against your son?"

"No one, in truth; but a mother has a twofold sight. I guessed all; I followed him this evening to the Opera, and have seen all."

"If you have seen all, madame, you know that the son of Fernand has publicly insulted me," said Monte-Cristo, with awful calmness.

"Oh! for pity's sake!"

"You have seen that he would have thrown his glove in my face, if Morrel, one of my friends, had not stopped him."

"Listen to me: my son has also guessed who you are; he attributes his father's misfortunes to you."

"Madame, you are mistaken, they are not misfortunes,—it is a punishment. It is not I who strike M. de Morcerf; it is Providence which punishes him."

"And why do you represent Providence?" cried Mercédès. "Why do you remember, when it forgets? What are Janina and its vizier to you, Edmond? What injury has Fernand Mondego done you in betraying Ali Tebelin?"

"And, madame," replied Monte-Cristo, "all this is an affair between the French captain and the daughter of Vasiliki. It does not concern me, you are right; and if I have sworn to revenge myself, it is not on the French captain, nor on the Count de Morcerf, but on the fisherman Fernand, the husband of the Catalan Mercédès."

"Ah! sir," cried the countess, "how terrible a vengeance for a fault which fatality made me commit! for I am the only culprit, Edmond; and if you owe revenge to any one, it is to me, who had not fortitude to bear your absence and my solitude."

"But," exclaimed Monte-Cristo, "why was I absent? And why were you alone?"

"Because you had been arrested, Edmond, and were a prisoner."

"And why was I arrested? Why was I a prisoner?"

"I do not know," said Mercédès.

"You do not, madame; at least, I hope not. But I will tell you. I was arrested and became a prisoner, because under the arbor of La Réserve, the day before I was to marry you, a man named Danglars wrote this letter which the fisherman Fernand himself posted."

Monte-Cristo went to a secrétaire, opened a drawer by a spring, from which he took a paper which had lost its original color, and the ink of which had become a rusty hue; this he placed in the hands of Mercédès. It was Danglars' letter to the *procureur du roi*, which the Count of Monte-Cristo, disguised as a clerk from the house of Thomson and French, had taken from the docket of Edmond Dantès on the day he had paid the two hundred thousand francs to M. de Boville. Mercédès read with terror the following lines:

"The *procureur du roi* is informed by a friend to the throne and the religious institutions of his country, that an individual named Edmond Dantès, second in command on board the *Pharaon*, this day arrived from Smyrna, after having touched at Naples and Porto-Ferrajo, has been the bearer of a letter from Murat to the usurper, and again taken charge of another letter from the usurper to the Bonapartist Club in Paris. Ample corroboration of this statement may be obtained by arresting the above-named Edmond Dantès, who either carries the letter for Paris about with him, or has it at his father's abode. Should it not be found in possession of either father or son, then it will assuredly be discovered in the cabin belonging to the said Dantès on board the *Pharaon*."

"How dreadful!" said Mercédès, passing her hand across her brow, moist with perspiration; "and that letter——"

"I bought it for two hundred thousand francs, madame," said Monte-Cristo; "but that is a trifle, since it enables me to justify myself to you."

"And the result of that letter——"

"You well know, madame, was my arrest; but you do not know how long that arrest lasted. You do not know that I remained for fourteen years within a quarter of a league of you, in a dungeon in the Château-d'If. You do not know that each day of those fourteen years I renewed the vow of vengeance which I had made the first day; and yet I knew not you had married Fernand, my calumniator, and that my father had died of hunger!"

"Can it be?" cried Mercédès, shuddering.

"That is what I heard on leaving my prison, fourteen years after I had entered it, and that is why, on account of the living Mercédès and my deceased father, I have sworn to revenge myself on Fernand, and—I have revenged myself."

"And you are sure the unhappy Fernand did that?"

"I am satisfied, madame, he did what I have told you; besides that is not much more odious than a Frenchman by adoption, having passed over to the English; a Spaniard by birth, having fought against the Spaniards; a stipendiary of Ali having betrayed and murdered Ali. Compared with such things, what is the letter you have just read? A lover's deception, which the woman who has married that man ought certainly to forgive, but not so the lover who was to have married her. Well! the French did not avenge themselves on the traitor, the Spaniards did not shoot the traitor; Ali, in his tomb, left the traitor unpunished; but I, betrayed, sacrificed, buried, have risen from my tomb, by the grace of God, to punish that man. He sends me for that purpose, and here I am."

The poor woman's head and arms fell; her legs bent under her, and she fell on her knees

"Forgive, Edmond, forgive for my sake, who love you still!"

The dignity of the wife stopped the enthusiasm of the lover and the mother. Her forehead almost touched the carpet, when the count sprang forward and raised her Then, seated on a chair, she looked at the manly countenance of Monte-Cristo, on which grief and hatred still impressed a threatening expression.

"Not crush that accursed race!" murmured he, "abandon my purpose at the moment of its accomplishment! Impossible, madame, impossible!"

"Edmond," said the poor mother, who tried every means, "when I call you Edmond, why do you not call me Mercédès?"

"Mercédès!" repeated Monte-Cristo, "Mercédès! Well! yes, you are right, that name has still its charm, and this is the first time for a long period that I have pronounced it so distinctly O Mercédès! I have uttered your name with the sigh of melancholy, with the groan of sorrow, with the last effort of despair: I have uttered it when frozen with cold, crouched on the straw of my dungeon, I have uttered it, consumed with heat, rolling on the stone floor of my prison Mercédès, I must revenge myself, for I suffered fourteen years,—fourteen years I wept, I cursed, now I tell you, Mercédès, I must revenge myself!"

The count, fearing to yield to the entreaties of her he had so ardently loved, recalled his sufferings to the assistance of his hatred

"Revenge yourself then, Edmond," cried the poor mother, "but let your vengeance fall on the culprits; on him, on me, but not on my son!"

Monte-Cristo groaned, and seized his beautiful hair with both hands.

"Edmond," continued Mercédès, with her arms extended toward the count, "since I first knew you, I have adored your name, have respected your memory. Edmond, my friend, do not compel me to tarnish that noble and fine image reflected incessantly on the mirror of my heart. Edmond, if you knew all the prayers I have addressed to God for you while I thought you were living and since I have thought you must be dead! Yes, dead, alas! I thought your dead body was buried at the foot of some gloomy tower; I thought your corpse was precipitated to the bottom of one of those gulfs where jailers roll their dead prisoners, and I wept! What could I do for you, Edmond, besides pray and weep? Listen; during ten years I dreamed each night the same dream. I had been told you had endeavored to escape; that you had taken the place of another prisoner; that you had slipped into the winding-sheet of a dead body; that you had been precipitated alive from the top of the Château-d'If; and the cry you uttered as you dashed upon the rocks first revealed to your jailers that they were your murderers. Well! Edmond, I swear to you, by the head of that son for whom I entreat your pity,—Edmond, during ten years I have seen every night men balancing something shapeless and unknown at the top of a rock; during ten years I have heard each night a terrible cry which has awoke me, shuddering and cold. And I, too, Edmond—oh! believe me—guilty as I was—oh! yes, I too, have suffered much!"

"Have you felt your father die in your absence?" cried Monte-Cristo, again thrusting his hands in his hair: "have you seen the woman you loved giving her hand to your rival while you were perishing at the bottom of a dungeon?"

"No," interrupted Mercédès, "but I have seen him whom I loved on the point of murdering my son."

Mercédès pronounced these words with such deep anguish, with an accent of such intense despair, that Monte-Cristo could not restrain a sob. The lion was daunted; the avenger was conquered.

"What do you ask of me?" said he,—"your son's life? Well! he shall live!"

Mercédès uttered a cry which made the tears start from Monte-Cristo's eyes; but these tears disappeared almost instantaneously, for, doubtless, God had sent some angel to collect them; far more precious were they in his eyes than the richest pearls of Guzerat and of Ophir.

"Oh!" said she, seizing the count's hand, and raising it to her lips; "oh! thank you, thank you, Edmond! now you are exactly what I dreamt you were, such as I always loved you. Oh! now I may say so."

"So much the better," replied Monte-Cristo; "as that poor Edmond will not have long to be loved by you. Death is about to return to the tomb, the phantom to retire in darkness."

"What do you say, Edmond?'

"I say, since you command me, Mercédès, I must die."

"Die! and who told you so? who talks of dying? whence have you these ideas of death?"

"You do not suppose, that publicly outraged in the face of a whole theater, in the presence of your friends and those of your son—challenged by a boy, who will glory in my pardon as in a victory — you do not suppose I can for one moment wish to live. What I most loved after you, Mercédès, was myself, my dignity, and that strength which rendered me superior to other men; that strength was my life. With one word you have crushed it, and I die."

"But the duel will not take place, Edmond, since you forgive?"

"It will take place," said Monte-Cristo, in a most solemn tone; "but instead of your son's blood which will stain the ground, mine will flow."

Mercédès shrieked, and sprang toward Monte-Cristo, but suddenly stopping: "Edmond," said she, "there is a God above us, since you live, and since I have seen you again, I trust to him from my heart. While waiting his assistance I trust to your word; you have said my son should live, have you not?"

"Yes, madame, he shall live," said Monte-Cristo, surprised that, without more emotion, Mercédès had accepted the heroic sacrifice he made for her. Mercédès extended her hand to the count.

"Edmond," said she, and her eyes were wet with tears while looking at him to whom she spoke, "how noble it is of you, how great the action you have just performed; how sublime to have taken pity on a poor woman who offered herself to you with every chance against her! Alas! I am grown old with grief more than with years, and cannot now remind my Edmond by a smile, or by a look, of that Mercédès whom he once spent so many hours in contemplating. Ah! believe me, Edmond, I told you, I too had suffered much; I repeat it, it is melancholy to pass one's life without having one joy to recall, without preserving a single hope; but that proves that all is not yet over. No; it is not finished, I feel it by what remains in my heart. Oh! I repeat it, Edmond, what you have just done is beautiful — it is grand, it is sublime."

"Do you say so, now, Mercédès, and what would you say if you knew the extent of the sacrifice I make to you? Suppose the Creator, after having made the world and vivified chaos, had stopped at the end of one-third of his work, in order to spare an angel the tears which the crimes of man would one day evoke from heavenly eyes; suppose that when all was prepared, ready, quickened, God at the time when he saw his work was good had extinguished the sun and kicked aside the earth into endless night, then you might have some idea of my sacrifice. But, no, no, you cannot imagine what I lose in sacrificing my life at this moment."

Mercédès looked at the count with an air which depicted at the same time her astonishment, her admiration, and her gratitude. Monte-Cristo pressed his forehead on his burning hands, as if his brain could no longer bear alone the weight of its thoughts.

"Edmond," said Mercédès, "I have but one word more to say to you."

The count smiled bitterly.

"Edmond," continued she, "you will see if my face is pale, if my eyes are dull, if my beauty is gone; if Mercédès, in short, no longer resembles her former self in her features, you will see her heart is still the same. Adieu, then, Edmond; I have nothing more to ask of Heaven — I have seen you again — and have found you as noble and as great as formerly you were. Adieu, Edmond, adieu, and thank you."

But the count did not answer. Mercédès opened the door of the cabinet and had disappeared before he had recovered from the painful and profound reverie into which his thwarted vengeance had plunged him.

The clock of the Invalides struck one when the carriage which conveyed Madame de Morcerf rolled away on the pavement of the Champs Elysées, and made Monte-Cristo raise his head.

"What a fool I was," said he, "not to tear my heart out on the day when I resolved to avenge myself!"

CHAPTER XC

THE MEETING

AFTER Mercédès had left Monte-Cristo, a gloomy shadow seemed to overspread everything. Around him and within him thought appeared stopped; his energetic mind slumbered, as does the body after extreme fatigue.

"What," said he to himself, while the lamp and the wax lights were nearly burned out, and the servants were waiting impatiently in the ante-room; "what! this edifice which I have been so long preparing—which I have reared with so much care and toil, is to be crumbled by a single touch, a word, even a slight breath! Yes, this self, of whom I thought so much, of whom I was so proud, who had appeared so worthless in the dungeons of the Château-d'If, and whom I had succeeded in making so great, will be but a lump of clay to-morrow. Alas, it is not the death of the body I regret; for that destruction of the vital principle is it not the rest to which everything is tending, to which every unhappy being aspires, the repose of matter after which I so long sighed, and which I was seeking to obtain by the painful process of starvation when Faria appeared in my dungeon? What is death for me but one step more toward repose? No, it is not existence, then, that I regret, but the ruin of our projects, so slowly carried out, so laboriously framed. Providence is now opposed to them, when I most thought it would be propitious. It is not God's will they should be accomplished. This burden, almost as heavy as a world, which I had raised, and I had thought to bear to the end, was too great for my strength, and I was compelled to lay it down in the middle of my career.

"Oh! shall I then again become a fatalist, whom fourteen years of despair and ten of hope had rendered a believer in Providence? And all this—all this, because my heart, which I thought dead, was only sleeping; because it has awoke and has beaten again; because I have yielded to the pain of the emotion excited in my breast by a woman's voice."

"Yet," continued the count, becoming each moment more absorbed in the anticipation of the dreadful sacrifice for the morrow, which Mercédès had accepted, "yet, it is impossible that so noble-minded a woman should thus, through selfishness, consent to my death when in the prime of life and strength; it is impossible she can carry to such a point maternal love, or rather delirium. There are virtues which become crimes by exaggeration. No, she must have conceived some pathetic scene; she will come and throw herself between us, and what would be sublime here will appear there ridiculous."

The blush of pride mounted to the count's forehead as this thought passed through his mind.

"Ridiculous?" repeated he; "and the ridicule will fall on me. I ridiculous! no, I would rather die."

Thus exaggerating to his own mind the anticipated ill-fortune of the next day, to which he had condemned himself by promising Mercédès to spare her son, the count at last exclaimed:

"Folly! folly! folly! to carry generosity so far as to place myself as a mark for that young man to aim at. He will never believe my death was a suicide; and yet it is important for the honor of my memory,—and this, surely, is not vanity, but a justifiable pride,—it is important the world should know that I have consented, by my free will, to stop my arm, already raised to strike, and that with that arm, so powerful against others, I have struck myself. It must be, it shall be."

Seizing a pen, he drew a paper from a secret drawer in his bureau, and traced at the bottom of that paper, which was no other than his will, made since his arrival in Paris, a sort of codicil, clearly explaining the nature of his death.

"I do this, O my God!" said he, with his eyes raised to heaven, "as much for thy honor as for my mine. I have during ten years considered myself the agent of thy vengeance; and it must not be that wretches, like a Morcerf, a Danglars, a Villefort, even that Morcerf himself, shall imagine that chance has freed them from their enemy. Let them know, on the contrary, that their punishment, which had been decreed by Providence, is only delayed by my present determination; and although they escape it in this world, it awaits them in another, and that they are only exchanging time for eternity."

While he was thus agitated by these gloomy uncertainties, these wretched waking dreams of grief, the first rays of twilight pierced his windows, and shone upon the pale blue paper on which he had just traced his justification of Providence.

It was just five o'clock in the morning, when a slight noise reached his ear, which appeared like a stifled sigh; he turned his head, looked around him, and saw no one; but the sound was repeated distinctly enough to convince him of its reality. He arose, and quietly opening the door of the drawing-room, saw Haydée, who had fallen on a chair, with her arms hanging down and her beautiful head thrown back. She had been standing at the door to prevent his going out without seeing her, until sleep, which the young cannot resist, had overpowered her frame, wearied as she was with watching so long. The noise of the door did not awaken her, and Monte-Cristo gazed at her with affectionate regret.

"She remembered she had a son," said he, "and I forgot I had a daughter." Then, shaking his head sorrowfully, "Poor Haydée!" said he, "she wished to see me to speak to me; she has feared or guessed something. Oh! I cannot go without taking leave of her; I cannot die without confiding her to some one."

He quietly regained his seat, and wrote under the other lines:

"I bequeath to Maximilian Morrel, captain, and son of my former patron, Pierre Morrel, shipowner at Marseilles, the sum of twenty millions, a part of which may be offered to his sister Julia and brother-in-law Emmanuel, if he does not fear this increase of fortune may mar their happiness. These twenty millions are concealed in my grotto at Monte-Cristo, of which Bertuccio knows the secret. If his heart is free, and he will marry Haydée, the daughter of Ali, Pacha of Janina, whom I have brought up with the love of a father, and who has shown the love and tenderness of a daughter for me, he will thus accomplish, I do not say my last order, but my last desire. This will has already constituted Haydée heiress of the rest of my fortune, consisting of lands, funds in England, Austria, and Holland, furniture in my different palaces and houses, and which, without the twenty millions, and the legacies to my servants, may still amount to sixty millions."

He was finishing the last line when a cry behind him made him start, and the pen fell from his hand.

"Haydée," said he, "did you read it?"

"Oh! my lord," said she, "why are you writing thus at such an hour? why are you bequeathing all your fortune to me? Are you going to leave me?"

"I am going on a journey, dear child," said Monte-Cristo, with an expression of infinite tenderness and melancholy; "and if any misfortune should happen to me——" The count stopped.

"Well?" asked the young girl, with an authoritative tone the count had never observed before, and which startled him.

"Well! if any misfortune happen to me," replied Monte-Cristo, "I wish my daughter to be happy." Haydée smiled sorrowfully and shook her head.

"Do you think of dying, my lord?" said she.

"The wise man has said it is good to think of death, my child."

"Well, if you die," said she, "bequeath your fortune to others; for if you die I shall require nothing"; and, taking the paper, she tore it in four pieces and threw it into the middle of the room. Then, the effort having exhausted her strength, she fell, not asleep this time, but fainting on the floor.

The count leaned over her and raised her in his arms; and seeing that sweet pale face, those lovely eyes closed, that beautiful form motionless, and to all appearance lifeless, the idea occurred to him for the first time that perhaps she loved him otherwise than as a daughter loves a father.

"Alas!" murmured he, with intense suffering, "I might then have been happy yet."

Then he carried Haydée to her room, resigned her to the care of her attendants, and returning to his cabinet, which he shut quickly this time, he again copied the destroyed will. As he was finishing, the sound of a cabriolet entering the yard was heard. Monte-Cristo approached the window, and saw Maximilian and Emmanuel alight. "Good!" said he; "it was time," and he sealed his will with three seals.

One moment afterward he heard a noise in the drawing-room, and went to open the door himself. Morrel was there, he had come twenty minutes before the time appointed.

"I am, perhaps, come too soon, count," said he, "but I frankly acknowledge I have not closed my eyes all night, nor any one in my house. I required to see you strong in your courageous assurance, to recover myself."

Monte-Cristo could not resist this proof of affection, he not only extended his hand to the young man, but flew to him with open arms.

"Morrel," said he, "it is a happy day for me, to feel I am beloved by such a man as you. Good-morning, Emmanuel; you will come with me, then, Maximilian?"

"Did you doubt it?" said the young captain.

"But if I were wrong——"

"I watched you during the whole scene of that challenge yesterday; I have been thinking of your firmness all this night, and I said, 'Justice must be on your side, or man's countenance is no longer to be relied on.'"

"But, Morrel, Albert is your friend?"

"HAYDÉE," SAID HE, "DID YOU READ IT?"

"A simple acquaintance, sir."

"You met on the same day you first saw me?"

"Truly, but I should not have recollected it had you not reminded me."

"Thank you, Morrel." Then ringing the bell once, "Look," said he to Ali, who came immediately, "take that to my solicitor It is my will, Morrel When I am dead, you will go and examine it."

"What!" said Morrel, "you dead?"

"Yes; must I not be prepared for everything, dear friend? But what did you do yesterday after you left me?"

"I went to Tortoni, where, as I expected, I found Beauchamp and Château-Renaud. I own I was seeking them."

"Why, when all was arranged?"

"Listen, count, the affair is serious and unavoidable."

"Did you doubt it?"

"No, the offense was public, and every one is already talking of it."

"Well?"

"Well! I hoped to get an exchange of arms, to substitute the sword for the pistol; the pistol is blind"

"Have you succeeded?" asked Monte-Cristo, quickly, with an imperceptible gleam of hope.

"No, for your skill with the sword is so well known."

"Ah! who has betrayed me?"

"The skillful swordsman, whom you have conquered."

"And you failed?"

"They positively refused."

"Morrel," said the count, "have you ever seen me fire a pistol?"

"Never."

"Well, we have time; look." Monte-Cristo took the pistols he held in his hand when Mercédès entered, and fixing an ace of clubs against the iron plate, with four shots he successively shot off the four sides of the club. At each shot Morrel turned pale. He examined the balls with which Monte-Cristo performed this dexterous feat, and saw that they were no larger than deer-shot.

"It is astonishing!" said he; "look, Emmanuel." Then turning toward Monte-Cristo "Count," said he, "in the name of all that is dear to you, I entreat you not to kill Albert! the unhappy youth has a mother."

"You are right," said Monte-Cristo, "and I have none" These words were uttered in a tone which made Morrel shudder

"You are the offended party, count."

"Doubtless; what does that imply?"

"That you will fire first"

"I fire first?"

"Oh! I obtained, or rather claimed that; we had conceded enough for them to yield us that."

"And at what distance?"

"Twenty paces." A terrific smile passed over the count's lips.

"Morrel," said he, "do not forget what you have just seen."

"The only chance for Albert's safety, then, will arise from your emotion."

"I suffer from emotion?" said Monte-Cristo.

"Or from your generosity, my friend; to so good a marksman as you are, I may say what would appear absurb to another."

"What is that?"

"Break his arm — wound him — but do not kill him."

"I will tell you, Morrel," said the count, "that I do not need entreating to spare the life of M. de Morcerf; he shall be so well spared, that he will return quietly with his two friends, while I ——"

"And you?"

"That will be another thing; I shall be brought home."

"No, no," cried Maximilian, not knowing how to endure himself.

"As I told you, my dear Morrel, M. de Morcerf will kill me."

Morrel looked at him in utter unconsciousness. "But what has happened, then, since last evening, count?"

"The same thing which happened to Brutus the night before the battle of Philippi; I have seen a phantom."

"And that phantom ——"

"Told me, Morrel, I had lived long enough."

Maximilian and Emmanuel looked at each other. Monte-Cristo drew out his watch. "Let us go," said he; "it is five minutes past seven, and the appointment was for eight o'clock."

A carriage was in readiness at the door. Monte-Cristo stepped into it with his two friends. He had stopped a moment in the passage to listen at a door, and Maximilian and Emmanuel, who had considerately passed forward a few steps, thought they heard him answer, by a sigh, a sob from within. As the clock struck eight, they drove up to the place of meeting.

"We are the first," said Morrel, looking out of the window.

"Excuse me, sir," said Baptistin, who had followed his master with indescribable terror, "but I think I see a carriage down there under the trees."

Monte-Cristo sprang lightly from the carriage, and offered his hand to assist Emmanuel and Maximilian. The latter retained the count's hand between his.

"I like," said he, "to feel a hand like this when its owner relies on the goodness of his cause."

"Truly," said Emmanuel, "I perceive two young men down there, who are evidently waiting."

Monte-Cristo drew Morrel, not aside, but a step or two behind his brother-in-law.

"Maximilian," said he, "are your affections disengaged?" Morrel looked at Monte-Cristo with astonishment. "I do not seek your confidence, my dear friend. I only ask you a simple question; answer it,—that is all I require."

"I love a young girl, count."

"Do you love her much?"

"More than my life."

"Another hope defeated!" said the count. Then, with a sigh, "Poor Haydée!" murmured he.

"In truth, count, if I knew less of you, I should think you were less brave than you are."

"Because I sigh when thinking of some one I am leaving? Come, Morrel, it is not like a soldier to be so bad a judge of courage. Do I regret life? What is it to me, who have passed twenty years between life and death? Moreover, do not alarm yourself, Morrel; this weakness, if it is such, is betrayed to you alone. I know the world is a drawing-room, from which we must retreat politely and honestly, that is, with a bow, and all debts of honor paid."

"That is to the purpose. Have you brought your arms?"

"I?—what for? I hope these gentlemen have theirs."

"I will inquire," said Morrel.

"Do, but no compromises—you understand me?"

"You need not fear." Morrel advanced toward Beauchamp and Château-Renaud, who, seeing his intention, came to meet him. The three young people bowed to each other courteously, if not affably.

"Excuse, me, gentlemen," said Morrel, "but I do not see M. de Morcerf."

"He sent us word this morning," replied Château-Renaud, "that he would meet us on the ground."

"Ah!" said Morrel. Beauchamp pulled out his watch.

"It is only five minutes past eight," said he to Morrel, "there is not much time lost yet."

"Oh! I made no allusion of that kind," replied Morrel.

"There is a carriage coming," said Château-Renaud. It advanced rapidly along one of the avenues leading toward the open space where they were assembled.

"You are doubtless provided with pistols, gentlemen?" said Morrel. "M. de Monte-Cristo yields his right of using his."

"We had anticipated this kindness on the part of the count," said Beauchamp, "and I have brought some arms which I bought eight or ten days since, thinking to want them on a similar occasion. They are quite new, and have not yet been used. Will you examine them?"

"Oh, M. Beauchamp," replied Morrel with a bow, "if you assure me M. de Morcerf does not know these arms, you may readily believe your word will be quite sufficient."

"Gentlemen," said Château-Renaud, "it is not Morcerf coming in that carriage; — faith, it is Franz and Debray!"

The two young men he announced were indeed approaching. "What chance brings you here, gentlemen?" said Château-Renaud, shaking hands with each of them.

"Because," said Debray, "Albert sent this morning to request us to come." Beauchamp and Château-Renaud exchanged looks of astonishment.

"I think I understand his reason," said Morrel.

"What is it?"

"Yesterday afternoon I received a letter from M. de Morcerf, begging me to attend the Opera."

"And I," said Debray.

"And I also," said Franz.

"And we, too," added Beauchamp and Château-Renaud. "Having wished you all to witness the challenge, he now wishes you to be present at the combat."

"Exactly so," said the young men; "you have probably guessed right"

"But, after all these arrangements, he does not come himself," said Château-Renaud; "Albert is ten minutes after time."

"There he comes!" said Beauchamp; "on horseback, at full gallop, followed by a servant."

"How imprudent!" said Château-Renaud, "to come on horseback to fight with the pistol, after all the instructions I had given him."

"And besides," said Beauchamp, "with a collar above his cravat, an open coat and white waistcoat? Why has he not painted a spot upon his heart? — it would have been more simple."

Meanwhile Albert had arrived within ten paces of the group formed by the five young men. He jumped from his horse, threw the bridle on his servant's arms, and joined them. He was pale, and his eyes were red and swollen; it was evident that he had not slept. A shade of melancholy gravity overspread his countenance, which was not natural to him.

"I thank you, gentlemen," said he, "for having complied with my request; I feel extremely grateful for this mark of friendship." Morrel had stepped back as Morcerf approached, and remained at a short distance. "And to you, also, M. Morrel, my thanks are due. Come, there cannot be too many."

"Sir," said Maximilian, "you are not perhaps aware that I am M. de Monte-Cristo's friend?"

"I was not sure, but I expected it. So much the better; the more honorable men there are here the better I shall be satisfied."

"M. Morrel," said Château-Renaud, "will you apprise the Count of Monte-Cristo that M. de Morcerf is arrived and we are at his command?"

Morrel was preparing to fulfill his commission. Beauchamp had meanwhile drawn the box of pistols from the carriage.

"Stop, gentlemen!" said Albert; "I have two words to say to the Count of Monte-Cristo."

"In private?" asked Morrel.

"No, sir; before all who are here."

Albert's seconds looked at each other; Franz and Debray exchanged some words in a whisper; and Morrel, rejoiced at this unexpected incident, went to fetch the count, who was walking in a retired path with Emmanuel.

"What does he want with me?" said Monte-Cristo.

"I do not know, but he wishes to speak to you."

"Ah?" said Monte-Cristo, "I trust he is not going to tempt me by some fresh insult!"

"I do not think such is his intention," said Morrel.

The count advanced, accompanied by Maximilian and Emmanuel; his calm and serene look formed a singular contrast to Albert's grief-stricken face, who approached also, followed by the four young people.

When at three paces distant, Albert and the count stopped.

"Approach, gentlemen," said Albert; "I wish you not to lose one word of what I am about to have the honor of saying to the Count of Monte-Cristo; for it must be repeated by you to all who will listen to it, strange as it may appear to you."

"Proceed, sir," said the count.

"Sir," said Albert, at first with a tremulous voice, but which gradually became firmer; "I reproached you with exposing the conduct of M. de Morcerf in Epirus, for, guilty as I knew he was, I thought you had no right to punish him; but I have since learned you have that right. It is not Fernand Mondego's treachery toward Ali Pacha which induces me so readily to excuse you, but the treachery of the fisherman Fernand toward you, and the almost unheard-of miseries which were its consequences; and I say, and proclaim it publicly, that you were justified in revenging yourself on my father; and I, his son, thank you for not using greater severity."

Had a thunderbolt fallen in the midst of the spectators of this unexpected scene, it would not have surprised them more than did Albert's declaration. As for Monte-Cristo, his eyes slowly rose toward heaven with an expression of infinite gratitude. He could not understand how Albert's fiery nature, of which he had seen so much among the Roman bandits, had suddenly stooped to this humiliation. He recognized the influence of Mercédès, and saw why her noble heart had not opposed the sacrifice she knew beforehand would be useless.

"Now, sir," said Albert, "if you think my apology sufficient, pray give me your hand. Next to the merit of infallibility which you appear to possess, I rank that of candidly acknowledging a fault But this confession concerns me only I acted well according to the laws of man, but you have acted according to those of God. An angel alone could have saved one of us from death — that angel came from heaven, if not to make us friends (which, alas! fatality renders impossible), at least to make us esteem each other."

Monte-Cristo, with moistened eye, heaving breast, and lips half open, extended to Albert a hand, which the latter pressed with a sentiment resembling respectful fear.

"Gentlemen," said he, "M. de Monte-Cristo receives my apology; I acted hastily toward him. Hasty actions are generally bad ones. Now my fault is repaired. I hope the world will not call me cowardly for acting as my conscience dictated But if any one should entertain a false opinion of me," added he, drawing himself up as if he would challenge both friends and enemies, "I shall endeavor to correct his mistake."

"What has, then, happened during the night?" asked Beauchamp of Château-Renaud; "we appear to make a very sorry figure here."

"In truth, what Albert has just done is either very despicable or very noble," replied the baron.

"What can it mean?" said Debray to Franz.

"The Count of Monte-Cristo acts dishonorably to M. de Morcerf, and is justified by his son! Had I ten Janinas in my family, I should only consider myself the more bound to fight ten times"

As for Monte-Cristo, his head was bent down, his arms were powerless; bowing under the weight of twenty-four years' reminiscences, he thought not of Albert, of Beauchamp, of Château-Renaud, or of any of that group; but he thought of that courageous woman who had come to plead for her son's life, to whom he had offered his, and who had now saved it by the revelation of a dreadful family secret, capable of destroying forever, in that young man's heart, every feeling of filial piety.

"Providence still!" murmured he, "now only am I fully convinced of being the emissary of God!"

CHAPTER XCI

MOTHER AND SON

THE Count of Monte-Cristo bowed to the five young people with a melancholy and dignified smile, and got into his carriage with Maximilian and Emmanuel. Albert, Beauchamp, and Château-Renaud remained alone. The young man's look at his two friends, without being timid, appeared to ask their opinion of what he had just done.

"Indeed, my dear friend," said Beauchamp, first, who had either the most feeling or the least dissimulation, "allow me to congratulate you; this is a very unhoped-for conclusion of a very disagreeable affair."

Albert remained silent and wrapped in thought. Château-Renaud contented himself with tapping his boot with his flexible cane.

"Are we not going?" said he, after this embarrassing silence.

"When you please," replied Beauchamp; "allow me only to compliment M. de Morcerf, who has given proof to-day of such chivalric generosity, so rare."

"Oh, yes," said Château-Renaud.

"It is magnificent," continued Beauchamp, "to be able to exercise so much self-control!"

"Assuredly; as for me, I should have been incapable of it," said Château-Renaud, with most significant coolness.

"Gentlemen," interrupted Albert, "I think you did not understand that something very serious had passed between M. de Monte-Cristo and myself."

"Possibly, possibly," said Beauchamp, immediately; "but every simpleton would not be able to understand your heroism, and sooner or later you will find yourself compelled to explain it to them more energetically than would be convenient to your bodily health and the duration of your life. May I give you a friendly counsel? Set out for

Naples, the Hague, or St. Petersburg — calm countries, where the point of honor is better understood than among our hot-headed Parisians. Seek quietude and oblivion, so that you may return peaceably to France after a few years. Am I not right, M. de Château-Renaud?"

Naples.

"That is quite my opinion," said the gentleman; "nothing induces serious duels so much as a fruitless one."

"Thank you, gentlemen," replied Albert, with a smile of indifference; "I shall follow your advice—not because you give it, but because I had before intended to quit France. I thank you equally for the service you have rendered me in being my seconds. It is deeply engraved on my heart, since, after what you have just said, I remember that only."

Château-Renaud and Beauchamp looked at each other; the impression was the same on both of them, and the tone in which Morcerf had just expressed his thanks was so determined that the position would have become embarrassing for all if the conversation had continued.

"Farewell, Albert," said Beauchamp suddenly, carelessly extending his hand to the young man, without the latter appearing to rouse from his lethargy; in fact, he did not notice the offered hand.

"Farewell," said Château-Renaud in his turn, keeping the little cane in his left hand, and bowing with his right.

Albert's lips scarcely whispered "Farewell," but his look was more explicit: it embraced a whole poem of restrained anger, proud disdain, and generous indignation. He preserved his melancholy and motionless position for some time after his two friends had regained their carriage; then, suddenly loosing his horse from the little tree to which his servant had fastened it, he sprang on it, and galloped off in the direction of Paris.

In a quarter of an hour he was entering the hotel of the Rue du Helder. As he alighted he thought he saw behind the curtain of the count's bedroom his father's pale face. Albert turned away his head with a sigh, and went to his own apartments. He cast one lingering look on all the luxuries which had rendered life so easy and so happy since his infancy; he looked at the pictures, whose faces seemed to smile, and the landscapes, which appeared painted in brighter colors. Then he took away his mother's portrait, with its oaken frame, leaving the gilt frame, from which he took it, black and empty. Then he arranged all his beautiful Turkish arms, his fine English guns, his Japanese china, his cups mounted in silver, his artistic bronzes, signed Feuchères or Barye; examined the cupboards, and placed the key in each; threw into the drawer of his secrétaire, which he left open, all the pocket-money he had about him, and with it the thousand fancy jewels from his vases and his jewel-boxes, made an exact inventory of all, and placed it in the most conspicuous part of the table, after putting aside the books and papers which encumbered it.

At the commencement of this work, his servant, notwithstanding his prohibition, came to his room.

"What do you want?" asked he, with a more sorrowful than angry tone.

"Pardon me, sir," replied the valet; "you had forbidden me to disturb you, but the Count de Morcerf had called me."

"Well?" said Albert

"I did not like to go to him without first seeing you."

"Why?"

"Because the count is doubtless aware that I accompanied you to the meeting this morning."

"It is probable," said Albert.

"And since he has sent for me it is doubtless to question me on what happened there. What must I answer?"

"The truth."

"Then I shall say the duel did not take place?"

"You will say I apologized to the Count of Monte-Cristo. Go."

The valet bowed and retired, and Albert returned to his inventory. As he was finishing this work, the sound of horses prancing in the yard, and the wheels of a carriage shaking his window, attracted his attention. He approached the window, and saw his father get into it, and it drove away. The door was scarcely closed when Albert bent his steps to his mother's room; and no one being there to announce him, he advanced to her bedroom, and, distressed by what he saw and guessed, stopped for one moment at the door.

As if the same soul had animated these two beings, Mercédès was doing the same in her apartments as he had just done. Everything was in order: laces, dresses, jewels, linen, money, all were arranged in the drawers, and the countess was carefully collecting the keys. Albert saw all these preparations; he understood them, and exclaiming, "My mother!" he threw his arms round her neck.

The artist who could have depicted the expression of these two countenances would certainly have made of them a beautiful picture. All these proofs of an energetic resolution, which Albert did not fear on his own account, alarmed him for his mother. "What are you doing?" asked he.

"What were you doing?" replied she.

"Oh, my mother!" exclaimed Albert, so overcome he could scarcely speak; "it is not the same with you and me — you cannot have made the same resolution, I have, for I am come to warn you that I bid adieu to your house, and — and to you!"

"I also," replied Mercédès, "am going, and I acknowledge I had depended on your accompanying me; have I deceived myself?"

"My mother," said Albert, with firmness, "I cannot make you share the fate I have planned for myself. I must live henceforth without rank and fortune, and to begin this hard apprenticeship I must borrow from a friend the loaf I shall eat until I have earned one. So, my dear mother, I am going at once to ask Franz to lend me the small sum I shall require to supply my present wants."

"You, my poor child, suffer poverty and hunger! Oh, say not so; it will break my resolutions."

"But not mine, mother," replied Albert. "I am young and strong, I believe I am courageous, and since yesterday I have learned the power of will. Alas! my dear mother, some have suffered so much, and yet live, and have raised a new fortune on the ruin of all the promises of happiness which Heaven had made them — on the fragments of all the hope which God had given them! I have seen that, my mother; I know that from the gulf in which their enemies have plunged them they have risen with so much vigor and glory that in their turn they have ruled their former conquerors, and have punished them. No, my mother; from this moment I have done with the past, and accept nothing from it — not even a name, because you can understand your son cannot bear the name of a man who ought to blush before another."

"Albert, my child," said Mercédès, "if I had a stronger heart, that is the counsel I would have given you; your conscience has spoken when my voice became too weak; listen to its dictates. You had friends, Albert, break off their acquaintance. But do not despair; you have life before you, my dear Albert, for you are yet scarcely twenty-two years old; and as a pure heart like yours wants a spotless name, take my father's — it was Herrera. I am sure, Albert, whatever may be your career, you will soon render that name illustrious. Then, my friend, return to the world still more brilliant from the reflection of your former sorrows, and if I am wrong, still let me cherish these hopes, for I have no future to look forward to; for me the grave opens when I pass the threshold of this house."

"I will fulfill all your wishes, my dear mother," said the young man. "Yes, I share your hopes; the anger of Heaven will not pursue us — you so pure, and me so innocent. But since our resolution is formed, let us act promptly. M. de Morcerf went out about a half an hour since; the opportunity is favorable to avoid an explanation."

"I am ready, my son," said Mercédès.

Albert ran to fetch a hackney-coach; he recollected there was a small furnished house to let in the Rue des Saint-Pères, where his mother would find a humble but decent lodging, and thither he intended conducting the countess. As the hackney-coach stopped at the door, and Albert was alighting, a man approached, and gave him a letter.

Albert recognized the bearer. "From the count," said Bertuccio. Albert took the letter, opened it, and read it, then looked round for Bertuccio, but he was gone.

He returned to Mercédès, with tears in his eyes and heaving breast, and, without uttering a word, he gave her the letter. Mercédès read:

"ALBERT. — While showing you that I have discovered your plans, I hope also to convince you of my delicacy. You are free, you leave the count's hotel, and you take your mother to your home; but reflect, Albert, you owe her more than your poor noble heart can pay her. Keep the struggle for yourself, bear all the suffering, but spare her the trial of poverty which must accompany your first efforts; for she deserves not even the shadow of the misfortune which has this day fallen on her, and Providence wills not the innocent should suffer for the guilty.

"I know you are going to leave the Rue du Helder without taking anything with you; do not seek to know how I discovered it; I know it — that is sufficient. Now, listen, Albert. Twenty-four years ago I returned, proud and joyful, to my country. I had a betrothed, Albert, a lovely girl, whom I adored, and I was bringing to my betrothed a hundred and fifty louis, painfully amassed by ceaseless toil. This money was for her; I destined it for her, and, knowing the treachery of the sea, I buried our treasure in the little garden of the house my father lived in at Marseilles, on the Allées de Meillan. Your mother, Albert, knows that poor house well. A short time since, I passed through Marseilles, and went to see the old house, which revived so many painful recollections, and in the evening I took a spade and dug in the corner of the garden, where I had concealed my treasure. The iron box was there — no one had touched it; it was under a beautiful fig-tree my father had planted the day I was born, which overshadowed the spot. Well, Albert, this money, which was formerly designed to promote the comfort and tranquillity of the woman I adored, may now, from a strange and painful circumstance, be devoted to the same purpose.

"Oh, feel for me, who could offer millions to that poor woman, but who return her only the piece of black bread, forgotten under my poor roof since the day I was torn from her I loved. You are a generous man, Albert, but perhaps you may be blinded by pride or resentment; if you refuse me, if you ask another for what I have a right to offer you, I will say it is ungenerous of you to refuse the life of your mother at the hands of a man whose father was allowed by your father to die in all the horrors of poverty and despair."

Albert stood pale and motionless to hear what his mother would decide after she had finished reading this letter. Mercédès turned her eyes with an ineffable look toward heaven.

"I accept it," said she; "he has a right to pay the dowry, which I shall take with me to some convent!"

Putting the letter in her bosom, she took her son's arm, and, with a firmer step than she even herself expected, she went downstairs.

CHAPTER XCII

THE SUICIDE

MEANWHILE Monte-Cristo had also returned to town with Emmanuel and Maximilian. Their return was cheerful. Emmanuel did not conceal his joy at having seen peace succeed to war, and acknowledged aloud his philanthropic tastes. Morrel, in a corner of the carriage, allowed his brother-in-law's gayety to expend itself in words, while he felt equal inward joy, which, however, betrayed itself only by his look.

At the Barrière du Trône they met Bertuccio, who was waiting there, motionless as a sentinel at his post. Monte-Cristo put his head out of the window, exchanged a few words with him in a low tone, and the steward disappeared.

"M. le Comte," said Emmanuel, when they were at the end of the Place Royale, "put me down at my door, that my wife may not have a single moment of needless anxiety on my account or yours. If it were not ridiculous to make a display of our triumph, I would invite the count to our house; besides that, he doubtless has some trembling heart to comfort. So we will take leave of our friend, and let him hasten home."

"Stop a moment," said Monte-Cristo, "do not let me lose both my companions; return, Emmanuel, to your charming wife, and present my best compliments to her, and do you, Morrel, accompany me to the Champs Elysées."

"Willingly," said Maximilian; "particularly as I have business in that quarter."

"Shall we wait breakfast for you?" asked Emmanuel.

"No," replied the young man. The door was closed, and the carriage proceeded. "See what good fortune I brought you!" said Morrel, when he was alone with the count. "Have you not thought so?"

"Yes," said Monte-Cristo, "for that reason I wished to keep you near me."

"It is miraculous!" continued Morrel, answering his own thoughts.

"What?" said Monte-Cristo.

"What has just happened."

"Yes," said the count, "you are right — it is miraculous."

"For Albert is brave," resumed Morrel.

"Very brave," said Monte-Cristo; "I have seen him sleep with a sword suspended over his head."

"And I know he has fought two duels," said Morrel; "how can you reconcile that with his conduct this morning?"

"All owing to your influence," replied Monte-Cristo, smiling.

"It is well for Albert he is not in the army," said Morrel.

"Why?"

"An apology on the ground!" said the young captain, shaking his head.

"Come," said the count, mildly, "do not entertain the prejudices of ordinary men, Morrel! Acknowledge, if Albert is brave, he cannot be a coward; he must then have had some reason for acting as he did this morning, and confess that his conduct is more heroic than otherwise."

"Doubtless, doubtless," said Morrel; "but I shall say, like the Spaniard, 'He has not been so brave to-day as he was yesterday.'"

"You will breakfast with me, will you not, Morrel?" said the count, to turn the conversation.

"No, I must leave you at ten o'clock"

"Your engagement was for breakfast, then?" said the count.

Morrel smiled, and shook his head.

"Still you must breakfast somewhere."

"But if I am not hungry?" said the young man.

"Oh!" said the count, "I only know two things which destroy the appetite; grief,— and as I am happy to see you very cheerful, it is not that,— and love. Now, after what you told me this morning of your heart, I may believe ——"

"Well, count," replied Morrel, gayly, "I will not dispute it."

"But you will not make me your confidant, Maximilian?" said the count, in a tone which showed how gladly he would have been admitted to the secret.

"I showed you this morning I had a heart; did I not, count?" Monte-Cristo only answered by extending his hand to the young man. "Well!" continued the latter, "since that heart is no longer with you in the Bois de Vincennes, it is elsewhere, and I must go and find it."

"Go," said the count deliberately, "go, dear friend, but promise me, if you meet with any obstacle, to remember that I have some power in this world; that I am happy to use that power in the behalf of those I love; and that I love you, Morrel."

"I will remember it," said the young man, "as selfish children recol-

The Place Royale.

lect their parents when they want their aid. When I need your assistance, and the moment may come, I will come to you, count."

"Well, I rely upon your promise. Farewell. Adieu, till we meet again."

They had arrived in the Champs Elysées. Monte-Cristo opened the carriage-door, Morrel sprang out on the pavement, Bertuccio was waiting on the steps. Morrel disappeared through the avenue of Marigny, and Monte-Cristo hastened to join Bertuccio.

"Well?" asked he.

"She is going to leave her house," said the steward.

"And her son?"

"Florentin, his valet, thinks he is going to do the same."

"Come this way." Monte-Cristo took Bertuccio into his cabinet, wrote the letter we have seen, and gave it to the steward. "Go," said he quickly. "Apropos, let Haydée be informed I am returned."

"Here I am," said the young girl, who, at the sound of the carriage, had run downstairs, and whose face was radiant with joy at seeing the count return safely. Every transport of a daughter finding a father, all the delight of a mistress seeing an adored lover, were felt by Haydée during the first moments of this meeting, which she had so eagerly expected. Doubtless, although less evident, Monte-Cristo's joy was not less intense; joy to hearts which have suffered long is like the dew on the ground after a long drought; both the heart and the ground absorb that beneficent moisture falling on them, and nothing is outwardly apparent.

Monte-Cristo was beginning to think, what he had not for a long time dared to believe, that there were two Mercédès in the world, and he might yet be happy. His eye, elate with happiness, was reading eagerly the moistened gaze of Haydée, when suddenly the door opened. The count knit his brow.

"M. de Morcerf!" said Baptistin, as if that name sufficed for his excuse. In fact, the count's face brightened.

"Which," asked he, "the viscount or the count?"

"The count."

"Oh!" exclaimed Haydée, "is it not yet over?"

"I know not if it is finished, my beloved child," said Monte-Cristo, taking the young girl's hands; "but I do know you have nothing more to fear."

"But it is the wretched ——"

"That man cannot injure me, Haydée," said Monte-Cristo; "it was his son alone there was cause to fear."

"And what I have suffered," said the young girl, "you shall never know, my lord."

Monte-Cristo smiled. "By my father's tomb!" said he, extending his hand over the head of the young girl, "I swear to you, Haydée, that if any misfortune happens, it will not be to me."

"WE SHALL FIGHT TILL ONE OF US IS DEAD."

"I believe you, my lord, as implicitly as if God had spoken to me," said the young girl, presenting her forehead to him Monte-Cristo pressed on that pure, beautiful forehead a kiss which made two hearts throb at once, the one violently, the other secretly.

"Oh!" murmured the count, "shall I then be permitted to love again? Ask M de Morcerf into the drawing-room," said he to Baptistin, while he led the beautiful Greek girl to a private staircase.

We must explain this visit, which, although Monte-Cristo expected it, is unexpected to our readers. While Mercédès, as we have said, was making a similar inventory of her property to Albert's, while she was arranging her jewels, shutting her drawers, collecting her keys, to leave everything in perfect order, she did not perceive a pale and sinister face at a glass door which threw light into the passage, from which everything could be both seen and heard. He who was thus looking, without being heard or seen, probably heard and saw all that passed in Madame de Morcerf's apartments From that glass door the pale-faced man went to the count's bedroom, and raised, with a contracted hand, the curtain of a window overlooking the court-yard He remained there ten minutes, motionless and dumb, listening to the beating of his own heart For him those ten minutes were very long It was then that Albert, returned from his rendezvous, perceived his father watching for his arrival behind a curtain, and turned aside The count's eye expanded; he knew Albert had insulted the count dreadfully, and that, in every country in the world, such an insult would lead to a deadly duel Albert returned safely — then the count was revenged.

An indescribable ray of joy illumined that wretched countenance, like the last ray of the sun before it disappears behind the mass of clouds which appear more like its tomb than its couch But, as we have said, he waited in vain for his son to come to his apartment with the account of his triumph. He easily understood why his son did not come to see him before he went to avenge his father's honor, but when that was done, why did not his son come and throw himself into his arms?

It was then, when the count could not see Albert, he sent for his servant, whom he knew was authorized not to conceal anything from him. Ten minutes afterward the General Morcerf was seen on the steps in a black coat with a military collar, black pantaloons, and black gloves He had apparently given previous orders, for, as he reached the bottom step, his carriage came from the coach-house ready for him The valet threw into the carriage his military cloak, in which two swords were wrapped; and, shutting the door, took his seat by the side of the coachman The coachman stooped down for his orders

"To the Champs Elysées," said the general; "the Count of Monte-Cristo's. Quickly!"

The horses bounded beneath the whip, and, in five minutes, they stopped before the count's door. Morcerf opened the door himself; and, as the carriage rolled away, he passed up the walk, rang, and entered the open door with his servant.

A moment afterward Baptistin announced the Count de Morcerf to Monte-Cristo; and the latter, leading Haydée aside, ordered the Count de Morcerf to be asked into the drawing-room. The general was pacing the room the third time, when, in turning, he perceived Monte-Cristo at the door.

"Eh! it is M. de Morcerf," said Monte-Cristo, quietly; "I thought I had heard wrong."

"Yes, it is I," said the count, whom a frightful contraction of the lips prevented from articulating freely.

"May I know the cause which procures me the pleasure of seeing M. de Morcerf so early?"

"Had you not a meeting with my son this morning?" asked the general.

"I had," replied the count.

"And I know my son had good reasons to wish to fight with you, and to endeavor to kill you."

"Yes, sir, he had very good ones; but you see, in spite of them he has not killed me, and did not even fight."

"Yet he considered you the cause of his father's dishonor, the cause of the fearful ruin which has fallen on my house."

"Truly, sir," said Monte-Cristo, with his dreadful calmness, "a secondary cause, but not the principal."

"Doubtless you made, then, some apology or explanation?"

"I explained nothing, and it is he who apologized to me."

"But to what do you attribute this conduct?"

"To the conviction, probably, that there was one more guilty than me."

"And who was that?"

"His father."

"That may be," said the count, turning pale; "but, you know, the guilty do not like to find themselves convicted."

"I know it. And I expected this result."

"You expected my son would be a coward?" cried the count.

"M. Albert de Morcerf is no coward!" said Monte-Cristo.

"A man who holds a sword in his hand, and sees a mortal enemy within reach of that sword, and does not fight, is a coward! Why is he not here, that I may tell him so?"

"Sir," replied Monte-Cristo, coldly, "I did not expect you had come here to relate to me your little family affairs. Go and tell M. Albert that, and he may know what to answer you."

"Oh, no, no!" said the general, smiling faintly, "I did not come for that purpose; you are right! I came to tell you that I also look upon you as my enemy! I came to tell you I hate you instinctively! That it seems as if I had always known you, and always hated you, and, in short, since the young people of the present day will not fight, it remains for us to do it. Do you think so, sir?"

"Certainly. And when I told you I had foreseen the result, it is the honor of your visit I alluded to"

"So much the better. Are you prepared?"

"Yes, sir."

"You know that we shall fight till one of us is dead!" said the general, whose teeth were clinched with rage.

"Until one of us dies," repeated Monte-Cristo, moving his head slightly up and down.

"Let us start, then, we need no witnesses"

"Truly," said Monte-Cristo, "it is unnecessary, we know each other so well!"

"On the contrary," said the count, "we know so little of each other"

"Indeed!" said Monte-Cristo, with the same indomitable coolness; "let us see. Are you not the soldier Fernand who deserted on the eve of the battle of Waterloo? Are you not the Lieutenant Fernand who served as guide and spy to the French army in Spain? Are you not the Captain Fernand who betrayed, sold, and murdered his benefactor, Ali? And have not all these Fernands, united, made the Lieutenant-General de Morcerf, Peer of France?"

"Oh!" cried the general, as if branded with a hot iron, "wretch! to reproach me with my shame, when about, perhaps, to kill me No, I did not say I was a stranger to you; I know well, demon, that you have penetrated into the darkness of the past, and that you have read, by the light of what flambeau I know not, every page of my life, but, perhaps, I may be more honorable in my shame than you under your pompous coverings. No—no, I am aware you know me; but I know you not, adventurer, sewn up in gold and jewelry. You have called yourself, at Paris, the Count of Monte-Cristo; in Italy, Sindbad the Sailor, in Malta, I forget what. But it is your real name which I want to know, in the midst of your hundred names, that I may pronounce it when we meet to fight, at the moment when I plunge my sword through your heart"

The Count of Monte-Cristo turned dreadfully pale, his eye seemed to burn with a devouring fire; he bounded toward a dressing-room near his bedroom, and, in less than a moment, tearing off his cravat, his coat and waistcoat, he put on a sailor's jacket and hat, from beneath which rolled his long, black hair.

He returned thus, formidable and implacable, advancing with his arms crossed on his breast, toward the general, who could not understand why he had disappeared; but who on seeing him again, and feeling his teeth chatter and his legs sink under him, drew back, and only stopped when he found a table to support his clinched hand.

"Fernand," cried he, "of my hundred names I need only tell you one, to overwhelm you! But you guess it now, do you not?—or, rather, you remember it? For, notwithstanding all my sorrows and my tortures, I show you to-day a face which the happiness of revenge makes young again—a face you must often have seen in your dreams since your marriage with Mercédès, my betrothed!"

The general, with his head thrown back, hands extended, gaze fixed, looked silently at this dreadful apparition; then, seeking the wall to support him, he glided along close to it until he reached the door, through which he went out backward, uttering this single mournful, lamentable, distressing cry:

"Edmond Dantès!"

Then, with sighs which were unlike any human sound, he dragged himself to the door, reeled across the court-yard, and falling into the arms of his valet, he said in a voice scarcely intelligible,—"Home! home!"

The fresh air, and the shame he felt at having exposed himself before his servants, partially recalled his senses; but the ride was short, and as he drew near his house all his wretchedness revived. He stopped at a short distance from the house and alighted. The door of the hotel was wide open, a hackney-coach was standing in the middle of the yard—a strange sight before so noble a mansion; the count looked at it with terror; but without daring to ask, he rushed toward his apartment.

Two persons were coming down the stairs; he had only time to creep into a cabinet to avoid them. It was Mercédès leaning on her son's arm and leaving the hotel. They passed close by the unhappy being, who, concealed behind the damask door, almost felt Mercédès' dress brush past him, and his son's warm breath pronouncing these words:

"Courage, my mother! Come, this is no longer our home!"

The words died away, the steps were lost in the distance. The general drew himself up, clinging to the door; he uttered the most dreadful sob which ever escaped from the bosom of a father abandoned at the same time by his wife and son. He soon heard the clatter of the

"EDMOND DANTÈS!"

iron step of the hackney-coach, then the coachman's voice, and then the rolling of the heavy vehicle shook the windows. He darted to his bedroom to see once more all he had loved in the world; but the hackney-coach drove on without the head of either Mercédès or her son

The Barrière du Trône.

appearing at the window to take a last look at the house of the deserted father or husband.

At the very moment when the wheels of that coach crossed the gateway a report was heard, and a thick smoke escaped through one of the panes of the window, which was broken by the explosion.

CHAPTER XCIII

VALENTINE

WE may easily conceive where Morrel's appointment was. On leaving Monte-Cristo he walked slowly toward Villefort's; we say slowly, for Morrel had more than half-an-hour to spare to go five hundred steps, but he had hastened to take leave of Monte-Cristo because he wished to be alone with his thoughts. He knew his time well — the hour when Valentine was giving Noirtier his breakfast, and was sure not to be disturbed in the performance of this pious duty. Noirtier and Valentine had given him leave to go twice a week, and he was now availing himself of that permission.

He arrived; Valentine was expecting him. Uneasy and almost wandering, she seized his hand and led him to her grandfather. This uneasiness, amounting almost to wildness, arose from the report Morcerf's adventure had made in the world; the affair of the Opera was generally known. No one at Villefort's doubted that a duel would ensue from it. Valentine, with her woman's instinct, guessed that Morrel would be Monte-Cristo's witness, and from the young man's well-known courage and his great affection for the count, she feared he would not content himself with the passive part assigned to him. We may easily understand how eagerly the particulars were asked for, given, and received; and Morrel could read an indescribable joy in the eyes of his beloved, when she knew that the termination of this affair was as happy as it was unexpected.

"Now," said Valentine, motioning to Morrel to sit down near her grandfather, while she took her seat on his footstool, "now let us talk about our own affairs. You know, Maximilian, grandpapa once thought of leaving this house, and taking an apartment away from M. de Villefort's."

"Yes," said Maximilian, "I recollect the project, of which I highly approved."

"Well," said Valentine, "you may approve again, for grandpapa is again thinking of it."

"Bravo!" said Maximilian.

"And do you know," said Valentine, "what reason grandpapa gives for leaving this house?" Noirtier looked at Valentine to impose silence,

but she did not notice him; her looks, her eyes, her smile, were all for Morrel.

"Oh! whatever may be M. Noirtier's reason," answered Morrel, "I will readily believe it to be a good one."

"An excellent one!" said Valentine. "He pretends the air of the Faubourg Saint-Honoré is not good for me."

"Indeed!" said Morrel; "in that M. Noirtier may be right; your health has not appeared good the last fortnight."

"Not very," said Valentine. "And grandpapa is become my physician; and I have the greatest confidence in him, because he knows everything."

"Do you then really suffer?" asked Morrel, quickly.

"Oh, it must not be called suffering; I feel a general uneasiness, that is all. I have lost my appetite, and my stomach feels to be struggling to become accustomed to something." Noirtier did not lose a word of what Valentine said.

"And what treatment do you adopt for this singular complaint?"

"A very simple one," said Valentine. "I swallow every morning a spoonful of the mixture prepared for my grandfather. When I say one spoonful, I began by one — now I take four. Grandpapa says it is a panacea." Valentine smiled, but it was evident she suffered.

Maximilian, in his devotedness, gazed silently at her. She was very beautiful, but her usual paleness had increased; her eyes were more brilliant than ever, and her hands, which were generally white like mother-of-pearl, now more resembled wax, to which time was adding a yellowish hue.

From Valentine the young man looked toward Noirtier. The latter watched with strange and deep interest the young girl, absorbed by her affection; and he also, like Morrel, followed those traces of inward suffering, which were so little perceptible to a common observer that they escaped the notice of every one but the grandfather and the lover.

"But," said Morrel, "I thought this mixture, of which you now take four spoonfuls, was prepared for M. Noirtier?"

"I know it is very bitter," said Valentine; "so bitter, that all I drink afterward appears to have the same taste." Noirtier looked inquiringly at his granddaughter. "Yes; grandpapa," said Valentine; "it is so. Just now, before I came down to you, I drank a glass of *eau sucrée;* I left half, because it seemed so bitter." Noirtier turned pale, and made a sign that he wished to speak.

Valentine rose to fetch the dictionary. Noirtier watched her with evident anguish. In fact, the blood was rushing to the young girl's head already, her cheeks were becoming red.

"Oh!" cried she, without losing any of her cheerfulness, "this is singular! A dimness! Did the sun shine in my eyes?" And she leaned against the window.

"The sun is not shining," said Morrel, more alarmed by Noirtier's expression than by Valentine's indisposition. He ran toward her. The young girl smiled.

"Comfort yourself!" said she to Noirtier. "Do not be alarmed, Maxi-

milian; it is nothing, and has already passed away. But listen! Do I not hear a carriage in the court-yard?" She opened Noirtier's door, ran to a window in the passage, and returned hastily. "Yes," said she, "it is Madame Danglars and her daughter, who are come to call on us. Good-bye! I must run away, for they would send here for me; or, rather, farewell till I see you again. Stay with grandpapa, Maximilian; I promise you not to persuade them to stay."

Morrel watched her as she left the room; he heard her ascend the little staircase which led both to Madame de Villefort's apartments and to hers. As soon as she was gone, Nortier made a sign to Morrel to take the dictionary. Morrel obeyed; guided by Valentine, he had learned how to understand the old man quickly. Accustomed, however, as he was, and having to repeat most of the letters of the alphabet, and to find every word in the dictionary, it was ten minutes before the thought of the old man was translated by these words:

"Fetch the glass of water and the decanter from Valentine's room."

Morrel rang immediately for the servant who had taken Barrois' situation, and in Noirtier's name gave that order. The servant soon returned. The decanter and the glass were completely empty. Noirtier made a sign that he wished to speak.

"Why are the glass and the decanter empty?" asked he; "Valentine said she only drank half the glassful."

The translation of this new question occupied another five minutes.

"I do not know," said the servant, "but the housemaid is in Mademoiselle Valentine's room; perhaps she has emptied them."

"Ask her," said Morrel, translating Noirtier's thought this time by his look. The servant went out, but returned almost immediately. "Mademoiselle Valentine passed through the room to go to Madame de Villefort's," said he; "and in passing, as she was thirsty, she drank what remained in the glass; as for the decanter, M. Edward had emptied that to make a pond for his ducks."

Noirtier raised his eyes to heaven, as a gambler does who stakes his all on one stroke. From that moment the old man's eyes were fixed on the door, and did not quit it.

It was indeed Madame Danglars and her daughter whom Valentine had seen; they had been ushered into Madame de Villefort's room, who had said she would receive them there. That is why Valentine passed through her room, which was on a level with Valentine's and only separated from it by Edward's. The two ladies entered the drawing-room with that sort of official stiffness which announced a communication. Between people of the world, a hint is soon caught. Madame de Villefort received them with equal solemnity. Valentine entered at this moment, and the formalities were resumed.

"My dear friend," said the baroness, while the two young people were shaking hands, "I and Eugénie are come to be the first to announce to you the approaching marriage of my daughter with Prince Cavalcanti." Danglars kept up the title of prince. The popular banker found it answered better than count.

"Allow me to present you my sincere congratulations," replied Madame de Villefort. "M. le Prince Cavalcanti appears a young man of rare qualities."

"Listen," said the baroness, smiling; "speaking to you as a friend, I would say, the prince does not yet appear all he will be. He has about him a little of that foreign manner by which French persons recognize, at first sight, the Italian or German nobleman. Besides, he gives evidence of great kindness of disposition, much keenness of wit, and as to suitableness, M. Danglars assures me his fortune is majestic—that is his term."

"And then," said Eugénie, while turning over the leaves of Madame de Villefort's album, "add that you have taken a great fancy to the young man."

"And," said Madame de Villefort, "I need not ask you if you share that fancy."

"I!" replied Eugénie, with her usual candor. "Oh, not the least in the world, madame! My wish was not to confine myself to domestic cares, or the caprices of any man, but to be an artist, and, consequently, free in heart, in person, and in thought."

Eugénie pronounced these words with so firm a tone that the color mounted to Valentine's cheeks. The timid girl could not understand that vigorous nature which appeared to have none of the timidities of woman.

"At any rate," said she, "since I am to be married whether I will or not, I ought to be thankful to Providence for having released me from my engagement with M. Albert de Morcerf, or I should this day have been the wife of a dishonored man."

"It is true," said the baroness, with that strange simplicity sometimes met with among fashionable ladies, and of which plebeian intercourse can never entirely deprive them,—"it is very true that, had not the Morcerfs hesitated, my daughter would have married that M. Albert. The general depended much on it; he even came to force M. Danglars. We have had a narrow escape."

"But," said Valentine, timidly, "does all the father's shame revert upon the son? M. Albert appears to me quite innocent of the treason charged against the general."

"Excuse me," said the implacable young girl, "M. Albert claims and well deserves his share. It appears that, after having challenged M. de Monte-Cristo at the Opera yesterday, he apologized on the ground to-day."

"Impossible!" said Madame de Villefort.

"Ah, my dear friend," said Madame Danglars, with the same simplicity we before noticed, "it is a fact! I heard it from M. Debray, who was present at the explanation."

Valentine also knew the truth, but she did not answer. A single word had reminded her that Morrel was expecting her in Noirtier's room. Deeply engaged with a sort of inward contemplation, Valentine had ceased for a moment to join in the conversation. She would, indeed, have found it impossible to repeat what had been said the last few min-

VALENTINE OVERPOWERED BY THE POISON.

utes, when suddenly Madame Danglars' hand, pressed on her arm, aroused her from her lethargy.

"What is it?" said she, starting at Madame Danglars' touch as she would have done from an electric shock.

"It is, my dear Valentine," said the baroness, "that you are, doubtless, suffering."

"I?" said the young girl, passing her hand across her burning forehead.

"Yes, look at yourself in that glass; you have turned pale and red successively, three or four times in one minute."

"Indeed," cried Eugénie, "you are very pale!"

"Oh, do not be alarmed! I have been so for some days." Artless as she was, the young girl knew this was an opportunity to leave; besides, Madame de Villefort came to her assistance.

"Retire, Valentine," said she; "you are really suffering, and these ladies will excuse you; drink a glass of pure water, it will restore you."

Valentine kissed Eugénie, bowed to Madame Danglars, who had already risen to take her leave, and went out.

"That poor child," said Madame de Villefort, when Valentine was gone, "she makes me very uneasy, and I should not be astonished if she had some serious illness."

Meanwhile, Valentine, in a sort of excitement which she could not quite understand, had crossed Edward's room without paying any attention to some trick of the child, and through her own had reached the little staircase.

She was at the bottom excepting three steps; she already heard Morrel's voice, when suddenly a cloud passed over her eyes, her stiffened foot missed the step, her hands had no power to hold the baluster, and, falling against the wall, she rolled down these three steps rather than walked. Morrel bounded to the door, opened it, and found Valentine extended on the floor. Rapid as lightning, he raised her in his arms and placed her in a chair. Valentine opened her eyes.

"Oh, what a clumsy thing I am!" said she, with feverish volubility; "I no longer know my way. I forgot there were three more steps before the landing."

"You have hurt yourself, perhaps," said Morrel. "What can I do for you, Valentine?"

Valentine looked around her; she saw the deepest terror depicted in Noirtier's eyes.

"Comfort yourself, dear grandpapa," said she, endeavoring to smile; "it is nothing — it is nothing; I was giddy, that is all."

"Another giddiness!" said Morrel, clasping his hands. "Oh, attend to it, Valentine, I entreat you."

"But no," said Valentine,—"no, I tell you it is all past, and it was nothing. Now, let me tell you some news; Eugénie is to be married in a week, and in three days there is to be a grand feast, a sort of betrothing festival. We are all invited, my father, Madame de Villefort, and I — at least, I understood it so."

"When will it, then, be our turn to think of these things? Oh, Valentine, you, who have so much influence over your grandpapa, try to make him answer — Soon."

"And do you," said Valentine, "depend on me to stimulate the tardiness and arouse the memory of grandpapa?"

"Yes," cried Morrel, "be quick! So long as you are not mine Valentine, I shall always think I may lose you."

"Oh!" replied Valentine, with a convulsive movement, "Oh! indeed, Maximilian, you are too timid for an officer, for a soldier who, they say never knows fear. Ha! ha! ha!"

She burst into a forced and melancholy laugh, her arms stiffened and twisted, her head fell back on her chair, and she remained motionless. The cry of terror which was stopped on Noirtier's lips, seemed to start from his eyes. Morrel understood it; he knew he must call assistance. The young man rang the bell violently; the housemaid who had been in Madmoiselle Valentine's room, and the servant who had replaced Barrois, ran in at the same moment. Valentine was so pale, so cold, so inanimate, that, without listening to what was said to them, they were seized with the fear which pervaded the house, and they flew into the passage crying for help. Madame Danglars and Eugénie were going out at that moment; they heard the cause of the disturbance.

"I told you so!" cried Madame de Villefort. "Poor child!"

CHAPTER XCIV

THE CONFESSION

AT the same moment M. de Villefort's voice was heard calling from his cabinet, "What is the matter?"

Morrel consulted Noirtier's look, who had recovered his self-command, and with a glance indicated the closet where, once before, under somewhat similiar circumstances, he had taken refuge. He had only time to get his hat, and throw himself breathless into the closet; the *procureur's* footstep was heard in the passage.

Villefort sprang into the room, ran to Valentine, and took her in his arms.

"A physician! a physician! M. d'Avrigny!" cried Villefort; "or rather I will go for him myself."

He flew from the apartment, and Morrel, at the same moment, darted out at the other door. He had been struck to the heart by a frightful recollection — the conversation he had heard between the doctor and Villefort the night of Madame de Saint-Méran's death recurred to him; these symptoms, to a less alarming extent, were the same which had preceded the death of Barrois. At the same time Monte-Cristo's voice seemed to resound in his ear, who had said, only two hours before: "Whatever you want, Morrel, come to me; I can do much."

Quicker than thought, he darted down the Rue Matignon, and thence to the Avenue des Champs Elysées.

Meanwhile Villefort arrived in a hired cab at d'Avrigny's door. He rang so violently that the porter came alarmed. Villefort ran upstairs without saying a word. The porter knew him, and let him pass, only calling to him:

"In his cabinet, *M. le Procureur du Roi* — in his cabinet!" Villefort pushed, or rather forced, the door open.

"Ah!" said the doctor, "is it you?"

"Yes," said Villefort, closing the door after him, "it is I, who am come in my turn to ask you if we are quite alone. Doctor, my house is accursed!"

"What!" said the latter, with apparent coolness, but with deep emotion, "have you another invalid?"

"Yes, doctor," cried Villefort, seizing with a convulsive grasp a handful of hair, "yes!"

D'Avrigny's look implied, "I told you it would be so." Then he slowly uttered these words: "Who is now dying in your house? What new victim is going to accuse you of weakness before God?"

A mournful sob burst from Villefort's heart; he approached the doctor, and seizing his arm:

"Valentine!" said he, "it is Valentine's turn!"

"Your daughter!" cried d'Avrigny, with grief and surprise.

"You see you were deceived," murmured the magistrate; "come and see her, and on her bed of agony entreat her pardon for having suspected her."

"Each time you have applied to me," said the doctor, "it has been too late; still I will go. But let us make haste, sir; with the enemies you have to do with there is no time to be lost."

"Oh! this time, doctor, you shall not have to reproach me with weakness. This time I will know the assassin, and will pursue him."

"Let us try first to save the victim before we think of revenging her," said d'Avrigny. "Come."

The same cab which had brought Villefort took them back at full speed, at the very moment when Morrel rapped at Monte-Cristo's door.

The count was in his cabinet, and was reading, with an angry look, something which Bertuccio had brought in haste. Hearing Morrel announced, who had left him only two hours before, the count raised his head. He, as well as the count, had evidently been much tried during those two hours, for the young man had left him smiling, and returned with a disturbed air. The count rose, and sprang to meet him.

"What is the matter, Maximilian?" asked he; "you are pale, and the perspiration rolls from your forehead." Morrel fell, rather than sat down on a chair.

"Yes," said he, "I came quickly; I wanted to speak to you."

"Is all your family well?" asked the count, with an affectionate benevolence, whose sincerity no one could for a moment doubt.

"Thank you, count—thank you," said the young man, evidently embarrassed how to begin the conversation; "yes, every one in my family is well."

"So much the better; yet you have something to tell me?" replied the count, with increased anxiety.

"Yes," said Morrel, "it is true; I have just left a house where death has just entered, to run to you."

"Are you then come from M. de Morcerf?" asked Monte-Cristo.

"No," said Morrel; "is some one dead in his house?"

"The general has just blown his brains out," replied Monte-Cristo, with great coolness.

"Oh! what a dreadful event!" cried Maximilian.

"Not for the countess, nor for Albert," said Monte-Cristo; "a dead father or husband is better than a dishonored one: blood washes out shame."

"Poor countess!" said Maximilian, "I pity her very much; she is so noble a woman."

"Pity Albert also, Maximilian; for, believe me, he is the worthy son of the countess. But let us return to yourself: you have hastened to me; can I have the happiness of being useful to you?"

"Yes, I need your help; that is, I thought, like a madman, you could lend me your assistance in a case where God alone can succor me."

"Tell me what it is," replied Monte-Cristo.

"Oh!" said Morrel, "I know not, indeed, if I may reveal this secret to mortal ears; but fatality impels me, necessity constrains me, count ——" Morrel hesitated.

"Do you think I love you?" said Monte-Cristo, taking the young man's hand affectionately in his.

"Oh! you encourage me! and something tells me there," placing his hand on his heart, "that I ought to have no secret from you."

"You are right, Morrel; God is speaking to your heart, and your heart speaks to you. Tell me what it says."

"Count, will you allow me to send Baptistin to inquire after some one you know?"

"I am at your service, and still more my servants."

"Oh! I cannot live, if she is not better."

"Shall I ring for Baptistin?"

"No, I will go and speak to him myself." Morrel went out, called Baptistin, and whispered a few words to him. The valet ran directly.

"Well, have you sent?" asked Monte-Cristo, seeing Morrel return.

"Yes, and now I shall be more calm."

"You know I am waiting," said Monte-Cristo, smiling.

"Yes, and I will tell you. One evening I was in a garden; a clump of trees concealed me; no one suspected I was there. Two persons passed near me — allow me to conceal their names for the present; they were speaking in an undertone, and yet I was so interested in what they said that I did not lose a single word."

"This is a gloomy introduction, if I may judge from your paleness and your shuddering, Morrel."

"Oh! yes, very gloomy, my friend! Some one had just died in the house to which that garden belonged. One of those persons whose conversation I overheard was the master of the house, the other, the physician. The former was confiding to the latter his grief and fear; for it was the second time within a month that death had entered suddenly and unexpectedly that house, apparently destined to destruction by some exterminating angel, as an object of God's anger."

"Ah! ah!" said Monte-Cristo, looking earnestly at the young man, and, by an imperceptible movement, turning his chair, so that he remained in the shade while the light fell full on Maximilian's face.

"Yes," continued Morrel, "death had entered that house twice within one month."

"And what did the doctor answer?" asked Monte-Cristo.

"He replied — he replied, that death was not a natural one, and must be attributed ——"

"To what?"

"To poison!"

"Indeed!" said Monte-Cristo, with a slight cough, which, in moments of extreme emotion, helped him to disguise a blush, or his paleness, or the intense interest with which he listened; "indeed, Maximilian, did you hear that?"

"Yes, my dear count, I heard it; and the doctor added, that if another death occurred in a similar way, he must appeal to justice."

Monte-Cristo listened, or appeared to do so, with the greatest calmness.

"Well!" said Maximilian, "death came a third time, and neither the master of the house nor the doctor said a word. Death is now, perhaps, striking a fourth blow. Count, what am I bound to do, being in possession of this secret?"

"My dear friend," said Monte-Cristo, "you appear to be relating an adventure which we all know by heart. I know the house where you heard it, or one very similar to it; a house with a garden, a master, a physician, and where there have been three unexpected and sudden deaths. Well! I have not intercepted your confidence, and yet I know all that as well as you, and I have no conscientious scruples. No, it does not concern me. You say an exterminating angel appears to have devoted that house to God's anger — well! who says your supposition is not reality? Do not notice things which those whose interest is to see them, pass over. If it is God's justice, instead of his anger, which is walking through that house, Maximilian, turn away your face, and let his justice accomplish its purpose."

Morrel shuddered. There was something mournful, solemn, and terrible in the count's manner.

"Besides," continued he, in so changed a tone that no one would have supposed it was the same person speaking — "besides, who says that it will begin again?"

"It has returned, count!" exclaimed Morrel, "that is why I hastened to you."

"Well! what do you wish me to do? Do you wish me, for instance, to give information to the *procureur du roi*?" Monte-Cristo uttered the last words with so much meaning, that Morrel, starting up, cried out.

"You know of whom I speak, count, do you not?"

"Perfectly well, my good friend, and I will prove it to you by putting the dots to the *i*, or, rather, by naming the persons. You were walking one evening in M. de Villefort's garden. From what you relate, I suppose it to have been the evening of Madame de Saint-Méran's death. You heard M. de Villefort talking to M. d'Avrigny about the death of M. de Saint-Méran, and that, no less surprising, of the marchioness. M. d'Avrigny said he believed they both proceeded from poison; and you, honest man, have ever since been asking your heart, and sounding your conscience, to know if you ought to expose or conceal this secret. We are no longer in the Middle Ages; there is no longer a Vehmgericht, or Free Tribunals; what do you want to ask these people? 'Conscience, what has thou to do with me?' as Sterne said. My dear fellow, let them sleep on, if they are asleep; let them grow pale in their drowsiness, if they are disposed to do so; and pray do you remain in peace, who have no remorse to disturb you."

Deep grief was depicted on Morrel's features; he seized Monte-Cristo's hand. "But it is beginning again, I say!"

"Well!" said the count, astonished at his persistence, which he could not understand, and looking still more earnestly at Maximilian, "let it begin again: it is a family of Atrides; God has condemned them, and they must submit to their punishment. They will all disappear, like the fabrics children build with cards, and which fall, one by one, under the breath of their builder, even if there are two hundred of them. Three months since, it was M. de Saint-Méran; Madame de Saint-Méran two months since; the other day it was Barrois; to-day, the old Noirtier, or young Valentine."

"You knew it?" cried Morrel, in such a paroxysm of terror that Monte-Cristo started; he whom the falling heavens would have found unmoved; "you knew it, and said nothing?"

"And what is it to me?" replied Monte-Cristo, shrugging his shoulders; "do you know those people? and must I lose the one to save the other? Faith, no; for between the culprit and the victim I have no choice."

"But I," cried Morrel, groaning with sorrow,—"I love her!"

"You love?—whom?" cried Monte-Cristo, starting on his feet, and seizing the two hands which Morrel was raising toward heaven.

"I love most fondly—I love madly—I love as a man who would give his life-blood to spare her a tear—I love Valentine de Villefort, who is being murdered at this moment! Do you understand me? I love her; and I ask God and you how I can save her?"

Monte-Cristo uttered a cry which those only can conceive who have heard the roar of a wounded lion. "Unhappy man!" cried he, wringing his hands in his turn; "you love Valentine!—that daughter of an accursed race!"

Never had Morrel witnessed such an expression—never had so terrible an eye flashed before his face—never had the genius of terror he had so often seen, either on the battle-field or in the murderous nights of Algeria, shaken around him more dreadful fire. He drew back terrified.

As for Monte-Cristo, after his ebullition, he closed his eyes, as if dazzled by internal light. In a moment he restrained himself so powerfully that the tempestuous heaving of his breast subsided, as turbulent and foaming waves yield to the sun's genial influence when the cloud has passed This silence, self-control, and struggle lasted about twenty seconds, then the count raised his pallid face.

"See," said he, "my dear friend, how God punishes the most thoughtless and unfeeling men for their indifference, by presenting dreadful scenes to their view I, who was looking on, an eager and curious spectator,— I, who was watching the working of this mournful tragedy,— I, who, like a wicked angel, was laughing at the evil men committed, protected by secrecy (a secret is easily kept by the rich and powerful), I am, in my turn, bitten by the serpent whose tortuous course I was watching, and bitten to the heart!"

Morrel groaned.

"Come, come," continued the count, "complaints are unavailing, be a man, be strong, be full of hope, for I am here, and will watch over you"

Morrel shook his head sorrowfully

"I tell you to hope Do you understand me?" cried Monte-Cristo. "Remember that I never uttered a falsehood and am never deceived. It is twelve o'clock, Maximilian; thank Heaven that you came at noon rather than in the evening, or to-morrow morning. Listen, Morrel!—it is noon; if Valentine is not now dead, she will not die"

"How so?" cried Morrel, "when I left her dying?"

Monte-Cristo pressed his hands to his forehead. What was passing in that brain, so loaded with dreadful secrets? What does the angel of light, or the angel of darkness, say to that mind, at once implacable and generous? God only knows.

Monte-Cristo raised his head once more, and this time he was calm as a child awaking from its sleep

"Maximilian," said he, "return home. I command you not to stir— attempt nothing; not to let your countenance betray a thought, and I will send you tidings Go!"

"Oh! count, you terrify me with that coolness. Have you, then, power against death?—Are you superhuman?—Are you an angel?"

And the young man, who had never shrunk from danger, shrank before Monte-Cristo with indescribable terror. But Monte-Cristo looked at him with so melancholy and sweet a smile, that Maximilian felt the tears filling his eyes

"I can do much for you, my friend," replied the count "Go; I must be alone"

Morrel, subdued by the extraordinary ascendency Monte-Cristo exercised over everything around him, did not endeavor to resist it.

He pressed the count's hand, and left. He stopped one moment at the door, for Baptistin, whom he saw in the Rue Matignon, and who was running.

Meanwhile, Villefort and d'Avrigny had made all possible haste, Valentine had not revived from her fainting-fit on their arrival, and the doctor examined the invalid with all the care the circumstances demanded, and with an interest which the knowledge of the secret doubled. Villefort, closely watching his countenance and his lips, waited the result of the examination. Noirtier, paler than even the young girl, more eager than Villefort for the decision, was watching also intently and affectionately.

At last d'Avrigny slowly uttered these words: "She is still alive!

"Still?" cried Villefort; "oh! doctor, what a dreadful word is that!'

"Yes," said the physician, "I repeat it; she is still alive, and I am astonished at it."

"But is she safe?" asked the father.

"Yes, since she lives."

At that moment d'Avrigny's glance met Noirtier's eye. It glistened with such extraordinary joy, so rich and full of thought, that the physician was struck. He placed the young girl again on the chair; her lips were scarcely discernible, they were so pale and white, as well as her whole face; and remained motionless, looking at Noirtier, who appeared to anticipate and commend all he did.

"Sir," said d'Avrigny to Villefort, "call Mademoiselle Valentine's maid, if you please."

Villefort went himself to find her, and d'Avrigny approached Noirtier.

"Have you something to tell me?" asked he. The old man winked his eyes expressively, which we may remember was his only way of expressing his approval.

"Privately?"

"Yes."

"Well, I will remain with you." At this moment Villefort returned, followed by the lady's-maid; and after her came Madame de Villefort.

"What is the matter, then, with this dear child?" the latter exclaimed; "she has just left me, and she complained of feeling unwell; but I did not think seriously of it."

The young woman, with tears in her eyes and every mark of affection of a true mother, approached Valentine and took her hand. D'Avrigny continued to look at Noirtier, he saw the eyes of the old man dilate and become round, his cheeks turn pale and tremble; the perspiration stood in drops upon his forehead.

"Ah!" said he, involuntarily following Noirtier's eyes, which were fixed on Madame de Villefort, who repeated:

"This poor child would be better in bed. Come, Fanny, we will put her in."

D'Avrigny, who saw that would be a means of his remaining alone with Noirtier, expressed his opinion that it was the best thing that could be done; but he forbade anything being given to her besides what he ordered.

They carried Valentine away, she had revived, but could scarcely move or speak, so shaken was her frame by the attack. She had, however, just power to give her grandfather one parting look, who, in losing her, seemed to be resigning his very soul. D'Avrigny followed the invalid, wrote a prescription, ordered Villefort to take a cab, go in person to a chemist's to get the prescribed medicine, bring it himself, and wait for him in his daughter's room. Then, having renewed his injunction not to give Valentine anything, he went down again to Noirtier, shut the doors carefully, and after convincing himself no one was listening:

"Do you," said he, "know anything of this young lady's illness?"

"Yes," said the old man.

"We have no time to lose, I will question, and do you answer me." Noirtier made a sign that he was ready to answer. "Did you anticipate the accident which has happened to your granddaughter?"

"Yes" D'Avrigny reflected a moment; then approaching Noirtier:

"Pardon what I am going to say," added he, "but no indication should be neglected in this terrible situation. Did you see poor Barrois die?" Noirtier raised his eyes to heaven

"Do you know of what he died?" asked d'Avrigny, placing his hand on Noirtier's shoulder.

"Yes," replied the old man

"Do you think he died a natural death?"

A sort of smile was discernible on the motionless lips of Noirtier

"Then you have thought Barrois was poisoned?"

"Yes."

"Do you think the poison he fell a victim to was intended for him?"

"No"

"Do you think the same hand which unintentionally struck Barrois has now attacked Valentine?"

"Yes."

"Then will she die, too?" asked d'Avrigny, fixing his penetrating gaze on Noirtier. He watched the effect of this question on the old man

"No!" replied he, with an air of triumph, which would have puzzled the most clever diviner.

"Then you hope?" said d'Avrigny, with surprise.

"Yes."

"What do you hope?" The old man made him understand with his eyes that he could not answer.

"Ah! yes, it is true!" murmured d'Avrigny. Then, turning to Noirtier,—"Do you hope the assassin will be tried?"

"No."

"Then you hope the poison will take no effect on Valentine?"

"Yes."

"It is no news to you," added d'Avrigny, "to tell you an attempt has been made to poison her?" The old man made a sign that he entertained no doubt upon the subject. "Then how do you hope Valentine will escape?"

Noirtier kept his eye steadily fixed on the same spot. D'Avrigny followed the direction, and saw they were fixed on a bottle containing the mixture which he took every morning. "Ah! ah!" said d'Avrigny, struck with a sudden thought, "has it occurred to you ——" Noirtier did not let him finish.

"Yes," said he.

"To prepare her system to resist poison?"

"Yes."

"By accustoming her by degrees ——"

"Yes, yes, yes," said Noirtier, delighted to be understood.

"Truly! I had told you there was brucine in the mixture I give you."

"Yes."

"And by accustoming her to that poison, you have endeavored to neutralize the effect of a similar poison?" Noirtier's joy continued. "And you have succeeded!" exclaimed d'Avrigny. "Without that precaution Valentine would have died before assistance could have been procured. The dose has been excessive, but she has only been shaken by it; and this time, at any rate, Valentine will not die."

A superhuman joy expanded the old man's eyes, which were raised toward heaven with an expression of infinite gratitude. At this moment Villefort returned.

"Here, doctor," said he, "is what you sent me for."

"Was this prepared in your presence?"

"Yes," replied the *procureur du roi.*

"Have you not let it go out of your hands?"

"No."

D'Avrigny took the bottle, poured some drops of the mixture it contained in the hollow of his hand, and swallowed them.

"Well," said he, "let us go to Valentine; I will give instructions to every one, and you, M. de Villefort, will yourself see that no one deviates from them."

At the moment when d'Avrigny was returning to Valentine's room, accompanied by Villefort, an Italian priest, of serious demeanor and calm and firm tone, hired for his use the house adjoining the hotel of Villefort. No one knew how the three former tenants of that house left it. About two hours afterward its foundation was reported to be unsafe; but the report did not prevent the new occupant establishing himself there with his modest furniture the same day at five o'clock. The lease was drawn up for three, six, or nine years by the new tenant, who, according to the rule of the proprietor, paid six months in advance.

This new tenant, who, as we have said, was an Italian, was called Il Signor Giacomo Busoni. Workmen were immediately called in, and the same night the passengers at the end of the faubourg saw with surprise carpenters and masons occupied in repairing the lower part of the tottering house.

CHAPTER XCV

FATHER AND DAUGHTER

WE have seen in a preceding chapter Madame Danglars coming formally to announce to Madame de Villefort the approaching marriage of Eugénie Danglars and Andrea Cavalcanti. This formal announcement, which implied, or appeared to imply, a resolution taken by all the parties concerned in this great affair, had been preceded by a scene to which our readers must be admitted. We beg them to take one step backward, and to transport themselves, the morning of that day of great catastrophes, into the beautifully gilded salon we have before shown them, and which was the pride of its owner, the Baron Danglars.

In this room, at about ten o'clock in the morning, the banker himself had been walking some minutes, thoughtful, and evidently uneasy, watching each door, and listening to every sound. When his patience was exhausted, he called his valet.

"Stephen," said he, "see why Mademoiselle Eugénie has asked me to meet her in the drawing-room, and why she makes me wait so long."

Having given this vent to his ill-humor, the baron became more calm; Mademoiselle Danglars had that morning requested an interview with her father, and had fixed on that drawing-room as the spot. The singularity of this step, and, above all, its formal character, had not a little surprised the banker, who had immediately obeyed his daughter by repairing first to the drawing-room. Stephen soon returned from his errand.

"Mademoiselle's lady's maid says, sir, that mademoiselle is finishing her toilet, and will be here shortly."

Danglars nodded, to signify he was satisfied. To the world and to his servants Danglars assumed the good-natured man and the weak father. This was one of his characters in the popular comedy he was performing; it was a physiognomy he had adopted, and which appeared as suitable to him as it was to the right side of the profile masks of the fathers of the ancient theaters to have a turned-up and laughing lip, while, on the left side, it was drawn down and sulky. Let us hasten to say that, in private, the turned-up and laughing lip descended to the level of the drawn-down and ill-tempered one; so that, generally, the indulgent man disappeared to give place to the brutal husband and domineering father.

"Why the devil does that foolish girl, who pretends to wish to speak to me, not come into my cabinet? and why, above all, can she want to speak to me at all?"

He was revolving this worrying thought in his brain for the twentieth time, when the door opened, and Eugénie appeared, attired in a figured black satin dress, her hair arranged, and gloves on, as if going to the Italian Opera.

"Well, Eugénie, what is it you want with me? and why in this solemn drawing-room when the cabinet is so comfortable?"

"You are right, sir," replied Eugénie, making a sign to her father that he could sit down; "and have proposed two questions which include all the conversation we are going to have. I will answer them both, and, contrary to the usual method, the last first, as being the least complex. I have chosen the drawing-room, sir, as our place of rendezvous, in order to avoid the disagreeable impressions and influences of a banker's office. Those cash-books, gilded as they may be, those drawers, locked like gates of fortresses, those heaps of bank-bills, come from I know not where, and the quantities of letters from England, Holland, Spain, India, China, and Peru, have generally a strange influence on a father's mind, and make him forget there is in the world an interest greater and more sacred than the good opinion of his correspondents. I have, therefore, chosen this drawing-room, where you see, smiling and happy in their magnificent frames, your portrait, mine, my mother's, and all sorts of rural landscapes and touching pastorals. I rely much on external impressions; perhaps, with regard to you, they are immaterial; but I should be no artist if I had not some fancies."

"Very well," replied Danglars, who had listened to all this preamble with imperturbable coolness, but without understanding a word, engaged as he was, like every man burdened with hidden thoughts, in seeking the thread of his own ideas in those of the speaker.

"There is, then, the second point cleared up, or nearly so," said Eugénie, without the least confusion, and with that masculine pointedness which distinguished her gesture and her language; "and you appear satisfied with the explanation. Now, let us return to the first?

You ask me why I have requested this interview; I will tell you in two words, sir; I will not marry M. le Comte Andrea Cavalcanti."

Danglars bounded from his chair, and with this motion raised his eyes and arms toward heaven.

"Yes, indeed, sir," continued Eugénie, still quite calm; "you are astonished, I see; for since this little affair commenced, I have not manifested the slightest opposition; sure, as I always am, when the opportunity arrives, to oppose to people who have not consulted me, and things which displease me, a determined and absolute will. However, this time, this tranquillity, this passiveness, as philosophers say, proceeded from another source; it proceeded from a wish, like a submissive and devoted daughter (a light smile was observable on the purple lips of the young girl), to try and practice obedience."

"Well?" asked Danglars.

"Well, sir," replied Eugénie, "I have tried to the very last; and now the moment has come, in spite of all my efforts, I feel it is impossible."

"But," said Danglars, whose weak mind was at first quite overwhelmed with the weight of this pitiless logic, marking evident premeditation and force of will, "what is your reason for this refusal, Eugénie? what reason do you assign?"

"My reason?" replied the young girl. "Well! it is not that the man is more ugly, more foolish, or more disagreeable than any other; no, M. Andrea Cavalcanti may appear to those who look at men's faces and figures a very good model. It is not, either, that my heart is less touched by him than any other; that would be a school-girl's reason, which I consider quite beneath me. I actually love no one, sir; you know it, do you not? I do not, then, see why, without real necessity, I should encumber my life with a perpetual companion. Has not some sage said, 'Nothing to excess;' and another, 'Carry everything with you!' I have been taught these two aphorisms in Latin and in Greek; one is, I believe, from Phædrus, and the other from Bias. Well, my dear father, in the shipwreck of life — for life is an eternal shipwreck of our hopes — I cast into the sea my useless baggage, that is all; and I remain with my own will, disposed to live perfectly alone, and, consequently, perfectly free."

"Unhappy girl! unhappy girl!" murmured Danglars, turning pale, for he knew, from long experience, the solidity of the obstacle he so suddenly encountered.

"Unhappy girl!" replied Eugénie, "unhappy girl! do you say, sir? No, indeed, the exclamation appears quite theatrical and affected. Happy, on the contrary; for what am I in want of? The world calls me beautiful. It is something to be well received; I like a favorable reception; it expands the countenance, and those around me do not then appear so ugly. I possess a share of wit, and a certain relative sensibility, which enables me to draw from general life, for the support of mine, all I meet with that is good, like the monkey who cracks the nut to get at its contents. I am rich, for you have one of the first fortunes in France: I am your only daughter, and you are not so tenacious as the fathers of La Porte Saint-Martin and La Gaîté, who disinherit their daughters because they will give them no grandchildren. Besides, the law in its foresight has deprived you of the power to disinherit me, at least, entirely, as it has also of the power to compel me to marry a particular person Thus, beautiful, witty, somewhat talented, as the comic operas say, and rich. Why, that is happiness, sir! Why do you call me unhappy?"

Danglars, seeing his daughter smiling, and proud even to insolence, could not entirely repress his brutal feelings, but they betrayed themselves only by an exclamation. Under the inquiring gaze of his daughter, before that beautiful black eyebrow, contracted by interrogation, he prudently turned away, and calmed himself immediately, daunted by the iron hand of circumspection.

"Truly, my daughter," replied he, with a smile, "you are all you boast of being, excepting one thing; I will not too hastily tell you which, but would rather leave you to guess it."

Eugénie looked at Danglars, much surprised that one flower of her crown of pride, with which she had so superbly decked herself, should be disputed. "My daughter," continued the banker, "you have perfectly explained to me the sentiments which influence a girl like you who is determined she will not marry, now, it remains for me to tell you the motives of a father like me, who has decided his daughter shall marry."

Eugénie bowed, not as a submissive daughter, but as an adversary prepared for a discussion.

"My daughter," continued Danglars, "when a father asks his daughter to choose a husband, he has always some reason for wishing her to marry. Some are affected with the mania to which you alluded just now, that of living again in their grandchildren. This is not my weakness, I tell you at once; family joys have no charm for me I may acknowledge this to a daughter whom I know to be philosophical enough to understand my indifference, and not to impute it to me as a crime."

"*A la bonne heure*," said Eugénie; "let us speak candidly, sir, I admire it"

"Oh!" said Danglars; "I can, when circumstances render it desirable, adopt your love of frankness, although it may not be my general practice. I will therefore proceed. I have proposed to you to marry, not for your sake, for, indeed, I did not think of you in the least at the moment (you admire candor, and will now be satisfied, I hope), but because I had need of your taking this husband, as soon as possible, on account of certain commercial speculations I am desirous of entering into" Eugénie became uneasy

"It is just so, I assure you, and you must not be angry with me; for you have sought this disclosure I do not willingly enter into all these arithmetical explanations with an artist like you, who fear to enter my office lest you should imbibe disagreeable or anti-poetic impressions and sensations. But in that same banker's office, where you very willingly presented yourself yesterday to ask for the thousand francs I give you monthly for pocket-money, you must know, my dear young lady, many things may be learned, useful even to a girl who will not marry. There one may learn, for instance, what, out of regard to your nervous susceptibility, I will inform you of in the drawing-room, namely, that the credit of a banker is his physical and moral life; that credit sustains him as breath animates the body; and M. de Monte-Cristo once gave me a lecture on that subject, which I have never forgotten. There we may learn that as credit sinks, the body becomes a corpse; and this is what must happen very soon to the banker who is proud to own so good a logician as you for his daughter."

But, Eugénie, instead of stooping, drew herself up under the blow. "Ruined!" said she.

"Exactly, my daughter; that is precisely what I mean," said Danglars, almost digging his nails into his breast, while he preserved on his harsh features the smile of the heartless though clever man; "ruined! yes, that is it."

"Ah!" said Eugénie.

"Yes, ruined! now it is revealed, this secret so full of horror, as the tragic poet says. Now, my daughter, learn from my lips how you may alleviate this misfortune, so far as it will affect you."

"Oh!" cried Eugénie, "you are a bad physiognomist, if you imagine I deplore, on my own account, the catastrophe you announce to me. I ruined! and what will that signify to me? Have I not my talent left? Can I not, like Pasta, Malibran, Grisi, acquire for myself what you would never have given me, whatever might have been your fortune, a hundred or a hundred and fifty thousand livres per annum, for which I shall be indebted to no one but myself; and which, instead of being given, as you gave me those poor twelve thousand francs, with pouting looks and reproaches for my prodigality, will be accompanied with acclamations, with bravos, and with flowers! And if I do not possess that talent, which your smiles prove to me you doubt, should I not still have that furious love of independence, which will be a substitute for all treasure, and which, in my mind, supersedes even the instinct of self-preservation? No, I grieve not on my own account, I shall always find a resource; my books, my pencils, my piano, all those things which cost but little, and which I shall be able to procure, will remain my own. Do you think that I sorrow for Madame Danglars? Undeceive yourself again; either I am greatly mistaken, or she has provided against

"WELL, EUGÉNIE, WHAT IS IT YOU WANT WITH ME?"

the catastrophe which threatens you, and which will pass over without affecting her; she has taken care for herself, at least I hope so, for her attention has not been diverted from her projects by watching over me; she has left me my entire independence by professedly indulging my love for liberty. Oh! no, sir; from my childhood I have seen too much, and understood too much, of what has passed around me, for misfortune to have an undue power over me, from my earliest recollections, I have been beloved by no one — so much the worse; that has naturally led me to love no one—so much the better; now you have my profession of faith."

"Then," said Danglars, pale with anger, which did not emanate from offended paternal love,—"then, mademoiselle, you persist in your determination to accelerate my ruin?"

"Your ruin? I accelerate your ruin! what do you mean? I do not understand you"

"So much the better, I have a ray of hope left: listen"

"I am all attention," said Eugénie, looking so earnestly at her father, that it was an effort to the latter to bear her powerful gaze.

"M. Cavalcanti," continued Danglars, "is about to marry you, and will place in my hands his fortune, amounting to three million livres."

"That is admirable!" said Eugénie, with sovereign contempt, smoothing her gloves out one upon the other.

"You think I shall deprive you of those three millions," said Danglars; "but do not fear it They are destined to produce at least ten. I and a brother banker have obtained a grant of a railway, the only speculation which in the present day offers any prospect of immediate success, like the chimerical Mississippi, which Law formerly supplied for the good Parisians, those eternal gulls in speculation. In my reckoning, a man now ought to have a millionth of a railway, as we used to have an acre of unimproved land upon the banks of the Ohio It is a hypothecation, which is an advance, as you see, since we gain at least ten, fifteen, twenty, or a hundred pounds of iron in exchange for our money. Well, within a week I am to deposit four millions for my share; these four millions, I promise you, will produce ten or twelve."

"But during my visit to you the day before yesterday, sir, which you appear to recollect so well," replied Eugénie, "I saw you enter in your accounts — is not that the term? — five millions and a half, you even pointed them out to me in two drafts on the treasury, and you were astonished that so valuable a paper did not dazzle my eyes like lightning."

"Yes, but those five millions and a half are not mine, and are only a proof of the great confidence placed in me; my title of popular banker has gained me the confidence of the hospitals, and the five millions and a half belong to the hospitals; at any other time I should not have hesitated to make use of them, but the great losses I have recently sustained are well known, and, as I told you, my credit is rather shaken. That deposit may be at any moment withdrawn, and if I had employed it for another purpose, I should bring on me a disgraceful bankruptcy. I do not despise bankruptcies, believe me, but they must be those which enrich, and not those which ruin. Now, if you marry M. Cavalcanti, and I touch the three millions, or even if it is thought I am going to touch them, my credit will be restored, and my fortune, which for the last month or two has been swallowed up in gulfs which have been opened in my path by an inconceivable fatality, will revive. Do you understand me?"

"Perfectly; you pledge me for three millions, do you not?"

"The greater the amount, the more flattering it is to you; it gives you an idea of your value."

"Thank you. One word more, sir; do you promise me to make what use you can of the report of the fortune of M. Cavalcanti will bring, without touching the sum? This is no act of selfishness, but of honesty. I am willing to help rebuild your fortune: but I will not be an accomplice in the ruin of others."

"But since I tell you," cried Danglars, "that with these three millions——"

"Do you expect to recover your position, sir, without touching those three millions?"

"I hope so, if the marriage should take place and confirm my credit."

"Shall you be able to pay M. Cavalcanti the five hundred thousand francs you promise for my dowry?"

"He shall receive them on returning from the town-hall."

"Well!"

"What next? what more do you want?"

"I wish to know if, in demanding my signature, you leave me entirely free in my person?"

"Absolutely!"

"Then, well, as I said before, sir, I am ready to marry M. Cavalcanti."

"But what are your projects?"

"Ah, that is my secret. What advantage should I have over you, if, knowing your secret, I were to tell you mine?"

Danglars bit his lips. "Then," said he, "you are ready to pay the formal visits, which are absolutely indispensable?"

"Yes," replied Eugénie.

"And to sign the contract in three days?"

"Yes."

"Then, in my turn, I will say, Well!"

Danglars pressed his daughter's hand in his. But it was extraordinary, neither did the father say, "Thank you, my child," nor did the daughter smile at her father.

"Is the conference ended?" asked Eugénie, rising.

Danglars motioned that he had nothing more to say. Five minutes afterward the piano resounded to the touch of Mademoiselle d'Armilly's fingers, and Mademoiselle Danglars was singing Brabantio's malediction on Desdemona. At the end of the piece Stephen entered, and announced to Eugénie that the horses were to the carriage, and the baroness was waiting for her to pay her visits. We have seen them at Villefort's; they proceeded then on their course.

END OF VOLUME IV.

CPSIA information can be obtained
at www.ICGtesting.com
Printed in the USA
BVHW040813120720
583181BV00006B/100

9 781340 381028